SEVILLE, CÓRDOBA, AND GRANADA

SEVILLE, CÓRDOBA, AND GRANADA

A CULTURAL HISTORY

Elizabeth Nash

OXFORD
UNIVERSITY PRESS

2005

OXFORD
UNIVERSITY PRESS

Oxford University Press, Inc., publishes works that further
Oxford University's objective of excellence
in research, scholarship, and education.

Oxford   New York
Auckland   Cape Town   Dar es Salaam   Hong Kong   Karachi
Kuala Lumpur   Madrid   Melbourne   Mexico City   Nairobi
New Delhi   Shanghai   Taipei   Toronto

With offices in
Argentina   Austria   Brazil   Chile   Czech Republic   France   Greece
Guatemala   Hungary   Italy   Japan   Poland   Portugal   Singapore
South Korea   Switzerland   Thailand   Turkey   Ukraine   Vietnam

Copyright © 2005 by Elizabeth Nash

Foreword © 2005 by Ian Gibson

Published by Oxford University Press, Inc.
198 Madison Avenue, New York, New York 10016

www.oup.com

Oxford is a registered trademark of Oxford University Press

Co-published in Great Britain by Signal Books

Library of Congress Cataloging-in-Publication Data
Nash, Elizabeth, 1949–
Seville, Córdoba, and Grenada : a cultural history / Elizabeth Nash.
    p. cm. — (Cityscapes)
Includes bibliographical references and index.
ISBN-13 978-0-19-518203-3; 978-0-19-518204-0 (pbk.)
ISBN 0-19-518203-0; 0-19-518204-9 (pbk.)
1. Seville (Spain)—Civilization. 2. Granada (Spain)—Civilization. 3. Córdoba (Spain)—
Civilization. 4. Seville (Spain)—Description and travel. 5. Granada (Spain)—Description and
travel. 6. Córdoba (Spain)—Description and travel. I. Title. II. Series.
DP402.S415N37 2005
946'.8—dc22   2004061728

Drawings by Yvonne St Clair

3 1984 00240 0719

9 8 7 6 5 4 3 2 1

Printed in the United States of America
on acid-free paper

Foreword: "The Marvel of Andalucia"

In November 1830 Richard Ford and his family embarked in Cadiz on the British-built paddle-steamer that was to bear them up the meandering River Guadalquivir to Seville, a distance of some sixty miles. Ford knew the rest of Europe inside out, but this was his first visit to Spain and he expected to be surprised. He was. The journey to Seville took several hours, and the light was fading by the time the Giralda tower, the tallest building in Spain, was sighted soaring high over the famed city. The reason for coming to Andalusia was the poor health of Ford's wife, Harriet, but why he opted to make Seville their base rather than, say, Malaga with its sea breezes, is not clear. Perhaps because he had decided that the city offered three outstanding advantages: it enjoyed a mild winter climate, it was the unchallenged capital of Andalusia and, should anything go wrong, Gibraltar was near at hand. At all events he never regretted the decision, nor should we. Although the original plan was to spend a year in Spain, the family remained for three, by which time Ford had travelled over much of the country. The result was the wittily entitled *A Hand-Book for Travellers in Spain and Readers at Home*, published by John Murray in two small-format volumes in 1845. It was, and it remains, one of greatest books ever written on another country by an Englishman, and in many ways, despite Ford's prejudices, it as valid today as when written.

If by the time the *Hand-Book* appeared Washington Irving had already put Granada on the map with his *Tales of the Alhambra*, it fell to Ford to make widely known the charms and peculiarities of Seville, termed "the marvel of Andalucía" in his opening phrase on the city. Since then Seville has never failed to exert her magic over travellers from the north, many of whom have felt the need to publish their impressions of the place and its people. Elizabeth Nash is the latest in a long line of enthusiasts, and her book, which pays due homage to Ford, will be found extremely useful and engaging by the modern tourist contemplating a visit.

With the discovery of America in 1492, Seville, to which the "The Catholic Monarchs," Ferdinand and Isabella, granted the monopoly of trade with the New World (thereby provoking great resentment in Barcelona), quickly became one of the most flourishing ports in Europe. But as Nash reminds us in her introduction, she was a thriving city long before falling to the Christians in 1248, twelve years after Córdoba. I say "she" with some confidence, for if ever there was a feminine city it is Seville, her gender symbolized by the fervor with which the inhabitants embraced the dogma of the Immaculate Conception, promulgated in 1854. The goddess who presides over Seville is the Virgin Mary, and she is loved with a passion, as a thousand shrines, statues, images and plaques attest. I like to believe that this feminine quality is also responsible for the musicality and lilt of Sevillian speech, so much easier on the ear than the often strident diction that prevails further north, or, for that matter, in some other areas of Andalusia, and which V. S. Pritchett once memorably described as "desert Latin." Moreover, if the *Sevillanos* talk softly they move harmoniously. Their favorite color is friendly *albero*, ochre, which is found, in combination with white, on almost all the buildings. And they are convinced that their city is not only the most beautiful in Spain but in the universe. Other Andalusians find them maddeningly boastful, complacent and unfriendly, always trying to be witty and score points, always strutting, and complain that, because the city is the seat of the Andalusian Regional Government, it gets most of the perks (one of the most obvious being the high-speed train from Madrid, the AVE, put in place for Expo 92). There is truth in all of this, and also jealousy, but who could blame the *Sevillanos* for feeling special? Moreover, have they not looked after their city far better than other Andalusians have theirs, to such an extent that the skyline of the center remains largely as it was centuries ago? Even during the Franco era, urbanistically disastrous for much of Spain, Seville managed to keep the speculators at bay. The result, as the Irish art historian Rosemary Mulcahy observed recently, is that this is one of the best-preserved cities in Europe.

I grew to love it in 2002, when for a period of some six months I was a guest on a weekly TV chat show. I always stayed in the slightly old-fashioned Hotel Inglaterra, where the top-floor room they kindly reserved for me afforded a glorious view of the Giralda and the massive gothic cathedral erected on the site of the Great Mosque. At night I would roam the streets, sometimes accompanied by friends but more often alone, and the following morning, before returning to my village near Granada, investigate churches and museums. Reading Elizabeth Nash has brought back the excitement of that experience of discovery.

Away from the main boulevards, the streets of Seville are narrow and twisting. You have the feeling that around every corner something unexpected may appear or happen. Another of the ornate baroque churches in which Seville specializes, perhaps, or a tiny, intimate square with a fountain and fringed by orange trees, or a secondhand bookshop or little bar inserted into an old Arab wall decked in jasmine and bougainvillea. The houses of the affluent, with their courtyards sometimes glimpsed through a door or grille, and the apparently endless convents, speak of secret, inner worlds, and remind us of the amatory prowlings of the city's most famous literary personage, Don Juan.

I am not a Holy Week man, more a partisan of the unashamedly pagan Spring Fair which follows hard on the heels of Seville's annual religious orgy. Elizabeth Nash has a lot to tell us about both occasions, and her account of the background to the processions that are another reason for the city's international fame will be found interesting and informative by those who are attracted by this aspect of the Andalusian capital.

Elizabeth Nash has felt compelled to round off her book with a chapter each on Córdoba and Granada, probably a good idea since the visitor to Seville will almost certainly feel the urge to spend a few days in both cities. While, in Córdoba, the great draw is the mosque, still one of the most impressive religious buildings in the world despite the Christian cathedral erected in its midst, Granada offers, as well as the Alhambra and Generalife, the haunting presence of its great poet, Federico García Lorca, murdered by the fascists at the beginning of the Civil War in 1936, and to whom the author devotes considerable space. For Lorca, who theorized endlessly about Andalusia, sea-level Seville, with its great river, symbolized freedom, the possibility of escape, of adventure. Whereas enclosed, mountainous Granada, the last bastion of Islam in Spain, lost its soul when the Christians took over in 1492 and almost immediately reneged on their promise to respect the religion and customs of the inhabitants. The contrast with Seville could hardly be more poignant.

For readers at home (to return to Ford) this book will act as potent stimulus to explore Seville for themselves and then, hopefully, strike out for Córdoba and Granada. Elizabeth Nash provides just the right balance of fact, on-the-spot observation and opinion. And her enthusiasm is infectious. ¡Olé!

Ian Gibson,
Restábal (Granada),
August 2004

Preface and Acknowledgments

I first visited Seville as a student: my university sent me to a language school, now defunct, that was lined with handsome blue-and-gold tiles but so dreary that after two days I never returned. Holy Week approached and my landlady doubled the rent, a development unforeseen by my sponsors, so I took a train to the next stop down the line. It was Utrera, packed like Seville with Easter visitors, where I found a hostel that proffered a mattress with lace-trimmed sheets laid on the cool terracotta floor. Penitents clanked their chains round the clock, trumpets wailed in the street, and along the corridor a young musician picked a rippling flamenco guitar all night long. The reason for this ill-prepared discovery of Andalusia was that my tutors thought I should learn Spanish before pursuing graduate studies in Buenos Aires. So Seville was for me—as for adventurers down the centuries—gateway to the Americas. For years I perceived the city as if from across the Atlantic.

I learned from that chaotic first visit to flee the sun, to enjoy crowds, and to relish olives eaten outdoors from a little white dish. Seville seemed a paradise of liberty and pleasure. But within hours I discovered that unrestricted bar-hopping produced a crashing headache, that Franco's civil guardsmen vigorously discouraged unseemly behavior, and that young men's glances carried danger rather than promise for an unwary northern female.

Exuberant Seville imposes its own discipline: cooling, sometimes lugubrious, antidotes to the city's excessive light and heat. Summer streets are roofed with jaunty canvas shades or *toldos* that are decorative but essential: without them you burn. An earlier age protected windows with wrought-iron bars for a comparable purpose: to curb passion rather than sunstroke. In Seville you step constantly between glare and gloom, from zestful enjoyment to obsession with death. The threshold is physical and spiritual. A moment, a person, swings from vibrancy to aloofness and back in the blink of an eye. Seville's flickering ambiguity is captivating, sometimes unnerving, sometimes unreal, as I hope this book conveys.

I owe special thanks to Lorna Scott Fox and Ian Gibson. Others who helped me rediscover Seville, Granada and Córdoba include Ann Bateson, Flora Botsford, Anunciación Bremón, Tom Burns, Eduardo Castro, Marcial Castro, Leslie Crawford, Juan Antonio Díaz, Diana Durán, Carlos Elordi, Gabriele Finaldi at the Prado Museum, Laura García Lorca, Francisco González, Mercedes Herránz, Jonathan and Isabel Holland, Javier León, Juan de Loxa, Steven and Rosina Mackey, Ignacio Merino, Duque de Segorbe, Hugh O'Shaughnessy, Terry Otero, Edward Owen, Sol Pérez de Guzman, Marcelo del Pozo, Maite Ramos, Paul Rigg, Bernhard Roters, Isabel Sanchez Gil at Turespaña, Yvonne St. Clair, Emilio Silva at the Association for the Recovery of Historical Memory, Giles Tremlett, Jane Walker, José Verdú, Antonio Zoido; and my colleagues at *El País* in Madrid and Seville, especially Miguel Angel Bastenier and Santiago Fuertes.

Thanks again to my colleagues on *The Independent* foreign desk, especially Leonard Doyle, who never stopped encouraging me; and to my editor James Ferguson for his many good ideas. Visiting a city is no substitute for living there, however, and I apologize for any mistakes, gaps and lapses; they are all my fault.

Elizabeth Nash
Madrid, September 2004

Contents

Chapter Ten

Chapter Eleven

SEVILLE, CÓRDOBA, AND GRANADA

Introduction
GOLDEN TOWER, GREAT RIVER

Flanked by a few palm trees, the twelve-sided Torre del Oro—Seville's golden tower—stands as if on sentry duty guarding the banks of the languid Guadalquivir. The unfussy, austere outline of the tower that glows with fiery splendour at sunset forms an instantly recognizable profile of Seville, and expresses elements that define the culture of Spain's ancient southern port. Which is paradoxical, because unfussy and austere are not words you often associate with this most exuberant and over-decorated city. But the Torre del Oro embodies a sober aesthetic that underpins Seville's more florid and frivolous personality. *Finos y fríos*—refined and cool—was how the Basque poet Miguel de Unamuno defined *Sevillanos*, the city's inhabitants, tapping a deeper truth behind the façade of relentless and noisy gaiety.

The silhouette of the tower, the palms and the lazy waterfront of what the English writer Laurie Lee called the "mirage-river", which shimmers in the afternoon heat, seem more North African than southern European, and suggest the extent to which Seville's style and culture were shaped by its Moorish history. Troops led by Tariq ibn Ziryab, governor of Tangier, crossed the strait and invaded Spain in 711, landing on the outcrop that he called Jabal Tariq (Tariq's rock) or Gibraltar. Muslims swept north to conquer most of the Iberian Peninsula, and ruled the city of Seville—Isbiliya, they called it—for five centuries. Under their rule, the city grew ever more prosperous and sophisticated, and Jews, Christians and Muslims cohabited, albeit each in their own neighbourhood, to produce a rich mixture of three cultures, a *convivencia* whose influence is still felt today.

Córdoba, sixty miles up the Wadi-al-Kabir ("Great River") was capital of the Muslim kingdom of al-Andalus. Al-Andalus extended far beyond southern Spain's present-day Andalusia: the Arab kingdom stretched throughout what is now Spain and Portugal up to the Pyrenees. Córdoba, ruled first by Omeyas who originated from Damascus in Syria then by Berber factions from North Africa, fell to the Christian re-conquest in 1236 after attaining levels of philosophical, literary and scientific sophistication unknown in the Christian world. *Reconquista* was the term applied centuries later to the gradual dismantling of Moorish supremacy that took nearly a millennium. And in Granada, the last Muslim city in Spain to fall to the Catholic monarchs Fernando and Isabella, Boabdil, king of the city's ruling Nasrids, held out until 1492, the year Christopher Columbus made his first landfall in the Americas.

The Torre del Oro was built by the Almohad governor of Seville, the warrior Abul-Ula, in 1221, as a fortified watchtower to guard the flourishing port and dockyards against invasion from ships advancing upriver. This was the sturdiest and most important of more than a hundred towers linked like beads on a necklace by a lime and pebblestone wall six feet thick that encircled the riverside city to protect it both from invaders and frequent flooding. The walls remained more or less intact until the nineteenth century, prompting the French writer Théophile Gautier's description: "Seville is girt with a ring of crenellated walls, flanked at intervals with great towers, several of which have fallen into ruin, and with moats which are now almost entirely filled up. These walls, which would be no defence against modern artillery, produce quite a picturesque effect with their jagged, saw-like Arab battlements."

The tower, whose battlements are similarly jagged and saw-like, provides a sweeping panoramic view upstream to the Andalusian hinterland that Seville dominated with its trade to and from the known world, and downstream to the sea and a maritime empire the city built and commanded. The tower "bathes its foundations in the Guadalquivir hard by the landing stage, and rises into the azure air from amid a forest of masts and rigging," wrote Gautier in the 1830s. Even in the age of decline, when the romantic imagination of visiting writers eagerly filled in the gaps left by a fading empire, the tower controlled the navigation of the river. Laurie Lee, in *As I Walked Out One Midsummer Morning*, a romantic account of his journey through Spain on the eve of the Civil War, sketched a verse in the river's honour. The Guadalquivir was "a curled furrow in the dust/a sun-dazed wanderer/staggering to the sea."

In Moorish times, heavy chains were flung across the Guadalquivir from the golden tower to a buttress of masonry, now disappeared, on the opposite bank in the neighbourhood of Triana. When pulled taut, the chains closed the port to enemy ships advancing upstream. The tower became a symbol of the city, a landmark which returning sailors spotted peeping above the horizon before the city as a whole came into view, and one of the last sights that departing voyagers glimpsed before they sailed across the world. "Seville's riverside/The Golden Tower./Tile of the shore/of the Moorish river", wrote the avant-garde twentieth-century Spanish poet Gerardo Diego. Seville was *puerto y puerta*—port and gateway—to the Indies, in the words of Spain's finest seventeenth-century playwright, Lope de Vega.

Typically, though, in a city long careless of the glories of its heritage, no one knows for sure why it is called the golden tower, its name since Moorish times. There are various explanations: that its façade was once clad with gilded tiles, the Moorish *azulejos* for which Seville became renowned; that the fortress tower was used to store ingots of precious metal brought from Latin America by the galleons; or that its russet walls reflected the blazing rays of the setting sun. Within 27 years of the tower being built, however, the Catholic King Fernando III besieged the city with his Castilian forces and conquered Seville's ruling Almohads. In 1248, the king's Cantabrian ships burst through the city's protective chains across the Guadalquivir, and broke into the city's port area. Fernando's advance exposed the pontoon bridge a little further upstream, where today the Triana bridge spans the river, to the assailants. That bridge— since 1170 a line of rickety boats strung together beneath a wobbly deck—was Seville's only contact with the fertile Aljarafe region to the west, a region that supplied the city with its staples and its luxuries: wheat, oil, oranges, dates, milk and honey. Isbiliya surrendered to the Catholic invaders because it was starving.

By 1271 Seville's Christian conquerors had transformed the tower from a proud sentinel of maritime traffic into a chapel. This was in accordance with the priorities of Spain's Catholic rulers, who always sought to stamp, sometimes stamp out, important Moorish sites with their own faith. King Pedro the Cruel in the fourteenth century used the golden tower to store his treasures, and as a debtors' prison— presumably not at the same time. He also, it is said, incarcerated his mistress Aldonza Coronel in the tower when she resisted his carnal demands. In 1652 artillery pieces were installed on the roof, to strengthen the city's defences, and at the beginning of the nineteenth century during Napoleon's conquest of Spain, gunpowder was stored there. In 1822, when the walls linking the tower to the Alcázar royal palace were being pulled down, the tower was treated as a handy shed for storing the tools for the demolition. Throughout these centuries, the tower withstood waves of earthquakes, floods, storms and wars which battered Seville.

City of the Picaresque

Down the centuries famine frequently afflicted the city, which, because of the multitudes of poor folk drawn from all over Spain to the bustling port, produced a huge, miserable underclass. The gulf between an enormously rich minority and the rest with nothing at all caused suffering, of course, but it also produced a rich and ironic literature of hunger. Spain's—that is, the world's—picaresque novel was born in Seville. The picaresque, a product of the city's sixteenth- and seventeenth-century Golden Age, owed its dynamism and wit to the clash between classes, in episodes typically concerning concubines, thieves and acts of deceit and skullduggery. A typical scenario for picaresque adventures was the Alameda de Hércules, built on foul-smelling bogs near the riverside in the sixteenth century when it was known as Duck Lagoon. The spot retains today a certain badlands reputation. Long associated with bullfighters, flamenco, prostitutes and lowlife generally, the Alameda became a fashionable strolling ground or *paseo*, where nobles idled amidst cooling springs. The leafy boulevard was perfect for cloak and dagger encounters: it was fashionable but also louche. All that remains of its past splendour are the twin columns, brought from a Roman temple in what is now the Calle Mármoles (Marbles Street) in the city centre, topped with statues of the patrons of Seville, Hercules and Julius Caesar.

Until recently a Sunday flea market sprawled along the Alameda de Hércules, and those who frequented it spread into the boisterous bars round about. But the area became dilapidated as well as disreputable. The ancient *álamos* or poplars that gave the promenade its name shrivelled and died, probably because the excavation of an underground car park savaged their roots. The lively market offered anything from cables for old computers to home movie kits, flamenco frocks, religious paintings, pairs of socks, bird cages, spanners and old mobile phones, all beadily monitored by slight gypsy girls with heavy earrings and babies in arms. Fat motorbikes gleamed, and cannabis spiked the air in a spectacle whose clientele and merchandise evoked southern, even Caribbean, frontier lands. It was recently shifted to a more remote spot upriver and lost much of its appeal. There remains only El Jueves, the Thursday flea market snaking along the Calle Feria nearby. The origin of this Aladdin's cave of colourful bric-a-brac, ranging from junk to old masters, is thought to date back to Moorish times, as the market was held on the day before Friday prayers. This is the place where Cervantes' pair of young rogues Rinconete and Cortadillo, in his novella of that name, went every Thursday to ply their trade of thieving, under cover of selling meat, fish, fruit and bread from baskets.

The proximity of El Jueves to the Alameda is said to have tainted the leafy boulevard with *pícaros* from the start. In 1782 the Inquisition left its gloomy castle headquarters in Triana on the riverbank, to move to a building along the Alameda. Cervantes refers to Seville frequently in his works, from his epic *Don Quijote* (1605)—which he is said to have conceived during his period of imprisonment in Seville's jail—to his *novelas*, mostly in connection with the city's teeming lowlife. Seville was "a shelter for the poor, refuge for the outcast, for in its vast expanse not only can the humble find a place, but the great are unable to make their presence felt," says the dog Berganza to his canine companion Scipio in Cervantes' *Coloquio de los perros* (The Dogs' Colloquy, 1613). Some goatherds whom Cervantes' sad knight, Don Quijote, meets on his travels "begged him to come with them to Seville, because it's just the place to find adventures—on every street and round every corner they're simply waiting for you, more of them than anywhere in the world. Don Quijote thanked them for the information and for their disposition to extend such courtesies to him, but said that for the time being he did not wish to go to Seville and indeed could not go there, until he had rid all those sierras of foul robbers with which they were said to be infested. In view of his firm intentions the travellers decided not to pester him any more."

Rinconete and Cortadillo, drawn to Seville by the prospect of fat purses to slit, "went to look at the city, and were amazed at the vast number of people by the river, because it was at the time when they were loading up the fleet. There were six galleys there, the sight of which made them sigh and dread the day when a mistake on their part would lead them to spend the rest of their lives in them."

Death of a Port

By 1757 the Torre del Oro was so ramshackle that the authorities nearly pulled it down. But they renovated it instead, and added a little lighthouse to the roof, topped with a gilded cupola. In 1866 they would have sold it at auction but for the personal intervention of the queen, who vetoed the sale. The navy took over the Golden Tower, and declared it a national monument that could neither be demolished nor sold, and in 1944 they turned it into a naval museum. It is a modest outpost of a bigger operation in Madrid that rehabilitates the handsome building as a symbol of the port in its prime.

The higher you mount the spiral steps that wind up the centre of the tower, the more you glimpse from the narrow embrasures at each level ever-widening expanses of river, city and flood plain. You can imagine barrel-bellied galleons laden with silver from the New World jostling along the riverbank, just as the old prints and paintings on display portray, often under the slogan: *Qui non ha visto Sevilla, non ha visto maravilla* (If you haven't seen Seville, you've missed a marvel). Historical scenes of a bustling port adorn the walls of this endearing little museum, in which maps of the American colonies, nautical charts, pompous portraits of naval commanders, flags, uniforms, skeins of rope, shipwrights' mallets and chisels, and fine brass navigational instruments are crammed together in cabin-like proximity.

The collection records a lost era, because the only vessels to tie up at the foot of the Torre del Oro these days are passenger launches ferrying tourists up and down a short stretch of the river, or—if you have a day to spare—downstream to Sanlúcar de Barrameda where you can eat shrimps and gaze across the Atlantic towards America. Laurie Lee summed up the contrast between today and yesterday:

> *The Seville quays were unpretentious, and seemed no more nautical than a coal-wharf in Birmingham. The Guadalquivir, at this point, was rather like the Thames at Richmond, and was about as busy as the Paddington Canal. Yet it was from this narrow river, fifty miles from the sea, that Columbus sailed to discover America, followed a few years later by the leaking caravelles of Magellan, one of which was the first to encircle the world. Indeed, the waterfront at Seville, with its paddling boys and orange boats, and its mossy provincial stones, was for almost five hundred years... history's most significant launching pad.*

While you wait for your pleasure launch, stroll along the Muelle del Sal, Salt Wharf. The name recalls the former activity of this stretch of riverbank where essential supplies were loaded for the fleet in the days of Rinconete and Cortadillo. Salt, as it happens, was an important source of tax for the Crown from around the fourteenth century, and Alfonso XI granted to Seville the privilege of trading salt, in exchange for an annual levy. Salt Wharf is now a car park mostly, in which a magnificent stone monument by the Basque sculptor Eduardo Chillida symbolizes "Tolerance". The massive curving stone blocks, which seem to represent an embrace, were installed to mark the 500th anniversary of Columbus' voyage to the Americas, in 1992. The sculpture stands foursquare amidst the encroaching vehicles but, like everything along this west-facing bank, becomes breathtakingly warm, handsome and irresistible towards sundown.

Taking one of the popular boat trips only confirms the extent to which this 400-mile "great river" has silted up and died. The Guadalquivir, which the Romans called Betis and plied as a highway to

Córdoba, is navigable now only from Seville downstream. When the river bed silted up to the point that cargo vessels could no longer reach the Torre del Oro, in 1717, Seville died as a port. All the maritime traffic, the trading and the riches, the dynamism and the prestige moved sixty miles downriver to Cadiz, only to fizzle out as the Spanish seaborne empire itself declined beneath the onslaught of rival powers, movements of colonial liberation, and an overall enfeeblement of Spain's political and economic operations overseas.

Itálica: Hills of Melancholy

Commercial vessels used to trade upriver as far as Córdoba in Roman times, according to the seventeenth-century historian of Seville, Rodrigo Caro. In the British crime writer Lindsey Davis' rollicking, historically accurate detective story *A Dying Light in Corduba* (1997), the Roman hero Didio Falco hazards an ill-fated journey downstream from Corduba, as the Romans called it, in a ship overloaded with amphorae of olive oil. Today boats cannot even push as far upstream as the Roman settlement of Itálica, just north of the modest little settlement of Hispalis, the Romans' Seville.

Founded in 206 BC by Scipio "The African", and the birthplace of Emperors Trajan and Hadrian, Italica was the first Roman city to be established outside Italy. It has long since been stranded on the flood plain, amidst the meanderings of the Betis. "The ruin of Itálica dates from the river having changed its bed, common trick in wayward Spanish and Oriental streams," sniffed the British traveller Richard Ford, who settled in Seville with his family in 1830 for three years. "The Moors soon abandoned the town and 'a land which the rivers had spoiled', and left Itálica for Seville; and ever since the remains have been used as a quarry." Ford noted that locals were forever finding old coins, and "with a view of recommending their wares, polish them bright, the sacred rust of twice ten hundred years. They do their best to deprive antiquity of its charming old coat."

"The ruins peep out amid the weeds and olive groves, like the grey bones of dead giants... the scene is sad and lonely," but for "glittering lizards which hurry into rusting brambles," Ford observed. The historian and scholar Rodrigo Caro wrote a poem entitled "A las ruinas de Itálica" (To the Ruins of Itálica): "Fields of solitude, hills of melancholy." The pillars, the patios and the mosaics, minute morsels of red, cream and grey stone set in curvilinear geometry, rest in sun-drenched silence broken only by the cooing of wood pigeons amidst the scent of cypresses and jasmine, and a field of olive trees stirred by the breeze.

The city was originally established as a settlement for veterans and wounded soldiers who, supplied with land and money at the end of their active service, married local women and mingled immediately with the local inhabitants. The little colony became a big city and, with its strategic position on the northern bank of the Guadalquivir, an important Roman economic thoroughfare and hub of a communications network that crisscrossed western Andalusia. From here was organized the Romanization of the whole of Hispania; two emperors, Trajan and Hadrian, came from noble families who settled in Itálica, and thanks to them the city became hugely influential.

Itálica reached the peak of its splendour in the second century, with spacious residential areas, luxurious public buildings including baths, theatres and a huge amphitheatre. The settlement attained such a degree of independence from Rome that it even drafted some of its own laws. Most of the city remains buried beneath the otherwise unremarkable ("miserable", Ford thought) village of Santiponce, but you can visit the main areas of the Roman city, including the forum and the baths. Marvel at the mosaic pavements, uncovered in 1799, those that have not been plundered in the meantime; while leading troops in the Peninsular Wars of the early 1800s the French leader Maréchal Nicolas Jean Soult and the British Duke of Wellington each came to Itálica in search of Roman artefacts. The giant amphitheatre, said to be one of the biggest of its kind in the world, can hold 25,000 spectators. Its huge size, far in excess of the needs of such a remote outpost, suggests that Itálica was a centre of rest and recreation for weary Roman legionaries.

Even in its origins, therefore, Seville devoted itself to enjoyment of leisure and idleness, and what Ford, with barely concealed disapproval, called "games of blood". Today's bullfights are said to originate in the contests between men and wild beasts that lured crowds to the amphitheatre of Itálica. No one knows when or why this great settlement was abandoned. Perhaps when it was cold-shouldered by the river. A tenth-century manuscript describes it as an abandoned city stripped of its fine marble. Many of the columns and mosaics found their way into noble palaces of present-day Seville. By the Middle Ages it had lost even its name, and was known only as Old Seville.

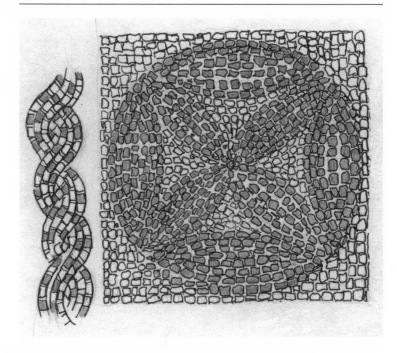

A City Divided

After the river silted up, and Seville turned inland for commercial contact, the advent of the railways in the nineteenth century opened up Spain's vast and inhospitable hinterland hitherto crossable only by mule or carriage, as early travellers painfully recorded. Trains steamed into Seville at the Córdoba station, a magnificent neo-Mudéjar pile that represents the triumph of the industrial age, imprinted with characteristically exuberant decoration recalling the city's Moorish past. Yet despite these small indicators of an industrial revolution, Seville was always more mercantile than industrial. Ford scoffed that the city's most dynamic trading activity was the sale of water along the Alameda. More likely it was begging.

The swanky station, meanwhile, has been demeaned somewhat by being turned into a shopping mall, with the usual retail outlets, but it still carries the proud swagger of the railway age. Up until a few decades ago, trains brought passengers from Madrid and Europe into the heart of the city, so that the visitor's first glimpse of Seville was the former military parade ground, or Plaza de Armas, by the Cacharro bridge. From here it is a short walk to a fin-de-siècle market hall with airy arching ironwork, a mini Les Halles by the Triana bridge, built by the French engineer Gustave Eiffel. It is now a cheery tourist information centre.

A stroll along the riverfront puts you in contact with all Seville's great historical moments, but the promenade, although pleasant, none the less feels on the margins of what is going on today. The railway tracks that once ran along the riverside, which in their day supplanted the maritime bustle of the portside, have in their turn been ripped up to make way for a motorway ring-road. Seville's main railway station of Santa Justa, the terminus for the Ave high-speed train linking this city to the rest of Spain, and Europe, is out on the eastern fringes. Traffic rushes along the riverside highway, but the city's driving force is no longer the river that impelled it to communicate with the wider world. Efforts have been made to revive the riverside, and especially to integrate the marshy zone known as La Cartuja on the western bank into the fabric of the city, which was the ambition of the 1992 World Exhibition. But Seville mostly turns its back on the watery thoroughfare that created both its baroque glory and its seamy underside, and brought currents of change and cascades of wealth from distant lands.

Today's Seville is inward-looking, stranded in solitary splendour, like an island: "widow of the sea, or rather, divorcee of the river", wrote the city's historian Francisco Morales Padrón in the 1980s. Laurie Lee spotted the trend, on the eve of bloody conflict: "This was a city absorbed in a boxed life of its own; strangers were few and almost ignored. Seville lived for itself, split into two halves, one riding on the back of the other." Andalusia's gulf between rich and poor ahead of the Civil War in 1936 was dissected by the British writer Gerald Brenan in his historical study *The Spanish Labyrinth* (1943). The grotesque inequality had its roots in the small numbers of extremely large landholdings or *latifundios*—a Roman name for a Roman legacy— which meant that the Civil War was particularly violent here. The victory of the powerful landowning class was swift and crushing, and resentments deep and long. Many of the large estates were uncultivated, many were devoted to bulls and horses. And many were olive groves.

Olives, Oranges and Flavours of the South

The olive groves and oil of Betica, the region around Seville, were celebrated by Roman historians. *Non alia maior in Bætica arbor:* "there is no better tree in Betica," wrote the historian Pliny. Arab historians praised the region's olive trees for "being plentiful, and very close together". Cervantes, who tramped the region extensively requisitioning tribute for the Crown, wrote: "These trees so fresh, so full, so beautiful; when they display their fruit, green, golden, and black, it is among the most agreeable sights one might see."

Olives are still the staple of Andalusia, Europe's biggest olive producer. They are cultivated in the Aljarafe around Seville, and especially further east upriver towards Córdoba and Granada, in what is called the *campiña*, a rolling countryside of spectacular beauty. Federico García Lorca wrote: "The field/of olives/opens and closes/like a fan." The road between Córdoba and Granada is impregnated with the fruity aroma of olive oil that hangs in the air, fills your nostrils, rises from the earth like intoxicating essences from a hot bath. The poet Antonio Machado grew up in Seville's palace of Las Dueñas, home of the Duchess of Alba, the grandest grandee of Spain. An admirer of Lorca, Machado wrote: "Over the olive grove,/you watched the owl/fly and fly./Fields, fields, fields./Amidst the olives,/the white country houses…" And again, "The grey olive trees/the white roads./The sun has sucked up/the heat of the fields:/and even your memory/is drying out/this soul of dust/of bad days."

Sevillanos will boast that the olive groves you can see from the top of the Giralda tower by the cathedral are those that produce the finest and fattest table olives in the world. You can believe this when you are casually handed a plateful to accompany a glass of chilled *fino*. These have not been beaten from the trees with sticks, but pulled by hand when just ripe in a gentle milking motion. They are further enhanced by being steeped in a dressing containing cumin, oregano, rosemary, thyme, bay leaves, garlic, fennel and a drop of vinegar. The olives are often served together with capers, huge green pods like pickled peppers.

The olive groves do not reach into the city, obviously. But the streets of Seville in spring are heavy with another evocative aroma, that of orange blossom. "Ever since childhood I'd imagined myself walking down a white dusty road through groves of orange trees to a city called Seville," wrote Laurie Lee, who left his native Cotswold village on a romantic quest to Spain at the age of nineteen. "In fact there was no white road, not even a gold-clustered orange tree, but Seville itself was dazzling—a creamy crustation of flower-banked houses fanning out from each bank of the river."

Seville oranges are well known to Britons who may know nothing else about the city. They are the bitter oranges for marmalade, part of the traditional British breakfast. All the many trees that line the streets of Seville (it is surprising that Lee never found one) and whose luscious fruit falls unpicked to the ground and squelches underfoot, are bitter oranges. I supposed they are somewhere cultivated for their fruit—the convent of Santa Paula near the city walls is renowned for its marmalade—but the produce must be mostly exported, since bitter orange marmalade to the British taste is not easy to find in Spain. They say marmalade was invented by accident when the shipper who carried oranges from Valencia to Scotland sealed them in a barrel of rum to preserve them on the journey. Storms shook the cargo into a flavoursome mush that had to be marketed somehow or be thrown

away. Spanish *mermelada* is feeble, sugary stuff to those habituated to the pungent fierceness of what connoisseurs consider real marmalade. I have, however, heard *Andaluces* swear that meat marinaded overnight in bitter orange juice is much improved.

The purpose of these lovely trees in the city is purely decorative. They look beautiful and the waxy creamy five-petalled flower which locals call *azahar*, which blossoms heavily amidst the glistening leaves, smells divine. The *azahar* blooms for just a fortnight in the spring, but so intoxicating and penetrating is the scent that you would swear it impregnates the city all year round. Orange blossom perfume has long been popular for cologne, of which southern Spanish men are very fond. A trail of flowery scent floating down the street behind a neat receding suit, often accompanied by the whiff of fierce black tobacco, evokes Spain for me, and a trace of either instantly recalls the Spain I first visited decades back in the dying days of Franco's rule. In the square outside the Museo de Bellas Artes more recently, I remember the thrill at spotting both orange and lemon trees in the same shady grove, although the two types of citrus are said not to be compatible.

There are thought to be more orange trees in Seville than in any other Spanish city. They not only line Seville's streets and fill its squares, they form an indispensable part of the voluptuous spirit of the place. The timeless tourist posters of simpering gypsy flamenco dancers invariably feature orange trees as a seductive backdrop. The bitter orange was brought to Seville by the Arabs from the Far East via Iraq around the tenth century, to beautify and perfume the patios of the mosques and the gardens filled with other fragrant flowers and trees that Moorish settlers cherished as small pieces of paradise on earth. King Badis of Granada banned the planting of orange trees since they were thought to bring bad luck, and symbolized a sedentary, decadent life, but other Arab rulers in al-Andalus prized them. Badis' grandson allowed them to be cultivated in Granada, a decision many blamed for the fall of the city into the hands of a rival faction. The sweet orange, by contrast, was brought in the sixteenth century by Christian traders from China.

Seville's Patio de Los Naranjos or Orange Tree Patio is, together with the Giralda tower, the only remaining part of the city's main mosque, obliterated in the fifteenth century to make way for the cathedral. This broad enclosed space was where Muslims performed

their rituals of purification. The irrigation channels crisscrossing the patio, and the fountain in the centre, recall its early history, although the fountain is not original. Later the Orange Tree Patio—being within cathedral precincts—became a sanctuary for miscreants, and Spain's first trading floor until the priests ejected the merchants from the temple. These orange trees, however, were a later addition, planted by Christians. The Muslims originally planted cypresses, bay trees and olives. But the concept of the patio—the enclosed inner courtyard between public street and the private house typical of Andalusia—was brought by the Arabs. They loved a fountain playing in the patio to cool the air and soothe the senses. "The Moorish occupation had bequeathed the affection for water around which so many of even the poorest dwellings were built—a thousand miniature patios set with inexhaustible fountains which fell trickling upon ferns and leaves, each a nest of green repeated in endless variation around this theme of domestic oasis," wrote Laurie Lee. "Here the rippling of water replaced the coalfire of the north as a symbol of home and comfort, while its whispering presence, seen through grilles and doorways, gave an impression of perpetual afternoon, each house turning its back on the blazing street outside to lie coiled around its moss-cool centre." The patio and the lemon tree formed for the poet Antonio Machado a precious childhood memory. In his poem "Portrait" he wrote: "My infancy are [sic] memories of a patio in Seville/a bright garden where the lemon tree grows." Throughout his life Machado referred with nostalgia to his lost childhood paradise.

Olives and oranges, along with saffron, almonds, garlic, onion, coriander and chocolate, are deeply embedded not just in the cooking but the entire popular culture of the region around Seville. These pungent and voluptuous scents and flavours cast a powerful spell on the northern visitor. Each flower, fruit and spice has deep historical roots that define them as *Andaluz*. The Romans, the Moors and the Christians all enjoyed, and wrote extensively about, the spiritual, medicinal or nutritional properties of products that still today seem exotic, even enchanting. The historian and commentator Gregorio Marañón attributed the region's celebrated sweetmeats to "the wisdom of the Moors who in addition to their wonderful monuments bequeathed us the art of sweets with their masterly use of almonds, eggs and honey, and on the other hand, the abundance of convents where nuns devoted hours of their time, their fervour and their skill to the confection of those products that seem to anticipate heavenly banquets..." Lope de Vega even defined the Spanish Moors as "people who eat rice, raisins, figs and couscous." The aromas cling to Seville like legends carrying echoes of every stage of its history.

✳ ✳ ✳

The Guadalquivir is sluggish and neglected now, but the sites through which it "trails like a ribbon of watered silk," as Gautier put it, all go towards the making of Seville. Defining the city, however, is a different matter. Antonio Machado's brother Manuel wrote a poem in praise of the provincial capitals of Andalusia, but Seville, he thought, spoke for itself:

> *Cadiz, salt-laden brilliance. Granada,*
> *hidden water that weeps.*
> *Roman and Moorish, silent Córdoba.*
> *Málaga flamenco singer.*
> *Almería, gilded. Silvered, Jaén. Huelva, the shore*
> *of the three caravels.*
> *And Seville.*

The scents of Easter lilies, *azahar*, candle wax and incense fuse to evoke the passionate, sometimes fanatical, Catholicism that fuels Seville's celebration of Holy Week. The event is a heady starting point to experience a city that the poet judged beyond words.

Chapter One
HOLY WEEK, HOLY OFFICE: CHRIST,
VIRGINS AND THE INQUISITION

Nothing prepares you for the magnificence, for the three-dimensional grandeur, of the spectacle of Holy Week in Seville. Hundreds of thousands of *Sevillanos*—the whole city it seems—jam the streets round the clock to express their adoration of their favourite gilded, bejewelled Virgin, or Christ, figure. In this deeply patrician city, where class differences are etched more sharply than anywhere else in Spain, this is the moment when the popular masses claim the streets in an annual explosion of emotion that is part devotion, part fiesta.

The passion with which Sevillians follow mobile altars bearing opulent life-size images around their city is difficult for outsiders to understand. Sceptics see the Easter week celebrations as an outmoded ritual sustained by fanatics and tourism. That perception is strengthened by long processions of caped, hooded penitents, including small children, who parade two by two in their pointed hats, bearing huge candles tilted from the hip.

The theatrical costume of long robes, tall conical cap and the mask covering the face but for two tiny eye holes was adopted by penitents in medieval Europe centuries before extremists in the American Deep South gave it today's sinister association with lynch mobs. It is curious to see the costumed figures hastening through town to their rendezvous. Federico García Lorca wrote in "Procession", one of his poems about Holy Week: "Down the lane come/strange unicorns./From which clearing,/of which mythological forest?/Close up,/they seem like astronomers./Fantastic Merlins..." Perhaps the contemporary echo of Seville's hooded men (only recently have women been admitted as very subordinate bit-players) pumps up the dramatic excitement of this religious street theatre for the Anglo-Saxon visitor.

Sevillians prepare for Semana Santa all year. Each of the countless churches dotted throughout the city has its own brotherhood or *hermandad* that organizes the social life of that parish. Locals confess

19

that the *hermandad* is one of the most powerful social or community bodies in the city. That it far surpasses the labour union, non-governmental organizations, trade or professional group, or other social group of power of influence, that it encompasses and supplants all these and is the only grouping to which ordinary folk feel clan loyalty. It might not beat, but easily matches, the power of birth and connections.

The *hermandad* spends months rehearsing its float's journey through the streets. Members load the mobile platform up with sandbags to match precisely the weight and dimensions of the real thing, play taped music to mark the rhythm and traipse round town perfecting the complicated manoeuvres. You may also glimpse, out of season, the bizarre sight of children "playing at Holy Week," with four youngsters crammed into a tiny cage covered with a cloth and topped with a cross, and the bossy one, often a girl exercising her only chance of authority, barking orders and rapping with a stick.

The *hermandad,* or *cofradía,* governs the life of most Sevillians from birth to death. New-born babes are registered with the *cofradía* before they are inscribed in the obligatory civil registry. This formidable instrument of social control is male-dominated. Women play no part in the power structure; their role is mostly limited to stitching the costumes and serving the men coffee and pastries during their planning meetings. The *cofradía* commands unconditional loyalty and imposes a social cohesion that is difficult to overestimate. You could compare this fusion of local, blood and emotional ties to the passion reserved for a football or baseball team, except that the *cofradías* in Seville interweave far more densely into the city's social fabric to perpetuate clan loyalties and traditional customs down the generations. Even those who love Semana Santa sigh wearily that tradition bears so heavily on the city that any sort of change or progress seems impossible to imagine.

Starting on Palm Sunday, marking Christ's entry to Jerusalem on a donkey, every church in Seville hoists its own images of Christ or the Virgin, and sometimes a scene from the gospels showing a moment of the passion, known as *misterio*, on to an elaborately decorated float or *paso*, which may weigh several tons. The *paso* is both a portable altar and a theatrical stage on which is depicted a lone Christ or a scene from Passiontide. It provides the hypnotic focus for a dramatic, emotion-packed spectacle.

On the dot of the appointed hour the float is carefully eased out of the church door—in a ceremony known as *la salida*—taken through the streets to Seville's cathedral and back to its church—*la recogida*. Processions and bullfights are said to be the only things in Spain to start on time. (Frequent visitors to Seville might be inclined to add the super-punctual high-speed Ave train from Madrid.) Each *paso* is preceded and followed by penitents who form up in hierarchical order with various sections (*tramos*) marked off by those carrying huge and elaborate silver crosses, candle sticks, insignia, silver bugles and other sumptuous regalia. The journey can last hours, sometimes all night until the flaming heat of the following afternoon. Each neighbourhood turns out en masse to support "its" procession or *cofradía*, with everyone dressed up and by tradition wearing new shoes, even though these may become extremely uncomfortable after hours of standing in the street. Locals prepare themselves as if for a gala outing to the opera, which in many respects this unique art form resembles.

Up to ten carefully staggered processions may crisscross the city at once, each with its retinue of penitents and supporters, presenting acute logistical problems that are always solved in a marvel of smoothly synchronized traffic-control rarely replicated in real traffic. For the spectator, the challenge is to hop from procession to procession, slipping through shortcuts, matching places and times so that you catch the highlights of each procession at the best moment, whilst seeking to avoid the impenetrable crowds that can immobilize you for more than an hour. Each procession carries two or three images. First out of the church comes the *Cristo*, then—sometimes—the *misterio* and finally, the big event, the *palio*, the canopied Virgin.

The ritual starts well before each procession sets off, with visitors touring the churches to admire the images draped in their Easter finery and decked with flowers and waxen falderals. Every minute annual addition or modification to the costumes and adornments is observed and commented upon. You carry with you *El Programa*, a detailed daily timetable issued by the city's newspapers complete with map showing where each *cofradía* and its hundreds or thousands of followers will be at every moment throughout the week. Aficionados know the timetable by heart. Sevillian boys absorb a rich knowledge of trivia about the colour of robes and sash, even the number of buttons of each costume of every *cofradía*. Experts steeped in Semana Santa lore since they were in the pram—and you often see tots enveloped in full regalia as miniature penitents being wheeled around in a buggy—consult the programme only to confirm, usually for the benefit of outsiders, the exact moment when they should make their way to see *la salida* or *la recogida*, the crossing of a bridge, or a square, the passage through a narrow alley, of their favourite float.

Baroque Beauty: Jesús del Gran Poder
The finest and most important figures date from the seventeenth century, carved and gilded by the master artists and embroiderers of Spain's Golden Age. The magnificent statue of Jesús del Gran Poder has pride of place behind the altar of the Church of San Lorenzo in a picturesque working-class neighbourhood. The church itself is an undistinguished twentieth-century pile reminiscent of a 1960s conference centre, but the lifelike, life-size, statue of Jesus was created in 1620 by the master carver Juan de Mesa. You can walk behind the figure, protected by a plate of glass except for a small hole cut around the heel, which female worshippers touch or kiss. Their menfolk usually kneel or cross themselves. But the most moving aspect of the sculpture is undoubtedly the face, whose tortured brow, agonized eyes and lips drawn with pain express vividly the suffering of Christ's journey to Golgotha.

The equally fine Jesús de la Pasión, which stands upon a base constructed of 400lb of finely carved silver in the Church of El Salvador, is the work of Mesa's teacher Juan Martínez Montañés, created around 1615. These Christ figures, each burdened with a heavy cross upon the shoulder, are so realistic that when carried through the street, the swaying movement of their flowing robes creates the illusion that the figure is striding towards his crucifixion. Martínez Montañés was born in the Andalusian town of Jaén in 1568, studied his craft in

Starting on Palm Sunday, marking Christ's entry to Jerusalem on a donkey, every church in Seville hoists its own images of Christ or the Virgin, and sometimes a scene from the gospels showing a moment of the passion, known as a *misterio*, on to an elaborately decorated float or *paso*, which may weigh several tons. The *paso* is both a portable altar and a theatrical stage on which is depicted a lone Christ or a scene from Passiontide. It provides the hypnotic focus for a dramatic, emotion-packed spectacle.

On the dot of the appointed hour the float is carefully eased out of the church door—in a ceremony known as *la salida*—taken through the streets to Seville's cathedral and back to its church—*la recogida*. Processions and bullfights are said to be the only things in Spain to start on time. (Frequent visitors to Seville might be inclined to add the super-punctual high-speed Ave train from Madrid.) Each *paso* is preceded and followed by penitents who form up in hierarchical order with various sections (*tramos*) marked off by those carrying huge and elaborate silver crosses, candle sticks, insignia, silver bugles and other sumptuous regalia. The journey can last hours, sometimes all night until the flaming heat of the following afternoon. Each neighbourhood turns out en masse to support "its" procession or *cofradía*, with everyone dressed up and by tradition wearing new shoes, even though these may become extremely uncomfortable after hours of standing in the street. Locals prepare themselves as if for a gala outing to the opera, which in many respects this unique art form resembles.

Up to ten carefully staggered processions may crisscross the city at once, each with its retinue of penitents and supporters, presenting acute logistical problems that are always solved in a marvel of smoothly synchronized traffic-control rarely replicated in real traffic. For the spectator, the challenge is to hop from procession to procession, slipping through shortcuts, matching places and times so that you catch the highlights of each procession at the best moment, whilst seeking to avoid the impenetrable crowds that can immobilize you for more than an hour. Each procession carries two or three images. First out of the church comes the *Cristo*, then—sometimes—the *misterio* and finally, the big event, the *palio*, the canopied Virgin.

The ritual starts well before each procession sets off, with visitors touring the churches to admire the images draped in their Easter finery and decked with flowers and waxen falderals. Every minute annual addition or modification to the costumes and adornments is observed and commented upon. You carry with you *El Programa*, a detailed daily timetable issued by the city's newspapers complete with map showing where each *cofradía* and its hundreds or thousands of followers will be at every moment throughout the week. Aficionados know the timetable by heart. Sevillian boys absorb a rich knowledge of trivia about the colour of robes and sash, even the number of buttons of each costume of every *cofradía*. Experts steeped in Semana Santa lore since they were in the pram—and you often see tots enveloped in full regalia as miniature penitents being wheeled around in a buggy—consult the programme only to confirm, usually for the benefit of outsiders, the exact moment when they should make their way to see *la salida* or *la recogida*, the crossing of a bridge, or a square, the passage through a narrow alley, of their favourite float.

Baroque Beauty: Jesús del Gran Poder

The finest and most important figures date from the seventeenth century, carved and gilded by the master artists and embroiderers of Spain's Golden Age. The magnificent statue of Jesús del Gran Poder has pride of place behind the altar of the Church of San Lorenzo in a picturesque working-class neighbourhood. The church itself is an undistinguished twentieth-century pile reminiscent of a 1960s conference centre, but the lifelike, life-size, statue of Jesus was created in 1620 by the master carver Juan de Mesa. You can walk behind the figure, protected by a plate of glass except for a small hole cut around the heel, which female worshippers touch or kiss. Their menfolk usually kneel or cross themselves. But the most moving aspect of the sculpture is undoubtedly the face, whose tortured brow, agonized eyes and lips drawn with pain express vividly the suffering of Christ's journey to Golgotha.

The equally fine Jesús de la Pasión, which stands upon a base constructed of 400lb of finely carved silver in the Church of El Salvador, is the work of Mesa's teacher Juan Martínez Montañés, created around 1615. These Christ figures, each burdened with a heavy cross upon the shoulder, are so realistic that when carried through the street, the swaying movement of their flowing robes creates the illusion that the figure is striding towards his crucifixion. Martínez Montañés was born in the Andalusian town of Jaén in 1568, studied his craft in

Granada and set up a workshop in Seville in 1587 where he led a productive life until his death in 1649. Montañés was famous for his ability to give human semblance to his sculptures and he became known as the "God of Wood". He founded a school of brilliant pupils, among them Juan de Mesa, born in Córdoba in 1583, who also settled in Seville and died in 1627. The baroque concept of religious imagery was to make the saints and Christ figures real flesh and blood creations, so that people would see them as examples to follow in their own lives. Guided by the Church, the artists' declared aim was to create figures of such beauty and emotional intensity that they would "incite people to pray."

Their images were designed essentially to awe, inspire and indoctrinate an illiterate people. Even the ascetic Englishman Gerald Brenan, who made an Andalusian village south of Granada his home in the 1920s, conceded that Seville's religious artistry "has a power of stirring the emotions and putting the mind into a state of confused exaltation and astonishment." The impact of Spanish baroque was described in similar terms by the art historian Roger Fry: "By the very superfluity and confusion of so much gold and glitter, guessed at through the dim atmosphere, the mind is exalted and spellbound. The spectator is not invited to look and understand, he is asked to be passive and receptive: he is reduced to a hypnoidal condition."

Mesa, Montañés and other sculptors vigorously interpreted the demands of the religious Counterreformation sweeping Europe after the Council of Trent in 1563. The Council recommended that artworks should have a didactic purpose and be clear, simple and readily comprehensible. Art was supposed to appeal to the senses rather than to reason, and to arouse religious fervour in the observer. Seville was at this time unbelievably rich, awash with wealth from gold and silver plundered from the Americas by the Spanish conquistadors. Those riches all passed through the city that was the only point of entry to Spain and Europe for trade with the Indies. In 1503 the Spanish Crown awarded Seville the monopoly of trade with the Americas, which it retained for almost two centuries. Conditions for the flowering of art and culture could not have been better. The city drew wealthy and discerning patrons from throughout Europe, eager to buy or commission religious artworks of high quality. In particular, they sought seductively beautiful three-dimensional images of the scriptures.

Some of Spain's finest painters, including Velázquez, Murillo and Zurbarán worked in Seville at this time, and although they too executed religious works, their paintings never tapped so deeply into popular emotions as did the startlingly lifelike sculptures. Sculptors like Mesa and Montañés, along with carvers, silversmiths and other craftsmen, set up studios in Seville offering apprenticeships to satisfy demand for their work. A thrilling artistic explosion occurred, which produced a sumptuous baroque decorative style whose legacy still infuses every corner of the city. The processional figures of Christ and the Virgin—with their agonized faces and expressive hands—are tangible objects of baroque religious art.

The essence of baroque Christianity, writes Juan Antonio Fernandez Bañuls, was the figurative representation of reality. The aim was to portray religious principles and Catholic dogma with maximum realism, to push the message home in the most powerful way possible. Semana Santa in Seville is the supreme example of how a Spanish popular fiesta has been absorbed and appropriated by the Catholic Church. In those years of warring religious factions, Semana Santa was the perfect way to promote the Counterreformation and combat the perceived heresy of Protestantism. Christians had long carried images of the crucifixion round the streets. But the *paso* assumed its present significance during the sixteenth century, and reached its high point then declined during the seventeenth, a period when master craftsmen were at their peak.

The Catholic hierarchy needed to win over and dazzle their flock with images of Christ's suffering, death and—something of an afterthought in Seville—resurrection. These requirements were met with dazzling effect by the baroque: the superimposition of layers of richness and the adornment of religious figures produced a theatrical sense of enchantment, even ecstasy. The baroque aesthetic defines Seville. In a sophisticated interplay between the real and the apparent, adornment is more important than the adorned. This notion sits comfortably with the doctrine that the natural world is mere illusion. The baroque ideal considered the direct presence of the image of the suffering Christ or the weeping Virgin, with human emotions etched upon the features, to be the most direct and effective didactic tool. The Virgins embodied the Counterreformation ideals of sensual beauty that the baroque developed into an elaborate and powerful illusion of reality.

The Virgin seems to dance; the Christ seems to stride. The illusion can catch your breath on a balmy night in Holy Week.

By 1700 the baroque era had blossomed and died, but the ideal persisted for centuries, long after the social, religious and artistic forces that produced it had fallen into ruin. Lesser artists tried to copy it, but mostly only parodied its emotional excesses, falling short of the brilliance and emotional integrity of the original. They produced instead a sickly religious kitsch that the austere Protestant ethic condemned as typical of overwrought self-indulgent Spanish Catholicism. See, however, the real thing in Seville and you will begin to appreciate its compulsive appeal. Sceptics remain unconvinced, but the beauty and sincerity of Seville's finest pieces of original baroque art are breathtaking and repay the effort of understanding how and why they came about. The impact of the hyper-realist carved figures and faces, and the decorated altars in the churches that house them for the 364 days in the year when they are not borne through the streets, constitute possibly the most emotionally powerful instrument of mass persuasion that Europe ever invented.

The beleaguered Catholic hierarchy, desperate to vanquish the forces of Protestantism in pan-European wars that raged for decades, could have mounted no stronger ideological campaign to win the hearts and minds of the humble masses. But costly wars against Protestant Low Countries and England brought the Spanish economy—so long focused upon Seville—to its knees, and dimmed the city's artistic brilliance. It was Seville that had absorbed the riches of Spain's intercontinental empire, providing the backdrop for a blazing cultural evolution, and Seville that then squandered it all.

Holy Week became the focus of intense ideological confrontation around the time of the Civil War when opposing camps used the Church as a battleground. Intimidation during the years of the Republic in 1932 and 1933 stopped the Holy Week processions, and this persecution of the Church did much to cement the unity of the right. Radical anti-clericalism prompted the burning of images all over working-class Seville just before the nationalist uprising of July 1936. With Franco's victory in 1939, after the Civil War, the management of Holy Week once more became a vehicle for ideology, and its exaltation a symbol of the victor's culture. Following the burnings, a huge and hurried substitution-of-images industry emerged in the years of the dictatorship to produce bland, homogenous replacements for images lost. The process marked a savage downgrading of the former grandeur, and art critics condemned the resultant images as being no better than dolls.

Solemn Processions

Early on Maundy Thursday men encased in dark suits and women wearing what they call "rigorous mourning" throng the city, often having come from far-flung villages to celebrate the high point of the week, which is Good Friday. The women's arresting black ensemble of velvet frock, lace gloves, high-combed mantilla fastened with a diamond clasp and fluttering to the ankles, may include high-heeled patent shoes more suitable for a tango bar than Seville's cobbled lanes.

I met María Luisa and her boyfriend Francisco, in full fig, sipping icy frothy beer and munching fried shrimp on the pavement outside the bar Las Dueñas next to the convent and palace of the same name belonging to the Duchess of Alba, along one of the procession routes. The young people held themselves with that self-conscious hauteur that Andalusians adopt on important occasions, lightened by their irrepressible appetite for having a good time. Francisco had been the day before a *costalero*. The *costaleros* are the invisible heroes of Semana Santa. They crouch beneath the heavy *paso* and bear it on their shoulders through the street. With their distinctive turbans (*costales*) wrapped round padded neck rolls (*morcillas*), they follow the orders of the *capataz* or foreman who raps on the *paso* with a hammer to guide the *costaleros'* steps. The foreman walks ahead throughout its journey, stepping backwards to ensure that the precious cargo does not put a foot wrong. Shouting orders and words of encouragement to the thirty or forty men huddled like galley slaves behind the *paso's* velvet skirts, he ensures that every movement is smooth and co-ordinated so that no corner ever has to bear the full weight. At the end of the long day, his voice is hoarse and his hair and shoulders mottled with molten candle wax and rose petals tossed from windows and balconies along the route.

Sometimes the church doors are low and crenellated, or streets so narrow and twisting that minute, painfully slow shuffles are necessary to make sure that the *paso* does not bump into anything, or that the curlicued canopies do not snag on an outcrop of fretted stonework. The aim is to make the movements imperceptible, as though the *paso* were moving of its own accord. These movements are conducted either in silence, or to the sound of loud drum rolls and trumpet marches, rousing or soothing, interrupted by moments of rest, when the gangs of *costaleros* change shift and wander to the bars for a cigarette and a beer. An atmosphere of tension and high drama builds up, in which onlookers feel themselves both audience and participants in the opera. Particularly elegant or skilful movements of a *paso* whose dimensions are perfectly calibrated to clear by inches the city's narrow streets and wrought-iron balconies are applauded. Knowledgeable habitués nod wisely to each other and comment on the merits of a particular *salida* or *recogida* as if they were assessing a virtuoso ballet solo, a diva's aria, or the pass of a bullfighter's cape.

The *costaleros* are usually sturdy pasty-faced young men said to have originated among the stevedores of Seville's once flourishing docks along the Guadalquivir, a legacy of the city's glory days as a prosperous port and shipyard. Francisco was actually a lawyer, but his experience beneath the heavy *paso* was common to all. He bent to show me the swollen red sore across his neck. "It's another world under there. You are aware only of the ground, the feet in front and the drum's beat. I put my heart into what I'm doing. When we hear the rap of the *capataz* and we hoist up the *paso* I feel as though I'm lifting up God."

La Macarena: Dancing Virgin

In addition to a *paso* bearing the *Cristo*, most *cofradías* also carry an image of the Virgen Dolorosa known as *el palio*, or canopy, which is for Sevillians the more important figure in the procession and always brings up the rear. The Virgin wears a golden crown that radiates out from the head, is enveloped in a long stiff embroidered cape encrusted with gold and jewels, and is surrounded by banked up flowers and heavily carved silver candelabra. In contrast to carved Christ figures, which may hang semi-naked on the cross, the only parts of the Virgin visible are her face and her hands. They express the most profound emotions, often accentuated with the addition of glycerine tears upon the face, and a rosary held between delicate fingers. It is difficult to believe that apart from these visible features, the Virgin is beneath her finery just a framework of sticks.

The most adored versions of the Virgin are La Esperanza Macarena and Nuestra Señora la Esperanza de Triana, each hailing from working-class neighbourhoods on either side of the river. La Macarena—housed in the Macarena basilica by the walls built by the Moors during the occupation—dates from some time in the seventeenth century and is attributed to the sculptress Luisa Roldán, daughter of the master sculptor Pedro Roldán. It was said that only a woman could have produced such a perfect image of female anguish. These two Virgins each make their long journeys throughout Thursday night until well into Good Friday. La Macarena is followed by thousands of penitents, who by the time they are making their homeward journey along the Calle Feria in the hot morning sun are staggering with fatigue, often virtually propped up by solicitous girlfriends plying them with water.

Guided by their foreman, the *costaleros* create the surreal effect of making the *palios* of the Virgins dance. This is perhaps the most breathtaking spectacle of the entire week. The Virgin is by convention sheltered beneath a fringed and swagged canopy (the *palio*) supported by twelve slender silver pillars. The canopy symbolically protects her—the images are always addressed as if they were real persons—and also marks her exalted status. When the drums roll and trumpets wail their sentimental marches, the *costaleros* slowly rock the *palio* from side to side in time with the music, making the supports sway and the fringes and tassels swing, and the Virgin shimmies voluptuously down the street. This is a breathtaking, sensuous movement that has adoring crowds transfixed, as well as critically attentive. They watch to make sure the backside does not wiggle: the float must dance all of a piece. There may be gorgeous changes of pace, even quick steps backwards.

Imagine this scene against the moonlit sky with the warm air drenched in the scent of orange blossom, candle wax, Easter lilies, incense and the occasional waft of Havana cigars. Or crossing a bridge as the sun rises over the Guadalquivir, when the early birds' dawn chorus competes with the trumpets; or negotiating a narrow alley where every sound is magnified as hushed onlookers crane from balconies, hold their breath, cross themselves and toss petals and orange-blossom the length of the street. At certain points along the route, when the heavy cargo is laid to rest for a moment, someone (usually hired for the occasion, but occasionally spontaneously) sings a *saeta*—literally an "arrow"—an improvised flamenco prayer to the Virgin. Then, when the *palio* has passed and the tension subsides, the crowd heads for bars which stay open all night for cups of hot chocolate and sticks of deep-fried batter.

Some processions cast their spell from a distance, like the *chicotá*, which you watch from afar as it slowly climbs a long stretch up the Cuesta de los Bomberos, then turns to cross the bridge, and you see it side on, etched against the night sky. Others are best viewed close up, when in the silence and the candle-lit dark all you see and hear—if flash-cameras do not ruin the atmosphere—is the dry, short rustle of the *costaleros'* footsteps as they shuffle stockinged feet along the cobbles. *Sevillanos* are wonderful in crowds. They wait for hours, endure the crush with a patience and good humour learned from birth, and calmly wait for *la bulla*, as they call the intense conglomerations of people, to disperse.

The Inquisition and the Castle of St. George

It is tempting to trace some of the fervour of Holy Week back to the fanaticism of the Spanish Inquisition, which was founded in Seville in 1481. The "Holy Office" was set up with Rome's approval to resolve the problem of Jews who had been baptized Catholics but who continued secretly to practise their own faith. The Inquisitors also turned their attention to suppressing Protestants, who instigated a revolt in the nearby monastery of San Isidoro del Campo in Santiponce, just north of Seville. The headquarters of the Inquisition were initially in the San Pablo Dominican friary in the centre, now the Church of Magdalena; later the Inquisitors occupied the medieval Castillo de San Jorge, or St. George's Castle, which looms over the riverbank in Triana.

The origins of the castle are obscure, but it is thought to have been built originally to guard the pontoon bridge that was Seville's only means of communication with the fertile Aljarafe region south of the Guadalquivir. The bridge linking the Triana quarter with the main city was established during the Arab occupation of the twelfth century. For centuries the only link between the two halves of the city, the bridge was a precarious swaying platform that rested on barges fastened together by a hefty iron chain, anchored at both ends by pillars sunk into the riverbed. The bridge was often swept away by floods, and hundreds of houses were destroyed each time the Guadalquivir broke its banks. But a fixed bridge was not built until the present Puente de Triana in the mid-nineteenth century.

Seville was the first Spanish city to hold mass Inquisition trials or *autos-da-fe*, events which did much to contribute to Spain's "black legend" notoriety in the Protestant world. St. George's Castle, to judge from numerous contemporary prints, was a beetling pile fortified by walls, a moat, a barbican and ten crenellated look-out towers. Within the castle walls were various courtyards and buildings where the Inquisitors lived, and a chapel of St. George, which gave its name to the adjacent street. The castle also housed secret dungeons and, beneath one of the towers, a torture chamber. The castle was not altogether convenient for the Inquisitors, who complained bitterly about the distance from the centre of the city, the stifling heat to which they were exposed while crossing the riverside Arenal quarter during the summer, and the cold and mud during the winter. When the river swelled, the crossing was hazardous, and sometimes the Inquisitors were cut off. Frequent floods not only left them incommunicado, but inundated the foundations and undermined the walls, which needed constant repair. In 1620, for example, there was a proposal to abandon the castle altogether, turn it into an arsenal, and transfer the courts of the Inquisition to the Alcázar royal palace in the heart of Seville. The Inquisitors wrote to Madrid that the floods were so regular and so great that they were cut off for up to two months at a time, "receiving supplies from boats that came alongside the rooftops." They even had to remove prisoners from the secret dungeons so that they did not drown.

Jews, Protestants and Moors were the main victims of the Inquisition in Seville, followed by blasphemers and bigamists. The office relied greatly on informers, who would report on suspicious evidence of Judaism such as wearing clean shirts or putting on clean bed linen on Saturday, and doing no work on that day. For Muslims, Friday was the telltale day for the sin of wearing clean shirts, as was slitting the throat of birds or animals to eat, or washing their dead and wrapping them in new linen before burial. Lutherans, as Protestants were called, could be spotted by their refusal to confess, or to pray before images or to accept Purgatory, "or their propensity to say that there should be no friars, nuns or monasteries."

The Inquisition also came down hard on so-called *solicitantes*, churchmen who profaned the sacrament of penitence by using the moment of confession as an instrument of seduction. Efforts were made to lift the moral level of a corrupt clergy by preventing the total isolation of the confessor and the penitent, who formerly met face to face. None the less, the figure of the *solicitante*, the priest who made some kind of invitation to his penitent to sin—*ad turpia*, as the texts say—occurs frequently in the Inquisitorial records, nearly always through the accusation of a female penitent. Yet those condemned never appeared in the public trials; the Inquisitors did not want to publicize scandalous behaviour that might cause people to lose respect for the Church. The Inquisitors themselves kept apart and rarely appeared in public. It was part of their image to isolate themselves, and give the impression that they were a different sort of beings.

The legacy of the Inquisition can still be seen in what is left of St. George's Castle, with its high walls and deep vaults. Extensive remains have been spectacularly restored alongside what is now a huge and cheerful fruit and vegetable market, decorated with the bright ceramics for which the Triana neighbourhood is famous. The ancient arched vaults, steps and massive chunks of surviving brickwork lead down to an underground car park. There is no explanation of what we are looking at, what this expanse of blank wall, windowless but for a tiny barred nook near the ceiling, might have been. Instead, just a notice advising you to pay first before attempting to move your car. More atmospherically, the sinister cobbled little Callejón de la Inquisición, Inquisition Alley, descends steeply and narrowly to the riverbank. You can imagine unfortunate heretics being hauled in fetters to be plunged into the castle's dungeons, or being manhandled down to a prison ship to begin a sentence of years as a galley slave. Or, worse still, borne bound, blindfold and facing backwards on a donkey across the swaying bridge to a mass open air trial and thence to the bonfire. The baleful influence of the Inquisition's omnipotent cruelty is said by some writers to account for a supposed coldness in the Sevillian psyche that continues to be much remarked upon: *finos y fríos* was how Miguel de Unamuno characterized the people from the city, in marked contrast to the impression of gregarious, impulsive bonhomie.

The *autos-da-fe* were held in the centre of Seville, the most important ones in the square in front of the Church of San Francisco, headquarters of Seville's Franciscans, whose ornate balconies embedded in baroque plateresque stonework offered civil dignitaries a grandstand view. The first one held here was on 24 September 1559 when nineteen

Lutherans were burned. Until 1549 *autos* were held on the steps of the cathedral. For the *auto-da-fe* of 11 March 1691, four militia companies were sent to accompany the procession from the castle and keep curious onlookers at bay. Black-caped churchmen from Triana's Santa Ana Church—the oldest in the city—led the cortege, carrying a cross draped in black and candle sticks holding unlit yellow candles. Then came the chief of the secret dungeons, penitents wearing the yellow *sambenito* or smock decorated with the asp of St. Andrew, accompanied by their families, followed by heretics with a crown of flames painted on their head to symbolize the fate that awaited them. Behind them came the senior court official with his ministers and the paraphernalia of the trial, the documents, the bells and the writing equipment. A coach carrying the Inquisitors brought up the rear. It took an hour to cross the river and reach the Plaza de San Francisco. The square is spacious, but the popularity of the event was such that spectators would reserve their place the day before and sleep on the street. Everything was carpeted, the records tell us, with a canopy over the throne of crimson velvet with froggings of gold, and in the centre an altar with all the necessary vestments for celebrating Mass. The condemned stood on rough planks, accompanied by the statues of absent convicts, or those condemned after death. Death did not interrupt the trial: the sentence fell upon their "memory and honour", affected their property, which was confiscated, and their descendants. The proceedings lasted hours, often until nightfall, with the lengthy reading of the sentences and trial extracts; officials took turns to relieve each other. Once condemned, the heretics, statues included, were then taken to the bonfire in the Prado de San Sebastián, near what is today the main bus station.

The Inquisition, in addition to purging the populace of Jews, zealously patrolled the coast around the port of Cadiz at the mouth of the Guadalquivir, searching incoming ships to prevent the entry of prohibited books from the Spanish colonies. Inquisitors also suppressed a Protestant insurrection in the nearby monastery of San Isidoro del Campo at Santiponce, a few miles north of Seville near the ancient Roman city of Itálica. This was a traumatic episode remembered with some shame in the city that today stresses its commitment to religious tolerance. Around the 1550s, San Isidoro monastery had become, in the words of the Inquisitors, a "hotbed of Lutheranism". Two Jeronymite friars, Casiodoro de Reina and Cipriano de Varela, became the community's spiritual leaders and enjoyed the support of a number of secular figures who sought to impose the doctrines of the Reformation in the city of Seville. The Inquisition launched its full wrath upon the two renegades and subjected them to an *auto-da-fe* in 1559. The prior of the monastery was burned at the stake, but the two monks were among several who fled abroad. The two went to Geneva, then Basle, where in 1569 they published the first Spanish-language Bible, known as the Bible of the Bear (*Biblia del Oso*) after the symbol of the monastery printed on the flyleaf. Casiodoro translated the work directly from Hebrew, Aramaic and Greek, and Cipriano revised the text. This is the version that remains the most widely read Spanish-language book in the world. It sells three million copies a year, outstripping even *Don Quijote*.

In November 2002, in a gesture of support for freedom of expression and religious tolerance, the latest edition of the Bible of the Bear was presented in the monastery that had generated it. It was a work "for which those in former times were put to death," Seville's culture secretary, Maria Isabel Montano, admitted. The occasion was celebrated with a cantata by Bach—"a committed Lutheran", as the monastery's authorities acknowledged. The monastery's statue of San Jerónimo is one of the finest works by the sculptor Montañés.

Perhaps the Inquisition was itself product of a city steeped from earliest times in religious fervour and extremism, where rival faiths clashed and superimposed themselves in extravagant demonstrations of victory in a political power struggle. Arabs seized the city from Christians and built a mosque. When the Christian King Fernando reconquered the city he simply placed the world's biggest cathedral in the mosque's Orange Tree courtyard, and appropriated its minaret as the Giralda, topped with a Renaissance weathervane.

La Macarena: Ojeda the Modernizer

Semana Santa seems timeless, but the truth is that it declined and languished for two centuries after the baroque Golden Age—heyday of the Inquisition at its most vengeful—ended around 1700. Enthusiasm for processions slackened in the eighteenth century, inhibited partly by restrictive sumptuary laws introduced by King Carlos III in accordance with austere tastes associated with the Enlightenment, even though these curbs on luxury and show were only half-heartedly observed. Then the ravages of the Peninsular Wars against Napoleon's invading troops in the early 1800s, followed by the dispossession of many Church properties in the 1830s, sapped the brotherhoods of disposable riches and damped down the wilder extravagances of Holy Week's glory days.

Not until the late nineteenth century did the festival revive, boosted by an upturn in prosperity and the astute awareness by local grandees that the spectacle could be a big attraction for increasing numbers of foreign travellers, especially northern Romantic visitors with deep purses who started to flock to this exotic corner of southern Europe, as a fashionable addition to the Grand Tour. By the 1870s the ostentatious display of public luxury was back in vogue. The overwrought artistic merits of the baroque were rediscovered and old treasures dusted off. New artists emerged to create new images in the baroque style, the originals were smartened up with elaborate new decorations, and the impression was confected that Semana Santa had continued unchanged since the Golden Age that produced it. The week-long celebration was subtly transformed from a fairly humble fiesta designed to impress and subdue the common folk into the sophisticated tourist attraction and self-conscious expression of the city's identity that it is today.

Among those responsible for the late nineteenth-century revival of Semana Santa was the master embroiderer Juan Manuel Rodríguez Ojeda, a flamboyant figure who, despite humble origins, loved tailor-made suits, never went without a hat and was passionately attached to the traditions and fiestas of his city. A member of the *cofradía* of La Macarena, Ojeda virtually reinvented the image of Esperanza de la Macarena, creating for her the impressive gilded head-dress inspired by paintings of saints and the Virgin by the city's Golden Age masters Velázquez and Murillo. Treated with some disrespect for his homosexuality and his exaggerated manners, Ojeda pioneered the art of "dressing the Virgin", a curious preoccupation with embroidery, elaborate cloths, jewels and female accessories that grips many Sevillian men. This exotic enthusiasm was influenced by the arts and crafts movement of the British progressive idealists William Morris and John Ruskin. Their flowing, decorative designs emphasized the spiritual values of natural forms and artisanal skills in contrast to the supposedly unnatural materialism of a mechanized industrial age.

Embroiderers' workshops revived, copying Morris-inspired designs of vigorous, free-flowing plant forms, bolstered by a late Romantic spiritual style of Christianity. In the early 1900s, Ojeda remodelled the Macarena and its *palio* into today's multi-layered, some would say grotesquely overloaded, decorative extravaganza. He introduced a wardrobe of velvet capes and gilded fringes, jewelled crowns and the proliferation of carved candelabra, waxen flowers and other artefacts piled in front of the Virgin. The extra weight of all this decoration slowed down the *paso's* movements and accentuated its languorous swing.

Ojeda also, in a gesture that some city fathers considered an extravagance too far, dressed La Macarena in full mourning for the procession of 1920 to mark the death, aged 25, of the city's best loved bullfighter, Joselito el Gallo, who, along with many important bull-breeding families, had contributed generously to Ojeda's improvements. *Sevillanos* applauded the theatrical gesture, and thought it entirely appropriate to their twin passions for their matador and their Virgin.

The Church of the Macarena sits by the most complete surviving stretch of the Arab walls that once surrounded the city, beside a high and handsome 1940s arch called the Macarena Arch. Holy Week's organizational triumph reaches its highest point with the procession of the Virgin of the Macarena. She leaves the church at midnight as Maundy Thursday moves into Good Friday, this moment marking the climax of the whole week. This all-night session is known as La

Madrugá, which is how locals pronounce *madrugada*, the hours before dawn. She makes a thirteen-hour journey to the cathedral and back, returning at 1pm precisely on Good Friday. During that time she, thousands of penitents and an escort of young men wearing fake armour to represent Roman legionaries, snake through the city, seeking to avoid at least five other processions heading in the same direction. Towards Friday midday the procession straggles its way through the narrow streets of the poor neighbourhood, en route for its 1pm rendezvous at the church.

A curious and unsolved mystery occurred in 2000 when an unprecedented panic gripped the hundreds of thousands in the streets before dawn on Good Friday. People claimed afterwards to have heard gunshots, or seen men advancing on them with knives. The panic started simultaneously at several points at about 5.30am. Crowds swarmed screaming down alleyways and broke into shops to cower under counters. *Costaleros* dumped their precious cargo and fled, *nazarenos* ran for their lives, hoisting up their long skirts. Afterwards there was talk of mischievous provocation copied from a recent film about a role-playing game going amok in Semana Santa, but the mayor blamed foreigners who did not understand how to behave in Holy Week crowds. What people thought were shots were later believed to have been the sound of the folding chairs which lined the route snapping shut. The chaos lasted for more than half an hour, and scores were injured. The outburst was a one-off. Remarkably, given the crush and people's exalted emotions, the event is almost always peaceful.

Virgen Dolorosa: Immaculate Conception

For painters, the most frequently demanded image in seventeenth-century Seville was the Immaculate Conception, reflecting the belief that the Virgin Mary had been conceived without original sin. Seville was the focus of Catholicism's cult of the Virgin Mary, a dogma stressing her role in the redemption of humanity. Apparently a Dominican friar in the early seventeenth century rashly declared in a sermon that the Virgin Mary had been "conceived like you and me and Martin Luther." Jesuits turned upon him, poets defended her purity in verse, the brotherhoods took a "blood vow" and the populace went on the rampage, with Sevillians charging round the streets crying "Conceived without original sin!"

The "Marian War" was waged with zealous fanaticism by the Virgin's supporters: jobs and pulpits were denied those who did not fervently uphold her divine conception. Artists produced a tidal wave of paintings of the Virgin. Finally, in 1617, the Papal Bull arrived in Seville defending the conceptionist view, and locals surged into the streets to celebrate with fireworks and bullfights. Further celebrations occurred in 1661 when the Pope decreed a special holiday in her honour and in 1700 when 8 December was made the Day of the Virgin—to this day one of Spain's most important religious festivals. In 1761, when she was proclaimed patron of Spain and the Indies, festivities lasted a year and a half. And in 1854 the Pope declared the Immaculate Conception to be a doctrine revealed by God. Little wonder that Seville is a city full of graven images of the Virgin, and that she, rather than the figure of Christ, is the star of the show.

For many younger, more sceptical Sevillians, the emotional intensity of the whole business is ultimately stifling: "Seville is so self-absorbed and complacent that all this theatrical display is a block on any kind of change or innovation. It's frustrating, suffocating. Mind you, I wouldn't live anywhere else," says Marcelo del Pozo, a young photographer, in a typical combination of exasperation and adoration that Sevillians feel for their home city. The city's historian Rafael Sánchez Mantero has said something similar about what happened after Seville's brief and glorious flowering during the sixteenth-century Golden Age: "The decline was rapid and irreversible and Seville—which dominated the Atlantic for two centuries—became just another city within the Kingdom. The cosmopolitanism of the Golden Age was to give way to old-fashioned provincialism, more concerned with lamenting its glorious past than building a future."

Seville continues to bask like a salamander in its glory, and the visitor risks being charmed into an intellectual trance, hypnotized and immobilized by a seductive power that soaks through every aspect of Sevillian art, literature and culture.

Chapter Two

CONQUEST AND SLAVERY: LAS CASAS AND CERVANTES

The Church of Santa María de la Magdalena dominates the corner of Calles San Pablo and Calvario, in the heart of old Seville. The main entrance is set back from the road, giving a fine view of the austere frontage, and there are even benches so you can admire the building from beneath the shade of tall plane trees. But the side street, Calvario, is narrow and hemmed in by high walls, and you must tip your head back to view the cream and ochre arched bell towers and watch the bells turn and turn in deafening peals.

This used to be the site of the thirteenth-century Dominican friary of San Pablo, home to a remarkable local priest who sailed with the conquistadors but turned against them to become the first and fiercest critic of Spanish colonialism in America. A plaque on the church wall explains: "In this former Dominican convent of San Pablo on 30 March 1544 the Sevillian Friar Bartolomé de Las Casas, Protector of the Indians of the New World, was consecrated Bishop of Chiapas." The spot—and the man—symbolize the intertwined history of this port city and the sea-borne empire it launched, the new world of the Americas which generated for the city and the Spanish Crown undreamed-of wealth and power. The Mexican region of Chiapas was, and remains, populated by a majority of indigenous Maya people who resisted the conquering Spaniards and their descendants. The plaque adds a further detail: "May 1966. Fourth centenary of the death of this Spaniard of America."

Fray Bartolomé wrote a passionate denunciation of the acts of genocidal cruelty inflicted upon indigenous Americans in the reckless pursuit of gold. His *Short Account of the Destruction of the Indies* of 1542 was banned by the Inquisition—not because it was untrue, but because it "said cruel and fierce things about Spanish soldiers." The Sevillian priest's reportage is still a blistering read more than 460 years on, and makes him one of the world's first human rights campaigners. He once refused to administer last rites to a colonial landowner until the dying man agreed to free his indigenous slaves.

The old friary was also where the Inquisition carried out its trials and executions. Little of it survives, but for a small chapel whose wooden cupola is decorated by carvings echoing the geometric shapes of an even earlier place of worship, a Moorish mosque. Today's Magdalena church was built in 1697 and is decorated inside with fabulously ornate baroque frescos, paintings, gilded wooden carvings and stucco flourishes. But there is a nod to the older, more austere friary. A fresco on a side wall shows a *trompe-l'oeil* arcaded passage off the nave receding into the distance. Guarding the apparent entrance to this long vaulted passage, so realistic that it tempts you to walk smack into the wall, is the life-size figure of a robed friar. He is standing to the side, reading a book. Perhaps he is meant to be Las Casas, or one of the Dominican brothers who have kept his memory alive down the centuries.

A handful of friars gathered here one evening in October 2002 to set Bartolomé de Las Casas on the road to sainthood. "Fray Bartolomé was a prophet of our times, sensitive to the injustices and marginalization of the downtrodden," said Padre Herminio de Paz Castano, of Seville's Dominican community, which had requested canonization two years previously. "His ideas are utterly timely. The problems of racism and the marginalization of immigrants turn up on our doorstep every day."

Lure of the Americas
Bartolomé's father, Pedro de Las Casas, was a baker whose bakery was on the corner of what are today Calles Rivero and Cuna in the central quarter of El Salvador. In 1493 Pedro left his wife and four small children to seek his fortune in the new land that the ambitious Genoese Christopher Columbus had "discovered". He joined Columbus' second voyage to Hispaniola, fired with enthusiasm for adventure. Las Casas *padre* had heard that roofs were tiled with gold, that precious spices grew by the roadside and that—as locals said at the time—dogs were leashed with strings of sausages. The legends of America were still bound up with fantasies about the Far East, which the voyagers initially thought they had reached by the western sea route, hence the historical confusion reflected in the words Indies and Indians. Bartolomé, the

eldest son, was nine, and had three younger sisters. But his father Pedro found gold to be scarce, and did not become rich. He returned home in 1499, having learned that the reality fell short of the promise, but with stories and memories of an exotic world filled with unknown plants and animals, brilliant birds and exquisite masks and belts encrusted with gold and jewels created by local people.

Doubtless inspired, when Bartolomé was eighteen and had acquired some elementary clerical qualifications, he too signed up for an expedition in 1502 that landed on the Caribbean island of Hispaniola (now Haiti and the Dominican Republic) where Columbus had first made landfall ten years before. Las Casas and his comrades searched for gold, but made only a modest living. The governor of the island, Nicolás de Ovando, with whom he had voyaged, declared the young man an *encomendero*, and granted him land and a hundred "Indios".

In the great novel *Don Quijote*, which was conceived, if not written, while the author was in prison in Seville, Miguel de Cervantes brilliantly satirized the character of Governor of an Island, perhaps reflecting the empty pretensions of many of the men who attained such titles. In Cervantes' novel, the rough squire Sancho Panza demands, and is promised, the governorship of an island in return for his loyalty to Don Quijote. Sancho is tempted to continue with his master's ludicrous and often painful adventures only by the assurance that he will one day be given an island to rule. Eventually he is duped in an elaborate ruse cooked up by a duke and duchess into believing he has actually been appointed governor and starts to act as if he is one. The satire is perfected by the fact that the unlettered but shrewd peasant displays a rare wisdom as governor. But Sancho wearies of excruciating protocol and painful battles against staged invaders, so saddles up his old donkey and prepares to go home. "Now make way gents and let me go back to my old freedom," he says to his supposed hangers-on:

> *Let me go and look for my past life, so that it can deliver me from this present death. I wasn't born to be governor or defend islands or cities from the enemies that choose to attack them. I know more about ploughing and digging, about pruning and layering vines, than about making laws or defending provinces or kingdoms. St Peter's all right in Rome—in other words each man's all right doing the job*

he was born for. It suits me better to have a reaper's sickle than a governor's sceptre in my hand. I'd rather guzzle my bread-and-meat soup than be in the clutches of a mean and meddling medical man who starves me to death, and I'd sooner be in the shadow of an evergreen oak in the summer and snuggle up inside a nice thick sheepskin coat in the winter and be free, than be tied down by being governor and lie between sheets of holland and dress up in savoury fur. Goodbye to you all, then, and tell my master the Duke that naked I was born, and naked I remain, so neither lose nor gain—in other words I hadn't got a penny when I was made governor and I haven't got a penny now I'm stopping being one, very different from governors of other islands.

Bartolomé returned home to visit his sisters and remained some months in Seville, where he entered the service of Bartolomé Colón, brother of Christopher Columbus. He then went with him to Italy, where Las Casas was ordained into the priesthood in 1507. He sailed again for America in 1512, this time as chaplain for the expedition that was to conquer Cuba. So far, then, so typical of the career of an ambitious young priest destined to use the protection of the Church to enrich himself in a conquered colony. But in 1514, aged thirty, Las Casas witnessed a savage massacre of indigenous Americans and the martyrdom of their leader. The experience changed his life. He renounced his land and his serfs, declaring the *encomienda* system of forced labour "a mortal pestilence that daily consumes these people". He decided to devote the rest of his life to defending them.

In his account he rails with passion and eloquence against the horrors he has witnessed. "I have seen with my own eyes these gentle, peaceful people subjected to the most inhuman cruelties that have ever been committed by generations of cruel and barbaric men, and for no other reason than insatiable greed, the hunger and thirst for gold on the part of our own people."

Las Casas was not the first to side with the local people. Some Dominican friars had already condemned the cruel treatment, especially one Friar Antonio Montesinos who in a sermon on Advent Sunday in the church of Santo Domingo in 1511 denounced before the island's authorities the slaughter of "Indios" by their *encomenderos*, their own masters. Those who were supposed to protect them worked them instead to death in the mines and the fields. In a tirade that has gone down in history Fr. Antonio threatened those who thus scorned Christ's teaching with the fires of hell. "By what right and with what justice do you keep these poor Indios in such cruel and horrible servitude? By what authority have you waged such detestable wars against these people who lived peacefully and gently on their own lands? Are these not men? Do they not have rational souls? Are you not obliged to love them as yourselves?"

Perhaps as a result of such denunciations, Spain's Catholic monarchs Fernando and Isabella, and later the powerful Indies Council—a sort of Spanish Ministry of America answerable to the Crown—introduced some humanitarian laws and reforms. But laws passed in Spain had no effect in the conquered lands of the New World. The law was "respected but not implemented," the *encomenderos* said, using a cynical formula that to this day describes Spain's bureaucratic resistance to unpopular reforms.

From the first moment of the conquest, however, doubts were raised among some clerics over whether Spain had a right to the lands of the New World. Their seizure was justified by the obligation to extend Christian religion and culture among pagans. Even Las Casas never challenged the legitimacy of Spanish rule in the Americas, convinced that the natives had, albeit in ignorance, voluntarily surrendered their sovereignty to the Spanish Crown.

Fired with the zeal of his conversion, Las Casas returned once more to Spain and in 1515 by his own account harangued the ageing King Fernando at length about the loss, destruction and greed that he had seen. "He informed the king of the perdition of these lands and violent death of their native inhabitants and the manner in which the Spaniards in their greed slew them, and how all died without having been baptized or having received the Sacraments and if, in brief, His Highness did not remedy the situation everything would become as a desert."

But Fernando, for whom the Americas were distant distraction from the more immediate threat facing Spain from enemies within Europe, referred the matter to the president of the Council of the Indies, Juan Rodríguez de Fonseca, Bishop of Burgos. When Las Casas informed the bishop that seven thousand children in Cuba had been killed in three months, the cleric replied, "And how does that concern me?"

When King Fernando died in 1516, Las Casas had to repeat his allegations to Cardinal Francisco Ximénez de Cisneros, the fanatical warrior priest and Grand Inquisitor who became Prince Regent on the death of the king. Cisneros sent three Jeronymite friars across the Atlantic to investigate Las Casas' allegations. They reported that the local people were a bunch of lazy malcontents whom the *encomenderos* treated better than they deserved. The three envoys are presumed to have been bribed by the *encomenderos* and their friends at court. Las Casas renewed his campaign with King Carlos V, and aroused the hostility of those at court who had enriched themselves in the Spanish colonies and who began to discredit him. He even tried to found peaceful settlements in northern Venezuela and in Guatemala, but the experiments collapsed amidst violence provoked by saboteurs, and irrevocably soured race relations.

Las Casas entered the Dominican order in 1522, and wrote his *Short Account* in 1542 as a passionate plea to King Carlos to right the wrongs perpetrated in his name. "I have time and again met Spanish laymen who have been so struck by the natural goodness that shines through these people that they frequently be heard to exclaim: 'These would be the most blessed people on earth if only they were given the chance to convert to Christianity.' He continues:

> It was upon these gentle lambs, imbued by the Creator with all the qualities we have mentioned, that from the very first day they clapped eyes on them the Spanish fell like ravening wolves upon the fold, or like tigers and savage lions who have not eaten meat for days. The pattern established at the outset has remained unchanged to this day, and the Spaniards still do nothing save tear the natives to shreds, murder them and inflict upon them untold misery, suffering and distress, tormenting, harrying and persecuting them mercilessly.

Las Casas describes what he calls "some of the many ingenious methods of torture they have invented and refined for this purpose." The reason for the murder of millions by Christians "is purely and simply greed", he writes. "They have set out to line their pockets with gold and to amass private fortunes so that they can then assume a status quite at odds with that into which they were born. Their insatiable greed and overweening ambition know no bounds; the land is fertile

and rich, the inhabitants simple, forbearing and submissive. The Spaniards have shown not the slightest consideration for these people, treating them (and I speak from first hand experience, having been there from the outset) not as brute animals—indeed, I would to God they had done and had shown them the consideration they afford their animals—so much as piles of dung in the middle of the road."

The *Short Account* was published in Seville in 1552 and swiftly translated into French, English, Dutch, German and Latin. The rapidity with which the account spread across Europe helped fuel a fierce propaganda campaign against Spain that came to be known as the "black legend". This was "a distorted Protestant-inspired record of Spanish atrocities and cruelties that was to darken every attempt to exonerate Spanish imperial ventures from the sixteenth to the eighteenth centuries," says the historian Anthony Pagden, in his introduction to a recent English-language edition of Las Casas' work. That edition is illustrated by gruesome engravings by the distinguished Flemish engraver Theodor De Bry which accompanied the sixteenth-century Dutch edition. They show horrors such as women and children being savaged by dogs, or being dismembered and roasted over a grill, or hung dozens at a time from gibbets over a fire, as if indeed they were less than animals.

Humans or Animals?

In 1548, between the completion of his report and its wider publication, Las Casas became embroiled in a curious theological debate over whether American Indians were human beings. A chaplain and chronicler to Carlos V, Juan Ginés de Sepúlveda, wrote a savage attack on native Americans whom he described as "homunculi in whom hardly a vestige of humanity remains. [They were]... like pigs with their eyes always fixed on the ground." They were brutish, uncultured, cowardly, cannibalistic and pagan, Sepúlveda wrote, insisting that God therefore intended them to be slaves to masters of "magnanimity, temperance, humanity and religion", i.e. the Spaniards.

The text was condemned as inflammatory by two prominent theologians who happened to be Dominicans and acquaintances of Las Casas, as well as by a jurist. Sepúlveda assumed that Las Casas was behind the condemnation, and complained to the Council of the Indies, which in August 1550 organized a "debate" between the two men. It was a curious encounter, because Las Casas had not read Sepúlveda's text "The Just Causes of the War against the Indians", but only a summary, and on no occasion did the two contenders actually meet. Each man read his objections to a panel of clerics. Las Casas read for days on end a rambling document that rebutted everything Sepúlveda ever wrote. The following April, Sepúlveda countered with twelve replies, to which Las Casas replied with twelve objections to the replies. And that was it. The clerics continued to regard Sepúlveda's text as subversive, and the Council of the Indies took no further action.

Inconclusive in other respects, the debate marked Las Casas' last significant clash with opponents at court and perhaps prompted him to publish the *Short Account* the following year. One of his central objections was that Sepúlveda maliciously distorted the nature of a society he had never visited. He had relied on the biased reports of a slaver and *encomendero* who was, in Las Casas' view, "a cruel enemy of the Indians". Hence the urgency with which the *Short Account* tries to press upon the reader the immediacy of the writer's experience and the honest integrity of his intentions.

But saintly though today's Dominicans consider their brother, Las Casas committed a serious lapse of judgement, which he was to regret for the rest of his life. At one point, while attempting to persuade

Carlos V to allow native Americans a voice in the governance of Spanish America, he suggested that supposedly more resilient black slaves be brought from Africa to substitute native Americans in heavier labour. Las Casas subsequently became aware that this proposal blew apart his own argument that America's native peoples were just as human as their European tormentors: nor did he ever try to explain why a "negro" was any less a child of God than an "Indio". The slip allowed opponents to accuse him of being a racist and an apologist for slavery. The export to America of slaves from Africa, meanwhile, developed into one of the most lucrative and sinister trades in imperial history, producing an underclass in Spanish America's stratified society even more oppressed than the continent's indigenous people.

There was much polemic, especially in the US, and particularly around the 500th anniversary of Columbus' landfall in 1992, about the over-heroic interpretation of the Admiral's achievement in the New World. Modern critics, echoing Las Casas, pointed out that the entire adventure of the "Discovery" was motivated by greed and Columbus' urgent need to repay the Spanish monarchs for the confidence, and the resources, they had given him. On one occasion, in 1495, Columbus is said to have resorted to importing to Spain a shipload of 1,200 Taino Indians from Hispaniola in his eagerness to convince the Catholic monarchs of the value of his discoveries. He suggested they be sold as slaves in Seville. Hundreds died en route and were tossed into the Atlantic.

The episode was recounted, somewhat shamefacedly, in the 1827 biography of Christopher Columbus by the American Romantic traveller and writer Washington Irving, who excused the action on the grounds that slave trading was already common practice. "It is repugnant to see the brilliant renown of Columbus sullied by such an ugly action, and the clear glory of his efforts darkened with a violation so flagrant of the rights of humanity," Irving wrote:

The customs of those times are the only justification. The Spaniards and the Portuguese had already long established the precedent in their African discoveries: slave trading was one of the richest sources of their profits. The highest authority, the church itself, sanctioned this practice; and the most learned theologians pronounced that all barbarous and infidel nations that closed their eyes to the truths of

Christianity were proper objects of war and pillage, captivity and slavery.

King Fernando himself had paraded captives in his war against the Moorish kingdom of Granada through the streets and sold them as slaves, Irving claimed. "These circumstances don't vindicate, but do palliate Columbus's conduct. He was working in conformity with the customs of his time, and the example of the sovereign he served sanctioned his actions."

As it happens, the Taino Indians adapted so badly to life and labour in Spain that some efforts were made to repatriate those who survived the twin ordeal of the voyage and of servitude.

Slavery on the Cathedral Steps

Seville was the port through which captive Africans were introduced into Spain, and from the fifteenth century the city became one of the main centres in Europe for the import and re-export of slaves. The human traffic was controlled by the Portuguese through their African colonies, and Portugal and Spain between them controlled the world's slave trade for centuries. Slaves from West Africa were shipped over to Seville from Lisbon. The debate over whether they were fully human persisted in the commercial language of the traffic, which referred to their human African commodities as "pieces". Apart from the chains the captives had to bear and the branding they endured, the particular humiliation that caused most unrest among slaves was that they were treated like animals and called "dogs". A seventeenth-century historian recounts the tale of Diego, a *morisco* (a Spanish Muslim of North African origin) slave to the priest of Seville's San Salvador Church. One day as Diego was measuring grain, the priest said to him "Measure it well, dog!" Diego in response turned on his master and killed him with a blow on the head with his scraper, for which crime he was hung, drawn and quartered.

Slaves were sold in a makeshift market set up on the steps of Seville's cathedral, and were housed in lodgings round about until the day of the sale. If they died in the meantime they were buried beneath the houses, or in outlying neighbourhoods, flung higgledy-piggledy into pits without coffin or shroud. We know this because archaeologists have found skeletons of Africans beneath streets near the cathedral. Moorish or Berber slaves from North Africa were common in Seville. The slave trade with Portugal flourished until halted by the outbreak of war between the Iberian neighbours in 1640. By then, slavery was entrenched in Seville and throughout Andalusia, where nobles, clerics, traders, professionals—even some artisans—had at least one slave. Many were freed in old age after spending all their life with a family, when they became more of a burden than a help to their masters. Others were freed out of gratitude from masters who had grown to appreciate them, or were granted freedom in their master's will. Still others were able to save up and buy their freedom. Freed slaves or *libertos* often married across racial barriers—despite fierce objections from the local religious authorities who were obsessed with *limpieza de sangre* or "clean bloodlines"—which gradually produced racial integration. But even freed, former slaves could never fully shake off their humble origins, even though some became slave owners themselves.

"Black Sevillians" no longer exist today, but throughout the Golden Age and the establishment of the American colonial empire, the separation between black and white was sharply delineated, making sixteenth-century Seville less a melting pot than "a chessboard", according to the expression of the time. Most slaves, and black free men and women, carried out domestic work or other service tasks; but others were set to hard labour in agriculture, loading and unloading, mining and the manufacture of soap. Black slaves, however, were considered favourably by the ecclesiastical authorities of the time, because their supposed "innocence" made them susceptible to Christian conversion—unlike Jews and Moors. Some even became clerics.

Sexual relations between races, "carnal intermingling" as it was called, was none the less condemned, both between slaves and non-slaves, and between free people. It is hardly surprising, therefore, that studies of eighteenth-century Andalusia show that those of West African origin often died childless. A very small minority of slaves were permitted to marry; many slave women were victim of their masters' sexual desires, and had to hand over their offspring to orphanages. Even so, genuine mixed-race love affairs were inevitable. Eighteenth-century records show that up to a third of babies handed into the orphanage were of mixed race.

One mid-eighteenth-century account of a priest's love for his *mulata* (mixed race) slave girl illustrates the outraged disapproval that such partnerships provoked. Pedro Morano Carrasco, from a village near Seville, lived openly with his slave Andrea for years, until a judge from the Archbishopric of Seville told them to separate "because of the great scandal caused in the neighbourhood" and ordered her to keep at least five leagues distance from him. They were denounced by neighbours who said the priest "behaved carnally with the said Andrea his slave." One day a witness saw that "said Pedro Morano taking a siesta and said Andrea his slave lying down in the same bed as the above-mentioned." Another witness testified that "every time she entered as a neighbour into the house of said Pedro Morano, she saw that the above-mentioned said to the said Andrea his slave 'what would you like, child?' bringing her and putting in front of her things that she requested while seated, and he putting the pot in front of her and sitting her down to eat." They had a daughter, who was neither sent to the orphanage nor hidden, as custom demanded. On the contrary, according to another witness: "The said Pedro Morano carries in his arms the little girl of the said slave and he loves her so much that he lets it be known she is his daughter, carrying her in his arms to the church for evening prayers, and around the neighbourhood, which has caused a serious scandal in the town." A priest who flaunted in the streets his daughter by his *mulata* slave girl clearly offered all the elements of behaviour that the Church hierarchy condemned as a breach of social and moral order.

A criminal case was opened in Seville in 1745 against a married woman who "constantly slept with different men of all classes" since her husband had left "because he could not support her [i.e. financially]." Her family and neighbours complained to the Archbishop's court that "she even slept with a negro slave... who had taken her virginity before she married." She also had relations with a Moorish slave "who never wanted to become a Christian." One witness "saw the said Moor seated on the lap of the above-mentioned while she combed his hair." In many cases the man in question was jailed or banished, the woman sent to a convent, and the offspring sent to an orphanage. This happened to a young woman Manuela Chacon who became friendly with Juan Fermin, "a negro dressed in rags with signs of branding on his face who is said to be a cook in a convent," according to the neighbour who denounced them. Manuela said they wanted to marry, and her mother had nothing against him. But the ecclesiastical court banished Juan from the city and ordered Manuela into a closed convent under guard, and ordered the child she was carrying to be put into an orphanage indefinitely. Seville's religious authorities created orphans, concludes Alessandro Stella, author of a study that turned up these examples of interracial affection.

The Royal Jail: Cervantes in Seville

In Cervantes' story *El celoso extremeño* (The Jealous Extremaduran, 1613), the author describes how the rich old man Filipo uses slaves to help protect his house in Seville against potential predators who might steal or corrupt his young wife Leonora. "At the street entrance which is called the 'house door' in Seville, he had a stable built for a mule, and above it a straw loft and a room for the man who was to be in charge of it, who was an old Negro eunuch." Filipo bought, in addition, "four white slave girls, whom he branded on the face, as well as two newly-imported Negro women." Cervantes describes the black slave women as *bozales*—which meant they had not yet learned Spanish, a derogatory term that came to signify something like "savage." Slaves were branded with an S on one cheek and a nail (*clavo*) on the other, whence apparently comes the Spanish word for slave, *esclavo*. The first Spanish language dictionary, that of Sebastian Covarrubias in 1611 and a later dictionary of 1732 suggest that the word *esclavo* derives "from the brand that was put on fugitives and rebels on both cheeks, that of the S and the nail."

Filipo was an "indiano", a Spaniard who had made his fortune in the Indies, i.e. the Caribbean, and would have been familiar with the slave market. In describing this character, Cervantes sketches what he says is a common fate of enterprising young men come down in the world:

> *After much wandering, his parents having died and his inheritance spent, he came to live in the great city of Seville, where he found plenty of opportunity to get through the little that he had left. So, seeing himself so short of money, and with few friends left, he had recourse to the solution to which many ruined people of that city are driven, namely that of going to the Indies, the refuge and shelter of all desperate folk in Spain, the sanctuary of bankrupts, the safe-conduct of murderers, the protection and cover of those gamblers*

known by the experts in the craft as sharpers, the general decoy for loose women, where many go to be deceived, and few find a way out of their difficulties. In short… embarking at Cadiz and saying good-bye to Spain, he set off with the fleet.

Filipo returns rich, and procures himself the young bride whom he obsessively protects.

In an even more dramatic evocation of Spanish slavery in its heyday, Cervantes in *Don Quijote* puts into the shape of the squire Sancho Panza the perfect caricature of the greedy and cynical slave trader. Sancho is persuaded in an elaborate ruse that a refined lady is the dispossessed princess of the African kingdom of Micomicona who seeks Don Quijote's aid in recovering it. Sancho urges his master Don Quijote to marry her and become king.

[Sancho] was only worried by the thought that this kingdom was in the land of negroes and that all the people he was going to be given as vassals would be black, but his imagination soon worked out a good solution, as he said to himself:

"Who cares if my vassals are negroes? All I'll have to do is ship them over here to Spain, sell them for hard cash, buy myself a title or some official position or other, and live at my ease for the rest of my days. Oh yes, I'm going to be caught napping, I am, and I won't have the wit or the savvy to see to things and sell thirty or ten thousand vassals in the twinkling of an eye, I won't! By God I'll shift them, as a job lot or however I can, and they can be as black as they like, I'll soon turn them into yellow gold and white silver! Come on, come on, I'm an innocent little thumbsucker I am!"

Cervantes was writing around 1604, at the height of Spain's slaving boom. The writer and former soldier had himself been captured into slavery in Algiers in 1575 and remained enslaved for five years. He made four attempts to escape, and was freed only following the painful efforts of his parents to scrape together a ransom. Cervantes returned to Madrid in 1580, aged 33, unknown, unpublished and impoverished. He even wrote to the king asking for a position in the Indies, an ambition that persisted for several years. But his request was turned down in a crushing letter of rejection that reads: *Busque por acá en qué se le haga merced* ("look around for something that suits you over here"). This discouraging document is conserved in Seville's Indies Archive. In 1587 he moved to Seville and obtained the ill-paid position of royal commissioner for supplies. For five years he crisscrossed Andalusia with the disagreeable duty of requisitioning from reluctant villagers oil and grain to supply the galleons of the royal naval fleet, the Armada which King Felipe II was preparing for his ill-fated expedition to invade England.

Cervantes was imprisoned at least twice in Seville's Royal Jail, accused of selling the requisitioned produce without permission, then finding himself unable to pay sums he owed because the bank where he had deposited the cash collapsed. He was jailed in 1592, 1597 and possibly 1602 or 1603. He then rejoined his family in Valladolid and never, to our knowledge, returned to Seville. One fanciful account by the local historian Antonio Cascales of the day that Cervantes walked free from jail, describes him leaving what is today a regional savings bank on Calle Sierpes, near the Town Hall. In this version of events, Cervantes, just freed, steps into the narrow alley of Entrecarceles (Between Prisons) which used to separate the Royal Jail from the even more sinister prison attached to the Church of San Francisco for those who fell foul of the Inquisition. Cascales has Cervantes clutching beneath his arm the precious manuscript of what was to become the first and most famous novel in the world. A plaque on the bank occupying the site of the former jail records the supposition that Cervantes' stay there inspired him to write *Don Quijote.* "Here he engendered for the amazement and delight of the world the ingenious nobleman Don Quijote de la Mancha," the inscription says.

There is no evidence that Cervantes wrote *Don Quijote* in jail, but equally none that he did not. "It is not impossible that there he heard the stories that moved him to write the novel. But that cannot have been the most propitious spot for literary creation," notes the Sevillian writer and novelist Antonio Burgos in his quirky *Guía secreta de Sevilla* (Secret Guide to Seville, 1991). Burgos then quotes a description of the prison made by the historian Alonso de Morgado in 1587: "The number of men that are held captive in the Royal Jail rarely drops below five hundred, and often rises to a thousand or fifteen hundred. Nearly all are free of fetters, for that is the custom of the Seville jail. But to see the rabble of so many prisoners, so disgusting, in rags, or naked, their stink, tumult and bawling appears nothing other than a true representation of hell on earth."

Once freed, Cervantes completed his masterwork in 1604, and published a collection of tales of Sevillian low life—his *Novelas exemplares* (Exemplary Stories)—nine years later. Cascales' engaging fictional account, which is based on the snippets of historical fact available, tracks Cervantes through the old streets of Seville to the lodging house of his friend Tomás de Gutiérrez in Calle Bayona in the Arenal district, near the port. Gutiérrez "asked him in a low voice, almost a flutelike warble, if he had written any play," Cascales writes.

The criminal looked under his arm as if searching for swallows in his armpits and seemed to discover there, at that moment, what he had held pressed beneath his entire arm since he set foot in the street, something that had accompanied him through leagues and leagues of requisitioning grain and enduring curses and stonings across the Andalusian countryside, a rectangular bundle which the criminal called scornfully his prophecy, although such a parcel did not hold money, nor half a slice of buttered bread for the road, but a bundle of paper, cut and trimmed, with its covers of Córdoban leather, bound together with a thick clasp, and containing a horn inkwell with a screw top, two goose quills, a penknife, all secured with six fine leather thongs, which had the same colour and appearance as the criminal's skin, the same smell of remote illnesses and riotous nights, the same lean hide, scored with miseries and stewed in lengthy heroic fevers.

Cervantes, in Cascales' account, takes a further turn about the city, ending up in the convent of Santiago de la Espada or de los Caballeros, where he thanks an aged prior for having sent him food in jail, and—even more precious to the prisoner—paper, pen and ink. In payment, he hands over to the old man a sheaf of pages "where the criminal had put down some reflections created in jail, on a past golden age of justice, which he hoped to include in the text of an unusual work that had been growing within him for some time." The story concludes with an extract from *Don Quijote*, in which the Sad Knight delivers a lyrical lament for lost age of innocence. Cervantes in his novel deprecates the knight's discourse as "a long harangue that could well have been dispensed with" and "useless arguments" intended to explain to a bunch of bemused goatherds why the hero of the tale has become a knight errant. The rough countrymen understand nothing, but they treat their eccentric guest kindly, and even administer an effective herbal remedy to the old man's ear, which had been injured in a battle with a Basque.

✳ ✳ ✳

The slave trade began to decline after 1640, and until 1800 there was a constant scarcity of "pieces", which accordingly became more expensive. Slavery survived in Spain until as late as 1886 and lingered still longer in the colonies. But blacks of African origin began to die out from the mid-nineteenth century. Today there is almost no trace of Seville's former racial "chessboard", except in the name of the Cofradía de Los Negritos—the colloquial name for the Brotherhood of the Virgin of the Angels, which still makes its procession through the streets of the city on the afternoon of every Good Friday. But Los Negritos have since 1888 been dominated by whites, without a black face to be seen.

By the year 1660, the works of the two writers whose lives were marked by Seville were enjoying contradictory fortunes: Cervantes' novel *Don Quijote* was heading for immortality, while Las Casas' *Short Account* was banned by the Inquisition. The "black legend" that Las Casas' reportage is said to have created by publicizing the cruelty of the Spanish empire was at its most vehement. Now, centuries on, the report is a classic work of polemic and reference. And the Vatican is being asked to repent its censorship of a man revered by his supporters, and to make the friar a saint. Canonization is long overdue, a fellow Dominican in Seville, Fr. Herminio, believes: "He's our brother, a free spirit who achieved glory."

Chapter Three
LA CARTUJA: FROM COLUMBUS TO CALATRAVA

When Spain's high-speed train, the Ave—an acronym that spells bird—glided from Madrid to Seville for the first time in 1992 in under three hours, the journey opened the way to the island of La Cartuja, the heart of the international exhibition of Expo 92.

The socialist government of the time, which happened to be led by Sevillians, probably knew in their hearts that it would have been more logical to build a high-speed link between Madrid and Barcelona, Spain's second city and the gateway to Europe. But when, more than a decade later, the Ave finally did advance towards Barcelona, they defended their original decision to make Seville the priority. If the Ave had gone first to Barcelona, the socialists argued, Andalusia would never have been connected to the fast track. Barcelona would inevitably get the Ave sooner or later, they explained, and Expo 92 was the perfect opportunity to connect an impoverished and remote corner of Spain with the national and international mainstream. Built to coincide with the Expo, the rail link had a branch line to shuttle visitors directly into the exhibition site. That plan was ephemeral: La Cartuja Island station lies abandoned and windblown, like many of the Expo's more extravagant conceits. But the Ave turned the international spotlight upon Seville with an intensity barely matched since the year Columbus set sail five centuries earlier.

Expo 92 was designed to celebrate the 500th anniversary of Columbus' landfall in the Americas. Commemorations of the "Year of Discovery" took place worldwide, especially in North and South America, and often with some acrimony. Seville, for its part, planned to seize the opportunity to revive an unprepossessing flood plain between two branches of the Guadalquivir on the city's north-western fringes, and integrate an unexploited area into a dynamic project of urban renaissance. Expectations of the Expo were enormous and encouraged to the maximum by a gung-ho government in Madrid, and it is hardly

surprising that the reality fell short of the hype. But the Ave survived and thrived as a popular, elegant and profitable means of transport that passengers overwhelmingly prefer to the plane. Seville's San Pablo airport, also built to coincide with the Expo, is still far too large for the limited traffic it handles. The Ave, by contrast, with its handsome Santa Justa station, built on a scale and with a brio befitting Paris or New York, immeasurably boosted the pride and self-confidence of the people of Seville, who are not anyway noted for their self-effacing modesty.

Another clear winner from the Expo is one small corner of the historic site that the authorities sought to reinvigorate. The island of La Cartuja covers a 1,100-acre stretch of sandy flats between the Guadalquivir and a sluggish offshoot, known as the San Jeronimo Meander. La Cartuja owes its name to a fifteenth-century Carthusian monastery later occupied by a British pottery firm in the nineteenth century. The spot represents centuries of Sevillian splendour, which by the 1980s seemed in terminal decline.

For centuries, potters from the Triana neighbourhood on the west bank of the coiling Guadalquivir headed up river to the silt-rich, swampy lands facing Seville, in search of clay. Triana is still the potters' quarter, the place to visit for traditional Sevillian ceramics whose rounded shapes and bright colours bear Roman and Moorish influences. Pots, tiles and ceramic fountains are laid out in cheerful warehouse-like shops lining the streets along the river bank, especially in the Calle Alfarería, Potters' Street. Kilns were established around here in perhaps the twelfth century—when the Moroccan warrior sect, the Almohads, ruled Andalusia—because of the high quality of the clay and its abundance. One day the potters said they saw a vision of the Virgin. It is supposed that the apparition occurred in one of the cavities gouged out for clay, giving rise to the name of the Virgin of the Caves. A magnificent painting of La Virgen de las Cuevas by Francisco de Zurbarán (1598-1664), celebrating the moment of the apparition, once hung in the monastery and is today one of the most important works in the city's Fine Arts Museum. The painting shows the protective figure of the Virgin extending her cloak and her arms over a host of kneeling white-robed friars, whose faces are suffused with tranquillity and adoration. Her hands rest on the heads of two of them. A Franciscan hermitage was built to mark the spot where the apparition occurred, and in 1399, the Archbishop of Seville, Don Gonzalo de

Mena, assigned more land to the site and founded the Carthusian monastery or La Cartuja.

The chapel of Santa Ana, just inside the entrance of the monastery grounds to the right, is a tall, vaulted, creamy building, lit by sun streaming through windows high in the cupola. Around about are baskets piled high with oranges and lemons grown in the vast orchard that the monks planted. This rustic detail adds to the feeling of peaceful enclosure. La Cartuja has suffered triumphs and crises down the centuries, and has been the focus of some of the most important moments in the history of Spain. Its low-lying riverside situation made it subject to annual floods, mosquitoes and damp air generally, and even today it remains rather an effort to get to. But La Cartuja symbolizes both ancient—pre-imperial—Seville and its most pressing avant-garde.

Christopher Columbus was a regular visitor. He spent time at La Cartuja preparing his second voyage to America in 1493, seeking refuge, some said, from the rivalries and intrigues threatening to sabotage his efforts. He worked away in the monastery's libraries and lodged in its vaults his most important personal documents and possessions, including his will, for safekeeping. Many of those precious objects are now held in the Columbine Library in the cathedral or in other archives of the city. After Columbus' death his bones lay there, together with those of his brother Diego, for almost thirty years, between 1509 and 1537. They were protected inside a lead box placed in the crypt down a small flight of steep steps set in the marble floor of the chapel. Outside, palm trees and billowing bougainvillea dot the area, giving it a languid, tropical air, and in the shade of a great spreading *ombú*, said to have been brought back by Diego from the third voyage to America, there is a statue of Columbus. The statue was put there by the "Marquesa, widow of Pickman" in 1888, according to the inscription in the classic blue-and-white tiles adopted by the English ceramicist who took over the monastery.

Painters and Art Thieves

The Carthusian Monastery of Santa María de las Cuevas, to give its full title, later offered spiritual comfort to Felipe II in the late sixteenth century and was a port of call for every Spanish monarch who passed through Seville. Important artworks by masters including Dürer, Montañés, Mesa, Murillo, Cano, Zurbarán and Pedro Roldán were held in the monastery, which evolved as a walled mini-city. It enclosed spacious gardens and orchards, and included handsome pavilions, retreats and look-outs. The monastery is particularly associated with Zurbarán. Son of a tradesman near Badajoz in Extremadura, he became apprenticed to the painter Pedro Diaz de Villanueva in Seville at 16, when the city was at its most artistically creative. He is considered inferior to his contemporaries Diego de Velázquez and Alonso Cano in handling perspective, and grouping figures. But his strength was in his realistic portrayal of objects like pots, and hair and skin tones, and intense and penetrating facial expressions. Some of Zurbarán's finest works, including *St. Hugo in the Refectory of the Carthusians*, also known as *The Miracle of St. Hugo*, painted in 1645-55, once hung here. The painting shows a tranquil, detailed scene of the monks' daily life, as they give thanks before an austere meal in the refectory. It represents the miracle carried out by the eleventh-century St. Hugo, founder of the order, who on a visit to a monastery found the monks eating meat, which was forbidden, so turned it into ashes. This painting, too, is on show at the Museo de Bellas Artes, one of the many art treasures taken before the monastery was dispossessed and sold. Zurbarán's paintings symbolized three of the most important Carthusian virtues: love of the Virgin, obedience and silence are represented respectively by *The Virgin of the Caves, St. Hugo*, and another important work, *St. Bruno before Pope Urban II*.

The monastery still exudes an air of protected, walled-in contemplation painfully recovered after the two centuries of hurly-burly that all but destroyed it. In particular, the arched and turreted Moorish *mirador*, or look-out, set amid the geometrically planted citrus and pomegranate orchards and olive groves, offers the best view in the whole city of the cathedral and the Giralda across the river. It is a timeless, almost medieval experience. Nearby is the Merendero, a little brick-built pavilion topped by an English-style weathercock, where monks could receive women visitors, who were barred from setting foot in the monastery buildings.

In 1810 Napoleon's troops who had invaded Spain seized the monastery and installed themselves there, building fortifications to defend the site. The soldiers, under the command of Maréchal Soult— who is still detested in Seville for the artworks he plundered—threw out the monks and took over their sacred chapels, halls and courtyards, using them as a barracks for his southern military command. Soult also established his personal headquarters in the Archbishop's Palace near the cathedral in the heart of the city. Armed with an authoritative guide to Spanish art, the *Historic Dictionary of the Most Illustrious Masters of Fine Art in Spain*, compiled by Juan Agustín Cean Bermúdez in 1800, Soult systematically sacked Seville of its finest treasures. "With Cean in his hand, he scoured the city looking for the names of artists mentioned in the dictionary, and everything cited by Cean he took. It was rape and pillage, but of a very discriminating and sophisticated kind," said Ignacio Cano Rivero, director of Seville's Museo de Bellas Artes. From the moment Soult arrived in February 1810 until his departure in 1812, he took his pick and stored his booty in the Archbishop's Palace. When he travelled through Madrid in March 1813 on his way back to France, the marshal was accompanied by a "caravan of carriages laden with paintings, Andaluz for the most part," wrote the historian of Spain's exiled art, Juan Antonio Gaya Nuño. Soult did not forget to strip the Archbishop's Palace itself. After the war ended, the author of one of the city's most comprehensive guides, José Amador de los Ríos, wrote sadly: "When at the beginning of this century the armies of Napoleon invaded Andalusia and took possession of Seville, Marshal Soult chose for his lodgings this building [i.e. the palace] and many of the excellent works that enriched it, both paintings and sculptures, disappeared." A large number of these works re-emerged in Paris when Soult died in 1852 and his vast collection went on sale. Some works catalogued in that sale disappeared without trace, but others, including a set of paintings by Valdés Leal celebrating the life of St Ambrose and commissioned for the Palace oratory, reappeared in the 1980s and 1990s. They were bought by the Prado Museum in Madrid and the Seville's Museo de Bellas Artes.

The French invaders who took over La Cartuja monastery even used the long high gabled refectory, depicted with such refinement and veneration by Zurbarán, for target practice. Bullet holes are still clearly visible in the carved wooden rafters. The monks fled to Portugal, returning only after Napoleon's defeat in 1812. But their repossession was brief. In 1836 they were expelled for good when a reforming government in Madrid dispossessed churches and monasteries throughout Spain. The abandoned monastery was bought in 1839 by Charles Pickman, a London pottery entrepreneur, who set the old site on a new road to prosperity.

Mr. Pickman the Potter

Pickman's family, originally pottery exporters from the English port of Liverpool, had close links with Andalusia. Charles' brother William opened a business importing foreign—that is, mainly English—pottery and glass into Seville and Cadiz in 1810. Charles inherited the firm when his brother died in 1822 and decided to expand the business by setting up his own pottery. When the monasteries were dispossessed, he looked to buy a vacant religious property, and settled on La Cartuja because of the abundance of water.

In 1841 Pickman produced his first trial kiln of pots, thus reviving the ancient tradition established by the Triana potters. He followed the style of English potteries like Wedgwood, Chelsea and Minton, which were already appreciated by Spain's rising middle class. So it was that the colourful, chunky pots produced in Triana for common use, whose rounded forms and bold, elaborate patterns can be traced back to Roman and Moorish traditions, came to coexist with fine dining sets, soup tureens and gravy boats, and tea services in the English style printed with hunting scenes and oriental gardens. Pickman's venture was encouraged by the authorities, eager to develop manufacturing in Spain. They much preferred that he boost local industry by making pots in Seville rather than importing them from abroad. Sevillians revered him for introducing the modern ideas and assembly-line production practices of the industrial revolution into a hidebound, somnolent and overwhelmingly agricultural society.

At first, the new owner tried to respect the buildings' original features as he put up huge brick kilns, chimneys and lodgings for the factory and its workforce, modelled on England's Staffordshire potteries. He brought 56 specialist master potters from England to train the young men and women from Triana, who, he was pleased to discover, were quick to learn and reached a high technical level. Between 400 and 500 workers were employed at a time, using modern techniques of mechanized and line production. In 1895 some 1,200 workers were employed, up to 400 of them women. A few years later a narrow gauge railway track linked up all the workshops with little trucks that trundled through all parts of the factory.

The walls by one entrance are covered with a stunning giant sampler of tiles. Further round, the main delivery entrance carries the pretty ceramic sign "1841, Pickman Sociedad Anónima", and is topped by a blue and white urn that looks like a teapot. Another entrance faces the river and has a road leading down to what used to be the company's landing stage, where boats loaded up the goods for shipment and brought in supplies. Above the entrance a sign says "La Cartuja. Factory of Ceramic Products" in black and white Triana tiles, all harmoniously in tune with the monastery's baroque style. But as Pickman's production increased, the giant funnel-shaped chimney stacks—known as "bottles"—and kilns bound by steel bands marched across the site, dwarfing, sometimes actually occupying, the original buildings. Many of these, including monks' cells, had to be destroyed to make room for the new industrial production. The cloisters, the church's nave, the refectory, the sacristy, the stables and the grain stores were taken over for making clay, and designing, painting, printing, glazing, gilding, storing, exhibiting and packing pots. Pickman built additional factory buildings, and lived on the site in a house he built around the prior's cell. His aim was to keep a close watch on the work, and also to enjoy the lovely orchards and flower beds of the old monastery garden, which he restored, including the elaborate irrigation system of geometrically arranged channels governed by little locks and dams.

Five of the giant "bottles" remain, soaring amidst the cypress trees and echoing their form. Topped with delicate blue and cream tiles, they give the ancient site a distinctive and dramatic skyline that can be seen for miles. Pickman continued to turn out pots—of "First Class Dinner Ware of Modern English Style" according to an advertising print I found in an antiques stall—until 1982, when the factory, which continues production to this day, moved to a suburb on the road to nearby Santiponce. My print is dated 1928, which marks just about the end of the company's years of splendour beginning around 1867. It illustrates the many international medals Pickman won, in London, Vienna, Paris and Philadelphia, and shows the Guadalquivir alongside the factory busy with vessels bringing in materials and being loaded up with produce for shipment. The factory supplied pots to rich houses and poor hostels throughout Spain.

In 1871 Charles Pickman was designated as provider of pots to the Spanish royal household. He was made a marquis in 1877 and died in 1883. His establishment became renowned and is celebrated in a local nineteenth-century couplet that has the unlikely refrain *Mi Novio es Cartujano*: "My sweetheart is a Carthusian,/painter of pots,/who paints washstands/a pretty pink." Today a footbridge, the Pasarela de La Cartuja, connects the factory to the city, partly fulfilling the Expo's ambition to bind together two ancient parts of Seville long divided by the meandering river.

In 1986 the Andalusian regional government took charge of the dilapidated cluster of buildings and started to restore them. They sought to reclaim La Cartuja's roller-coaster history and celebrate its incongruous evolution from monastery through barracks to factory. The restored site was to be the focal point of Expo 92. To crown the renovation effort, planners installed a modern art gallery, the Centro Andaluz de Arte Contemporáneo, and built within the ancient walled precincts the Expo's Fifteenth-Century Pavilion, a less successful enterprise. The pavilion, like many of the ephemeral structures built for the Expo, is now derelict, surrounded by dead trees shrivelled in their fallen pots, the cracked concrete of the courtyard choked with tumbling weeds, the odd whisky bottle tossed over the wall. Even when it was first built, the Fifteenth-Century Pavilion was little more than a flimsy pastiche, a grotesque attempt to recreate a 500-year-old building amidst the battered but still dignified remains of the real thing.

The 1929 Expo and Romantic Park

Seville had once before undergone the experience of planning and mounting an international exhibition, the Hispano-American Exhibition of 1929. This was a bold attempt to restore confidence and international prestige after the disaster of 1898 when Spain lost the Philippines, Puerto Rico and Cuba, the last of its colonies. That humiliating defeat at the hands of the United States marked the culmination of Spain's prolonged imperial decline that had begun more than 200 years earlier. The purpose of the 1929 exhibition was to re-launch Seville as a bridge across the Atlantic, to renew and reaffirm its historic connection with the New World. This was a theme that neatly dovetailed 63 years later with the "Discovery" motif of Expo 92. Seville had been chosen in 1910 for its first international exhibition after a close contest with the northern industrial port of Bilbao, which was also enjoying a golden age of prosperity, and the event was planned for 1914.

A Centre of Americanist Studies was founded in 1911 based in the Indies Archive and producing its own bulletin, and a Hispano-

American university was proposed. The First World War put everything on hold, but some of the urban reforms were set in train, and buildings representing the three great periods of Sevillian art—the Islamic, the Renaissance and the baroque—started to go up in and around the Parque María Luisa to the south of the city. Among them was the ornate Mudéjar Pavilion, with its triple-arched entry portal flanked by towers, but its inauguration was inauspicious. It was immediately used as an emergency hospital to tend the wounded of the disaster at Annual, a Moroccan battle of 1921 that marked the end of Spanish dominion over the Maghreb region of North Africa.

The Hispano-American Exhibition finally went ahead in 1929, only to coincide with the world financial crash, which dealt it a terrible blow. The city struggled throughout the depressed 1930s to pay off the debts. None the less, the effort achieved the lasting success of folding an untended stretch of land into the fabric of the city. New urban vistas were laid out, and important new buildings raised, in particular the opulent Hotel Alfonso XIII, designed to house the illustrious international visitors to the great event in palatial luxury. The most extravagant remnant of this effort to impress is the Plaza de España, a semicircular space 600 feet wide, complete with lagoon and four bridges representing each of the four ancient Spanish kingdoms. The whole square is flanked by the two enormous brick towers that formed the Spanish Pavilion. This was the site for the inauguration ceremony. More than fifty ceramic benches along the long curve illustrate every province of Spain with maps and historical scenes, exuding a colourful *joie de vivre* that invites the visitor to stroll and admire. At the side of each bench are little niches that once held books relating to each province. The area is particularly romantic at night.

The venture marked a final flourish of Miguel Primo de Rivera's dying dictatorship and reflected a society in decomposition. Conceived before the First World War, developed during the prosperous twenties—in Spain they call them "the happy twenties"—the 1929 exhibition was enthusiastically promoted by Primo de Rivera, who was from Jerez and sought to boost his home region. But it was a failure. One commentator singled out the Exhibition's Casino (now the Teatro Lope de Vega) as "a faithful reflection of an epoch that stretched from the end of the 1898 war (known in Spain as El Desastre) and the economic collapse of 1929." Sir Peter Chalmers-Mitchell, a former secretary of the London Zoological Society, passed through Seville shortly after the exhibition closed and went to look at the "deserted and faded glory of the unsuccessful Great Exhibition." He reflected: "Few things are more tragic than tattered splendour, whether it be of bright dresses or of painted pavilions." Another critic cynically remarked in 1930 that "the only creatures who ate as a result of the Exhibition were the pigeons in the Plaza de América." The white doves in the square at the southern limit of the park are still a great attraction, especially for children who can buy bags of feed for them.

During the Second Republic, declared in 1931, grumbles mounted about the debts that had accumulated, and it was even proposed to celebrate a new "Republican" exhibition that would avoid committing the mistakes of the original. Debate was extinguished by the outbreak of the Civil War in 1936. Giménez Fernández, the man described by the Sevillian-based national newspaper *ABC* as the "critical conscience" of the exhibition, summed it up thus: "A marvellous garden, expensive to maintain, and a collection of buildings as beautiful as they are useless, many of them badly constructed… The exhibition was a failure, but in spite of that the fundamental riches of the city have been increased."

The densely wooded, jungle-like Parque María Luisa is one of the most successful legacies of the 1929 Exhibition. It originally formed private gardens donated to the city by the Infanta María Luisa Fernanda of Orléans in the nineteenth century. The space was remodelled for the 1929 Expo and houses most of its buildings. Pavilions of some of the twenty participating countries that remain, most of them very handsome indeed, have been gradually converted into consulates or university annexes. They are wonderful in their playful, outlandish variety: the tiny box covered with blue and white Maya motifs, from Guatemala, and—at the other end of the scale—the bizarre eclecticism of the Peruvian pavilion, a massive building whose details—woodwork, ironwork, stonework—are a unique specimen of Inca Art Deco.

The 100 acres of park running along the riverside form a leafy oasis in a hot and densely urban city, and contain gardens inspired by Muslim, Italian, French and Andalusian traditions. It is a bit of a step to walk around, especially in high summer—although this part of town is noticeably cooler than the built-up centre—and you might not want to venture too far alone. But a horse-drawn carriage hired by the steps of the cathedral—perhaps the last remaining vestige of what was Seville's focus for trade of all kinds—is the perfect way of exploring the area, and in keeping with its romantic traditions. And, fortunately, one of the park's most important cultural landmarks is near the entrance.

Gustavo Adolfo Bécquer: Lovelorn Poet

The sentimental monument to the Sevillian poet Bécquer is probably better known today through being reproduced on tourist literature than is his work itself, although he is judged to have been Spain's leading nineteenth-century poet. The monument in his honour encircles a tall water cypress planted in 1870, the year Bécquer died at the age of 34, and is a glorification of the poet and a meditation on love. A striking group of three women in long frilly frocks bear expressions of wistfulness, rapture and sadness, which indicate respectively Hopeful Love, Consummated Love and Lost Love. Further round the circular structure is the sombre figure of Bécquer himself set high on a pedestal, with two allegorical bronze figures at his feet: of wounded love, and love that wounds. The monument, enclosed by a protective wrought-iron balustrade, is hailed as one of Spain's most outstanding public memorials, although its creator, the sculptor Lorenzo Coulart Varela, is barely remembered. Sheltered by tall ancient trees, the monument is sweetly, perhaps over-sweetly, melancholic, which befits a poet who was unhappy in love, disastrously married, and often ill and poor.

Bécquer, born in 1836, published almost nothing in his short life, and might have been forgotten but for the dedication of a handful of admirers who published a posthumous edition of a single, slender collection of poems, *Las Rimas*. Written with the directness and succinctness of traditional Andalusian folk *coplas* or couplets, *Las Rimas* became the most popular volume of Spanish verse until García Lorca published his *Romancero gitano* (Gypsy Ballads) in 1928.

Bécquer's works have been recently re-issued in popular paperback editions, an event that the critic Rafael Fernández Bermejo hailed as "offering a panorama of an author sarcastic, bold and, above all, still relevant." Fernández Bermejo wrote in *Babelia*, the cultural supplement of *El País* newspaper: "Bécquer knew the bitterness of love, lived it intensely day by day and recounted it without age or epoch. Hence his work remains imperishable… it transmits enthusiasm and emotion with a simple style that encompasses feelings of despair and eternal youth."

Here are three translated examples. "I didn't even know in those terrible hours/what I was thinking or what happened to me/I only remember that I wept and cursed,/and that that night I aged." (*Rima* XLIII)

"But oh! From a heart I reached the abyss/and I leaned over a moment,/and my soul and my eyes seized up:/so deep it was and so black!" (*Rima* XLVII)

"Awake I tremble to glance at you;/sleeping I dare to watch you;/so, soul of my soul, /I'll watch while you sleep." (*Rima* XXVII)

A descendant of Dutch nobles who had settled in Seville in the sixteenth century, Bécquer was orphaned at nine and taken in by his godmother, in whose library the young boy became inspired by English, French and especially German Romantic writers. He was educated, briefly, at the distinguished Nautical College in the San Telmo Palace opposite the Parque Maria Luisa. The building, built between 1628 and 1734, is considered one of Seville's finest baroque palaces, though purists argue that while the façade is unadulterated baroque, the building itself is rather neoclassical. It was created to train Spain's first pilots and navigators. The college insisted that its pupils be "orphans, poor and of noble birth", and aimed to teach them "the manners of well educated people, the formulas for greetings and conversations, how to behave with superiors, inferiors and equals, showing smooth sweetness to everyone, modesty and circumspection, prudence in speaking and keeping silent, cleanliness in eating and dressing." Bécquer benefited only two years from this useful education before the school closed in 1848 and the Duke of Montpensier bought the palace. The building later became a seminary, which it remains. Twelve statues of famous Sevillians, including Velázquez and Murillo, Mañara and Las Casas were sculpted by the Sevillian artist Antonio Susillo and installed on the roof of the north façade in 1895.

Bécquer started off as a painter—the profession of his father, uncle and brother—and his decision to take up poetry shocked his godmother who reputedly complained: "The English will always buy Andalusian scenes, but who will buy verses?" He left his native Seville aged 18 to try his luck as a writer in Madrid. He never saw his works published in his lifetime, managing only to sell newspaper articles and

adaptations of plays and light opera under a pseudonym. His poems about love, especially frustrated love, are abstract and elusive. But they capture Seville's ambivalent mood, mingling sweetness and sensuality, laced with sadness. *Las Rimas* suggest that the poet is struggling with the wreckage of own life and trying to express intangible human experiences and suffering. Up to a few years ago, a guard at the site of the monument in the park would hand a copy for anyone to read on request. In addition to writing poems, Bécquer also contributed articles between 1858 and 1864 to the conservative Madrid newspaper *El Contemporáneo* and other magazines.

One of his stories, or "legends", *La venta de los gatos* (Cats' Inn) conveys the sense of the yearning, some might say self-indulgent melancholy, typical of his work. It is a tragic tale set in a modest spot in a street across the river from La Cartuja which still bears the story's name. The *venta*, or tavern lodging house, a low stone hovel, according to a grainy photo in Burgos' *Guía secreta*, survived until the 1970s. The story begins:

> *In Seville, midway along the road towards the San Jerónimo convent from the Puerta de la Macarena, there is, among other well-known little taverns, one which, because of the place it occupies and the special circumstances that occurred there, could be said to have been, if it is no longer, the most characteristic of all Andalusian taverns.*

The author encounters an idyllic scene amidst the olive groves, the ancient monastery and the river's languid current:

> *Imagine this landscape animated by a multitude of figures, of men, women, urchins and animals, forming groups ever more picturesque and typical; here the innkeeper, plump and rosy, sitting in the sun on a low chair, pulling apart in his hands the tobacco to roll his cigarette and with the paper in his mouth; there an aficionado of the Virgin of the Macarena, who sings with his eyes upturned, accompanying himself on the guitar while others keep time by clapping their hands or striking the table with their glasses; further on a group of young girls with their gauzy kerchiefs of a thousand colours, an entire flowerpot of carnations in their hair, playing the tambourine, and shrieking and laughing as they push madly at a swing slung between*

two trees, and the inn boys who come and go with trays of manzanilla and plates of olives... the oil that boils and spits in the pan that is frying fish; the crack of the coachmen's whips as they arrive raising a cloud of dust; sounds of songs, castanets, laughter, voices, whistles and guitars, and thumps on the table, clapping, and the crash of wine jugs breaking, and thousands of strange and discordant noises that form a happy clamour impossible to describe. Imagine all this in a mild and gentle afternoon of one of those most beautiful days of Andalusia, and you will have some idea of the spectacle before me...

The narrator discovers a story of young love between the innkeeper's son and Amparo, a girl the family had adopted from an orphanage as a baby. The pair were to marry and tend a market garden that the boy's father planned to give them. The son tells the author of his hopes for happiness as he accompanies him back to town at nightfall. The narrator leaves Seville and returns years later, eager to revisit the happy scene, but finds tragedy: a rich family claimed Amparo as their lost daughter and swept her away to be a fine lady. The girl pined away and died, and her lovelorn swain went mad with grief. "Night began to fall, dark and infinitely sad. The sky was black and the land the same. From the branches of the tree still hung the rope for the swing, semi-rotten, moved by the breeze. It seemed to me the cord of a noose, still swinging after a criminal had been cut down... In my memory there remained of this fantastic scene of desolation nothing more than confused impressions, impossible to reproduce." The once cheery innkeeper has dwindled into a stricken old man, caring for his son who stays in a dark room, barely eats, no longer weeps, and only opens his lips to murmur the following quatrain: "In the cart of the dead/that passed by here,/a hand was visible,/and that's how I recognized her."

There is a dashing portrait of the young Bécquer, by his brother Valeriano, owned by the Ybarra family and often put on public show and widely reproduced. He fixes you with an arresting sidelong glance. With tumbling black curls, finely curved mouth, a floppy white collar and enveloping black cape, he cuts the perfect figure of the suffering, sensitive romantic Spanish hero.

The Return of the Admiral

In 2002 the curiosity of a Sevillian schoolteacher brought La Cartuja back into the limelight, and refocused world attention on Admiral Columbus. As a result of the efforts of local historian Marcial Castro Sánchez, scientists plan to exhume Christopher Columbus' supposed remains in the cathedral to make sure they are really his. They think the remains held aloft by four sculpted figures representing the ancient kingdoms of Spain might, in fact, be those of his son Diego, who was buried in the Dominican Republic and whose bones were then removed centuries ago by mistake. A team led by a professor of legal medicine at the University of Granada proposed to compare the DNA with the remains of another son, Hernando, who is certainly buried in the cathedral. A positive result would end 125 years of dispute over whether Columbus truly rests in Seville, or in Santo Domingo, where he made his historic landfall in the New World.

The idea was put forward by Castro Sánchez, a genealogist and history teacher at a secondary school near Seville, who was inspired by the work of the Oxford-based geneticist Brian Sykes on the use of DNA testing across generations to resolve unanswered historical questions. "I realized this technique could be applied to Christopher Columbus, so I went with 18 of my pupils to visit José Antonio Lorente Acosta at his Laboratory of Genetic Identification at Granada University, and he was delighted to help," he said. "The Professor had pondered the problem for years but hadn't known how to solve it."

Columbus, we know, died in the Spanish city of Valladolid in 1506, and his body was buried in the Santa Ana chapel of La Cartuja in 1509. Then, in 1537, his remains, together with those of his son Diego—an admiral like his father and Governor of the Indies, who died in 1526—were shipped across the Atlantic and buried in the cathedral of Santo Domingo on the island then known as Hispaniola, in accordance with the request of Columbus' daughter-in-law, Diego's widow. There Columbus' body remained until 1795, when the Caribbean island fell temporarily into French hands. Spaniards decided to rescue the body from its tomb behind the altar and ship the remains to nearby Havana, in Cuba, which was still a Spanish colony. "But since Christopher was buried very near Diego, it is possible that the wrong remains were removed," said Castro. Doubts emerged, and in 1877 the dispute over where the bones of Columbus really lay began when builders who were replacing the paving slabs of Santo Domingo cathedral uncovered a lead box bearing the inscription: "Illustrious and enlightened male Don Cristóbal Colón". The casket contained 41 bone fragments and a bullet, possibly received during the explorer's adventurous youth. The people of Santo Domingo insist that these are Columbus' real remains, and that the Spaniards took away those of his son Diego by mistake. Next to that tomb was another box inscribed with the name of Luis, Christopher Columbus' grandson, who died in Oran, Algeria, and whose remains, some experts say, could never have reached the Caribbean.

In 1898 when the Spanish colony of Cuba fell to the Americans, Spaniards again salvaged Columbus' supposed remains from Havana, brought them to Seville and buried them in the cathedral beneath the monumental tomb. His son Hernando, who died in 1539, is buried in a different tomb in the cathedral. He is the only direct relative whose burial place is not in doubt, as he has always been there.

Dr Lorente Acosta had made a name for himself by his work in identifying remains of people found in unmarked graves in Chile and Argentina, and is now doing the same for victims of Franco's dictatorship in Spain. He heads the team seeking to solve the mystery of Columbus' bones by making an analysis of nuclear DNA to reveal connections between direct family members, and an analysis of mitochondrial DNA, which could establish links with maternal descendants. "Even if we found it wasn't him, it would not matter because his tomb would be just as important as a cenotaph in his honour. And there should not be any difficulty about exhuming the remains. After all, he has been dug up nine times already," said Castro.

Not until 1930 was the Columbus family vault discovered beneath the stone flags of La Cartuja's Santa Ana chapel, where Christopher, his son Diego and his younger brother Diego had initially been buried. When the vault was opened in 1950, only the bones of his brother remained—Columbus and his son having been shipped centuries before to the Caribbean. In 1961 the remains were disinterred for forensic examination and stored within the Cartuja-Pickman grounds until 1977 when they were put in a cellar. In 2000 the leaden box was buried in the garden of the present factory in Santiponce, which is where it was opened on a rainy September afternoon in 2003, its lid peeled back like a tin of sardines. This was the box containing the remains of Diego, the admiral's younger brother who was a priest (not to be confused with his son Diego, a seafarer and an admiral like his father, who was buried in Santo Domingo). Analysis of Diego's DNA was to be the first step in trying to find out where Christopher's bones lie. But key to the mystery is Hernando. "His could be the most valuable remains of the whole Columbus family. They are the only ones that can confirm or discount theories about the Admiral's origins and clarify if they are brothers of both mother and father or just one of them. In addition, the genetic identification will determine whether the authentic remains of Columbus are in Seville or the Dominican Republic," said Castro.

The next step is to exhume the contents of the two tombs in the cathedral, supposedly of Christopher and his son Hernando. The historian Anunciada Colón, a descendant of the Admiral and author of a book about the mysteries surrounding Columbus's death and subsequent resting place, is convinced the Spaniards made no mistake in 1795 when they evacuated the Caribbean island and took her forebear's remains to Cuba. But Francisca Espinel, consul in Seville of the Dominican Republic, is in no doubt that the real tomb is in her country. The historian Marcial Castro, too, is convinced that Christopher Columbus's bones are in Santo Domingo, and that those of his son were brought by mistake back home to Seville. La Cartuja continues to make history, and Expo 92 was right to focus international interest on Columbus.

Expomania

Expo 92, like its predecessor, fell short of expectations but it succeeded in projecting Seville worldwide for a dazzling six months, and in bequeathing to the city some lasting—in some cases spectacular—benefits. In particular, six new bridges were built to link La Cartuja to the city, symbolizing the great re-encounter between Seville and the Guadalquivir, the fount of its erstwhile glory.

For centuries the only link that spanned the banks between Seville and Triana was an unsteady pontoon suspended on boats along which workers streamed to enter the city through the Triana gate. It was often submerged by floods. Not until 1852 did an iron bridge replace it, which remained for further decades the only crossing point. The new bridges are, from north to south: the spectacular Puente Alamillo, with its gravity-defying leaning support tower, by the Valencian architect Santiago Calatrava. (Calatrava planned the bridge as one of a pair, each of which would span an arm of the river. But even as he was explaining to the city fathers how laser lights would visually unite the highest points of the twin structures, money-minded officials were sabotaging his vision.) The next is the striking Puente de la Barqueta, the great steel arc created by the engineers Juan José Arenas and Marcos Pantaleón. Then comes the slender La Cartuja *pasarela* or footbridge, followed by the Cachorro with its tilted canvas canopies or *toldos*, which replaces an artificial dam that once blocked the river's natural course. The bridge was built before the blockage was cleared away, which is logical, but prompted sarcastic locals to scoff that first the engineers built the bridge, and only then did they install the river. The whole urban stretch of the river is now an artificial canal, where international boat teams come to train, the "real" river having been diverted to the west. The Cachorro is the only bridge to be built by a local architect, José Luis Manzanares. The Delicias is a dual-level mobile bridge for road and rail, by Leonardo Fernández Troyano and Javier Manterola. The central section lifts to allow the passage of ships. Finally there is the huge Puente del V Centenario, at 1,800 feet the longest in Spain, by José Antonio Fernández Ordóñez. The only construction in Seville taller than the Giralda, it was criticized at the time for being both grandiose and structurally flimsy. The Puente de la Barqueta and the footbridge each replaced ancient ferries.

Perhaps it was fanciful to imagine that Seville, with its unsurpassed southern talent for partying and display, could mount a world fair that would have transformed La Cartuja into a humming technopolis of scientific research. Despite various post-Expo efforts to revive the abandoned area, the reclaimed island of La Cartuja has a limp melancholy air that could not be more alien to Seville's vibrant personality. The last effort, launched in 1997, to build an adventure theme park on the concept of the "magic island", a Tintinesque vision of Central America, was gasping its final breaths by the turn of the millennium. The most successful projects were the creation of swooping temporary tent-like structures of the ephemeral kind the city has always favoured.

Critics say huge sums were squandered on the extravagant show by a Sevillian-led socialist government eager to cut a dash internationally.

The expected profit of 18bn pesetas ended up being a staggering 60bn peseta loss. Environmental campaigners complained that the Expo failed to bring lasting benefits because it did not solve the region's chronic problems of unemployment, lack of water and poor housing. "Unemployment was unaffected except for a short spell during the building works. Many of the hotels and offices remained empty and were sold off. Few homes were built and the slums remained as bad as ever," said the leader of the anti-Expo campaign Pepe García Rey. "After years of drought, water gushed during the Expo, but the minute it ended, water was rationed. The authorities hadn't given a thought to investing in new pipes or reservoirs." The Expo area, pocked by vacant plots where temporary pavilions were long cleared away, is crisscrossed by overgrown pergolas whose tangled greenery fails to soften a harsh concrete landscape. At night and at weekends it is deserted, as remote from the city's pumping heart as when the monks founded their contemplative community. Juan Gómez Puiggrós, spokesman for Cartuja 93, a body which sought to develop the site as a technology park, defends the project, saying it was important to have attracted the research and development departments of the Seville University. Many firms preferred to buy plots in the competing technology park in Málaga than rent from the authorities in Seville. But Puiggrós says that if they had not kept La Cartuja in public hands, "it would have become a victim of speculative development." Rey, for his part, claims that the high-tech plan, then the theme park scheme, were all improvised after the event. The entire university, much of which lies outside the city and in the old Tobacco Factory, could have been relocated to the site and the rest of the island laid out as a park, saving money and providing Sevillians with much-needed green space.

Actually, much of the area is now a wooded parkland of great beauty, the Alamillo Park, and a new generation of tens of thousands of anti-globalization environmental campaigners camped there to mount a huge protest during the European Union summit in Seville in 2002, many of them having arrived from all over Europe on the Ave high-speed train.

Chapter Four

PORT AND GATEWAY TO AMERICA

The Lonja de Mercaderes, or Merchants' Exchange, sits between Seville's two most important monuments: the Alcázar and the cathedral. This illustrious setting is not accidental, for the Lonja symbolizes Seville's link with the Americas, source of the city's imperial grandeur. One historian observed that this position is entirely appropriate for an institution that interposed the rule of Money between that of Church and State. The Lonja is a sombre and austere building that once had eleven doors open to the street on all four sides, as befitted its public function. The building's original purpose is indicated by a tall stone cross that stands outside the façade opposite the cathedral, almost within its bulky shadow. The cross, easy to overlook unless you seek it out, is the Cruz del Juramento, where traders sealed their contracts with a sworn promise, their word of honour.

Today the foursquare Lonja houses the Archivo General de Indias, the Indies Archive, a huge collection of documents recording every administrative detail of Spain's conquest of the Americas, and the activities of Spain's New World colonies. The story of how the archive was founded in 1785 is a fascinating saga of enlightened political opportunism. But the Lonja itself was built more than two centuries earlier for a different purpose, reflecting Seville's privileged status as monopolist of trade with the Americas.

Eleven years after the Discovery, in 1503, the Spanish Crown granted Seville the monopoly of Spain's trade with the New World. This decision effectively made the city the capital, albeit a distant one, of the newly conquered lands, a focus of adventure and opportunity that drew people high and low from throughout Europe. Some 60,000 people are reckoned to have lived in the city at the beginning of the sixteenth century, while by 1587 when Cervantes returned, the population had boomed to 150,000. Everything centred on the chartering of ships, supplying Spanish settlers in the Americas with essentials and luxuries, then taking delivery of the treasures brought from the Indies.

This prodigious transatlantic operation was orchestrated by the Casa de Contratación, or Trading House. As an institution dependent on the Crown, the Casa was housed in a magnificent room on the site of a former Arab palace within the Alcázar. You can still see it if you ask the doorman at the region's Public Works department, now occupying the site, to let you in from the Plaza de Contratación— Contract Square. But the hands-on trading, the shouting, the haggling, the contracts and the striking of deals took place around the cathedral. Traders called out their offers and counteroffers in the Patio de los Naranjos, Orange Tree Patio, and on the cathedral steps, *las gradas*. So intense was the activity that when it rained or when the sun beat down too fiercely, traders took shelter inside the cathedral itself, still shouting their business, to the great displeasure of the priests, who repeatedly threw them out. In the Orange Tree Patio, a relic of the mosque that once stood here, is a relief sculpture depicting the Biblical episode of Jesus evicting the merchants from the temple. Finally, in 1572, an exasperated Archbishop Sandoval y Rojas pleaded with King Felipe II to let the intrusive merchants have a building of their own. The clerics even erected a fence of chains around the cathedral and forbade the traders from crossing inside. The chains are still there, slung at around shoulder height between fat stone columns, marking off the holy territory.

The Indies Route

The entire purpose of the conquest and of the great expeditions of discovery was to open up new routes for communication and trade. This follow-up to the pioneering voyages of a handful of daring conquistadors and navigators in their tiny ships was carried out by a second wave of ships and men, most of whom remain anonymous. Colonization and establishing regular contacts with the metropolis needed a massive infrastructure of hundreds of vessels and thousands of crew-members. Seville was picked as the hub of an intercontinental maritime traffic carrying goods and people between the Philippines and Europe via the Americas though shipping lanes in the Atlantic and the Pacific every year for nearly two centuries. Contemporaries dubbed this ambitious operation, the orchestration of an unending round of ships that bound Seville to the Americas, the *Carrera de Indias*—the Indies Route.

Seville was chosen because it was a populous inland port, in a region where several grand families influential at court had their power base. It had also already established itself as a medieval trading centre within the Mediterranean. Thanks to its command of the Gibraltar Strait, Seville controlled the navigation routes established by Italian republics with northern Europe. Genoese bankers and merchants had installed themselves as prosperous members of Seville society, with their own neighbourhood in Calle Génova near the cathedral, eager to seize the opportunities presented by the transatlantic adventure. Moreover, the city had a fertile agricultural hinterland that produced oil, wheat and wine; it enjoyed a sophisticated artisan tradition, with shipyards, a banking system and a naval university. The upriver port, some 55 miles from the coast, was easily defended against pirates or enemy powers. And the coast was dotted with villages whose seafaring folk were used to sailing to the Canaries, which became a favoured port on the route to the Indies.

Seville had only one disadvantage as the navigational heart of intercontinental trade: the Guadalquivir was too shallow to allow heavily laden vessels to sail all the way upstream to the city. This meant that bulky war galleons and large merchant ships had to drop anchor downstream, either in the river's anchorage at Las Horcadas, in Sanlúcar de Barrameda at the river estuary, or in a port in the nearby bay of Cadiz. The river became less navigable as years passed: ships were built bigger and heavier, and accidents caused by the intense traffic left sunken boats the length of the river, creating a hazardous hidden obstacle course for the rest. To add to these navigational difficulties, silt gradually raised the level of the riverbed. So ships increasingly docked in Cadiz, causing that modest little port to grow rapidly, until at the beginning of the seventeenth century it surpassed Seville as the destination for Spanish transatlantic shipping.

But initially, at least, Seville became a trading and maritime powerhouse. The Sevillian writer and historian Francisco Morales Padrón describes one man's experience:

> *The year in which the German Nicolas Federman embarked in Seville for the second time, 1534, a companion of his, a witness, recalled that every traveller wanting to sign up had to present himself at the Casa de Contratación accompanied by witnesses who certified that the aspiring mariner was not among those listed as 'prohibited persons'. Once his name was registered, he lined up with others carrying flags (of the emperor, of the house of Welser, of the German governor who had brought them) and marched in military fashion, preceded by pipers, bagpipers and clerics bearing candles. Among those marching were soldiers with greyhounds and other fierce dogs, horsemen, torchbearers, musketeers, ensigns and shield-bearers decked with all their paraphernalia and, in the rear, the mule trains with luggage, surgeons and various ships' craftsmen. They crossed the bridge of little boats to attend mass in a monastery of Triana, where the flags were blessed, and then immediately boarded ship.*

The fleets that left Seville for the New World were bound both for trade and imperial rule, bent on the dual acquisition of riches and power. Ships carried governors destined to rule the overseas possessions, soldiers and cannon to defend the power of the Spanish Crown against enemies, plus trunks of letters and orders signed by the king to impose royal authority upon an empire that was to become as bureaucratically ordered as Spain under the obsessively methodical Habsburgs. The ships also transported emigrants, some 2,000 a year, who sought to *hacer las Américas* (to make it in America). So relentless was this outward flow of men that the Ambassador of Venice, Navagiero, wrote in 1525: "Seville is the place where so many people head out to the Indies that the city itself is depopulated, and left almost entirely in the hands of women."

Most ships, despite carrying passengers, mainly operated as floating warehouses of merchandise, particularly of precious metals. The prime purpose of fleets sent forth from Seville was to bring back gold and silver. The silver, in particular, spread throughout Europe because Spanish merchants used it to buy commodities they needed from abroad, or to pay off royal debts contracted with European bankers. This torrent of gold and silver was an important stimulus for the development of European capitalism. The precious metals also stimulated trade with the East. China was interested only in gold and silver, since the rudimentary products of European industry were far too crude to appeal to the world's finest craftsmen. Much of the silks, porcelains, and spices from the Far East were bought with American silver.

The quantity of precious metal shipped into Seville soared after 1536, doubled after 1560, and peaked at the turn of the century. The sixteenth-century historian Alonso de Morgado wrote: "A thing of admiration not seen in any other port is the sight of carts dragged by four oxen which, when the fleets come in, carry the silver and gold bars from the portside to the Trading House of the Indies. No less marvellous is the sight of the enormous riches accumulated in many streets in Seville inhabited by merchants from Flanders, Greece, Genoa, France, Italy, England and other parts, and from the Indies and Portugal. There is gold, silver, crystal, precious stones, enamels, coral, silks, brocades, rich cloths, all kinds of silken fabrics and fine linens. The area is full of silversmiths, jewellers, sculptors, silkweavers and haberdashers of immense wealth. The Royal Trading House [i.e. Casa de Contratación] of the Indies, if all the wealth that entered it were afterwards put to public use, could pave the streets of Seville with bricks of gold, silver and precious stones instead of bricks of clay."

Outgoing ships were laden with goods that settlers needed to exchange for silver mined by indigenous labour. Most of the silver arriving in Seville came from this barter. The rest—some 25 per cent— was taken by the king as tax, sent directly to the metropolis by governors in America. Settlers were particularly keen to be supplied with good quality fine clothing, so they could cut a dash in the New World and present themselves as equals to their metropolitan rulers. Andalusian wine and oil were also appreciated, plus iron bars or tools, and mercury, used in the extraction of silver. In general, only expensive goods were carried on the Indies Route. With the long voyages, the huge crews, and the enormous costs of loans and insurance to fund the trips, only top-price merchandise made the enterprise profitable. In addition, the precious convoys had to be protected from pirates and rival European naval ships. Piracy, especially, was used by competing European powers to try to break through Spain's exclusive command of the lands and seas of the New World. Two fleets a year set sail from Seville, each escorted by warships, bound for Veracruz in Mexico and Cartagena de las Indias in Colombia, known at the time as Nueva Granada. These ships did not themselves ply the Pacific: ships from Peru bearing silver from Potosí docked in Panama, those from Manila in the Philippines sailed to Acapulco, both on the Pacific coast. The goods were carried overland on mules or along rivers to Atlantic ports. Spain wanted to keep the Pacific a closed ocean, a sort of Spanish lake sealed off from competitors. All this required an administrative machinery of enormous sophistication, plus a constant supply of qualified sailors and navigators.

Lonja de Mercaderes: New World Moguls
This was the work of the Casa de Contratación, the Trading House installed in the Alcázar. In 1508 the Italian navigator Amerigo Vespucci, the man who gave his name to the new continent, was appointed Chief Navigator of the Trading House, which was responsible for making maps of the New World and examining those who wanted to go there as pilots. The monarchs received would-be navigators and explorers, including Columbus, in what are today the sumptuous Admiral's Rooms of the Alcázar. Wall hangings display the coats of arms of Spain's most distinguished admirals, and a chapel is dominated by the retable "The Virgin of the Navigators", created by Alejo Fernández between 1531 and 1536. In this magnificent work, venerated by mariners, the Virgin extends her hands in blessing over the heads of great men of the age of discoveries: Columbus, Vespucci, and others, kneeling in prayer before setting off. The foreground details the frail-looking ships in which they crossed the world.

The pilots' main task was to produce illustrated maps based on the information handed over by returning navigators, which formed the primary source for the creation of navigational charts. The Casa also operated as an examination board for pilots, and then went on to create a nautical school, where professors of cosmography and mathematics gave courses of six or three months. These courses were compulsory for anyone wanting to graduate as a pilot on the Indies Route. This intense scientific work produced a large number of nautical books published by the Casa and containing all the latest knowledge of the epoch. The books were mostly written by people attached to the institution, either as chief navigators or cosmography professors, or specialists in various aspects of the Indies Route. Some of them became bestsellers, and within a few years were reprinted dozens of times in most important European languages. Through these specialist manuals, seafarers throughout Europe gained access to the accumulated knowledge of the pioneering navigators of Spain and Portugal.

In one striking example of how this cutting-edge information was useful to Spain's enemies, the buccaneering English explorer Francis Drake used on his round-the-world trip the English version of Martín Cortés' *Brief Treatment of the Globe and the Art of Navigation.* Another of these master works, the *Arte de Navegar* (The Art of Navigation, 1545) by Pedro de Medina, was hailed as an example of its kind by cosmographers of the royal court in France.

To complement the work of the official Trading House, the Consulado de Comercio (Trade Consulate) was founded in 1534. The Consulado, a private institution, provided a swift-acting court to settle commercial disputes among traders, and came to represent the interests of the big merchants who ran the colonial traffic. This group's enormous strength was based on loans they made to the king, which ensured that they effectively funded the naval policy of the Crown and hence controlled the coming and going of the fleets. The handsome Lonja was built so that these powerful moguls would cease bothering the archbishop by sullying the precincts of the cathedral, and to provide them with a suitably imposing home of their own.

Felipe II contracted the great Renaissance architect Juan de Herrera, the man who created the gigantic palace of El Escorial north of Madrid, to design the Lonja. The building was started in 1582 and not completed until 1646. But even in 1603 it merits a mention in Lope de Vega's play *El Arenal de Sevilla.* In scale and geometric austerity the Lonja echoes the Escorial, with a similarly vast inner patio surrounded by vaulted galleries. But despite its imposing appearance, by the time it started operating as a trading house Seville's spectacular boom was already tailing off. The flow of gold and silver had slackened, Spain's trade monopoly was attacked from all sides by English and Dutch imperial rivals, and the city entered a decline that lasted for centuries: Seville never recovered the splendour of those years. In the end the global military machine was too much for a stricken economy to support, and the whole elaborate edifice of the Indies Route fell apart.

Seville's monopoly of American trade slipped in favour of the rival city of Cadiz. In 1717 the Casa de Contratación was moved from the Alcázar and transferred to Cadiz until it was abolished in 1790. By 1700 the ships that had once lined the portside of Seville and defined the city's skyline for centuries were gone. The horizon was instead dotted with crosses and steeples. Religious orders flocked to Seville during its glory years in pursuit of clientele, and set up convents and monasteries that still today dominate every corner of the city.

Murillo: Painter of Urchins

As the Lonja's role declined, the building emptied but for a few officials who rattled around its vast salons. The upper floor was divided up for apartments. Among the tenants who moved in upstairs was the artist Bartolomé Esteban Murillo who established his studio in one corner and founded a Public Painting Academy. Murillo (1618-82) is best known in Spain for his religious paintings, which in many cases still adorn the churches in Seville that had originally commissioned them. But Murillo became internationally celebrated during his lifetime for his secular—what Spaniards call his "profane"—paintings, his portrayals of ordinary people and particularly street urchins. Murillo pioneered the portrayal of children in art. No one before him had conveyed the experience of children, and few did so afterwards. Infancy remained until the present day a subject all but untouched in Spanish art. Art experts are baffled by the mystery, but suspect it might have to do with the extremely precarious life of young children for centuries in Spain. At the time Murillo was painting and picaresque authors were portraying young boys as their subjects, only one or two children might survive from a family of eight or nine.

Murillo's portraits were eagerly snapped up by prosperous and cultured northern European traders who followed Seville's artistic flowering with enthusiasm. At least one important Dutch trader from Rotterdam, Joshua van Belle, commissioned Murillo to paint his portrait, despite the political enmity between Holland's Protestant provinces and Catholic Spain. A Flemish merchant called Nicolas

Omazur, who arrived in Seville in 1669, became Murillo's main client; he commissioned and bought works from the artist off the easel. Which is why Murillo's assorted imps, scamps and ragamuffins are found mostly in British or German galleries rather than Sevillian churches or grand Spanish houses.

Hugely popular in the eighteenth and nineteenth centuries, when he was compared with Michelangelo and Raphael, Velázquez and Goya, Murillo fell out of favour in the twentieth century when his work was considered to be over-sentimental. His portraits of scallywags with filthy feet scoffing bread or fruit with a beguiling naturalism were seen as a tidied up and sweetened visual counterpart to the picaresque literature of the time. Picaresque stories were fictional autobiographies of impoverished and marginal anti-heroes who lived in the street and used their wits to survive. The literary genre pioneered in Seville became universal, and the precursor to the modern novel.

Murillo worked within a short stroll of the city's poorest quarters around 1650—a period when the city was reeling under the impact of plague and famine—when the streets teemed with homeless orphans, so he is bound to have come across scenes of child poverty. He even joined a religious brotherhood founded by Miguel de Mañara dedicated to helping the poor. But his paintings of young urchins, despite their torn rags and dirty fingernails, are not scenes of wretchedness. His street boys are rougher and more insolent than his idealized paintings of the infant Christ, in the *Good Shepherd* or *St John the Baptist*. Murillo's street children have a rough-and-tumble lust for life, and that life seems not too harsh, even though no adult appears to care for them. They are unwashed and hungry, but have bright eyes, a ready smile and rounded limbs and features. Some of the models are said to have been Murillo's own sons. The painter does not scorn or ridicule his humble subjects, as artists often did at the time. He evokes scenes of Sevillian street life in a way that appeals to our sympathy and compassion. For his purpose was to encourage Christian charity; it seems as though he did not want to repel people by presenting too brutal a realism, nor charm them with something so sanitized that they failed to get the message.

The Murillo expert Peter Cherry, writing in the catalogue of a recent exhibition at the Prado in Madrid, believes that most of Murillo's child models were not beggars, but had some sort of modest employment, as servants or delivery boys, carrying baskets of fruit, jars of oil or water from the market to private houses, or selling fruit on the street. Typically, though, they are never shown actually working, only resting and lounging about, enjoying their leisure, and sating their hunger. These boys are not *pícaros*, writes Cherry, but *chulitos*, which in the low Sevillian argot of the time, meant boy or kid. Omazur used the term to describe the subjects of the paintings he bought. Hunger is a constant preoccupation, as it is in picaresque literature and was in real Seville, but the boys do not beg for food. In Murillo's artistic world, only the dogs beg.

The Arenal: Lowlife Quarter

Ships provided the lifeblood of Seville, and galvanized the stretch of sandy terrain that descended from the city walls to the riverbank. This area was known as the Arenal. From the Salon del Almirante in the Alcázar palace to what was the Casa de Contratación next door, it is a short walk across the Plaza de la Contratación. This takes you to what is today the Avenida de la Constitución through the Arco del Postigo—a former postern for the busy coming and going of servants and supplies—down to the Arenal. All the operations necessary to supply the ships were carried out in this once-soggy marginal no-mans-land pressed against the city walls. The area contains streets or quarters named after makers of barrels (Toneleros), carts (Carretería) and baskets (Cestería), and after the secondhand market (Baratillo). Baratillo used to have a mound, which, when levelled in the eighteenth century, revealed a huge pile of broken and discarded pots and other junk, testifying to the activities that once took place on the spot. The Arenal was long renowned as a centre of dubious trading to judge by an evocative passage in Cervantes' short story, *Rinconete and Cortadillo* (1613), in a scene that might easily have inspired Murillo. The two young *pícaros* or ne'er-do-wells of the title had somehow secured themselves jobs as servants to a group of travellers headed for Seville.

> *Cortado and Rincon contrived to serve the travellers so well that they carried them on their horses for most of the way, and although they had some chances to rob the bags of their temporary masters, they didn't take them, so as not to lose the splendid chance of the journey to Seville, where they very much wanted to go. All the same, as they*

were going through the Aduana gate into the city at prayer time,
Cortado, taking advantage of the inspection and the payment of duty
could not refrain from cutting the bag or valise that a certain French-
man in the company was carrying on the crupper of his mule. So, with
his yellow-handled knife he gave it such a long and deep wound that
its insides were open for all to see, and he neatly took from it two good
shirts, a sundial and a little memo book, things which they didn't
much like the look of...

They had taken their leave of the party who had supported them
so far on their journey before performing this robbery, and the next
day they sold the shirts in the second-hand shop near the Arenal gate,
and made twenty reales out of them. After this they went to look at
the city, and were amazed at the size and splendour of its cathedral
and the vast number of people by the river, because it was at the time
when they were loading up the fleet. There were six galleys there, the
sight of which made them sigh and dread the day when a mistake on
their part would lead them to spend the rest of their lives in them.
They saw the vast number of basket-boys who were running about
there, and they inquired of one of them what sort of business they were
engaged in, if it was hard work, and what they made out of it. An
Asturian boy, who was the one they questioned, said it was an easy
trade and that you didn't pay any duty, and that some days he made
five or six reales profit. With that he could eat, drink and live splen-
didly without needing to look for a master to whom he would have
to give guarantees; and knowing that he could eat at any time he
wished, for he could find food at all times of the day in any cheap
eating house in the city.

As you walk through the Arenal down towards the high and
handsome Arab shipyards—the Atarazanas—recently opened to the
public, you can see on the right the old warehouses with their thick
columns and low arched ceilings. These are now atmospheric taverns,
and still exude a faintly louche portside flavour. The Atarazanas
themselves, built of brick and now floored with golden *albero* sand
occupy a high arched space of astonishing beauty. The huge complex
was until recently used as a military barracks, but the Atarazanas are
now restored, opened up, and destined as a contemporary arts centre
for exhibitions and performances. The galleon in which Don John of

Austria fought against the Turks at the battle of Lepanto in 1571 is supposed to have been built here.

Seventeenth-century Seville was a place of terrible poverty, the underside of the wealth and glory produced by the Indies Route, and in the 1660s the local nobleman Miguel de Mañara resolved to found a hospital for the poor. He took some of the land of the Ataranzas on which to build it, and asked Murillo, who joined his charitable brotherhood, to decorate it.

The Arenal, a huddle of hovels and workshops built higgledy-piggledy against the city wall, was beyond the pale. Among its rough swampy neighbourhoods, in what is today Calle Castelar, was La Mancebía or the brothel, and the prostitutes' quarter. You can still see in Plaza de Molviedro the chapel for fallen women. Not until you take a little side street that opens out to the Puerta de Triana, Triana Gate—whose original location is marked out by four palm trees—can you return directly to the heart of the city. Anyone wanting to reach the portside had to cross the Arenal, but when maritime trade flagged, the area lost its purpose and became a sluggish backwater leading nowhere. The city duly turned its back on the area, for it was not a part of town to pass through unless one had business there, presumably shady.

The Arenal was too swampy to develop until it was drained in the eighteenth century, but is now completely built up. It remains a rather poor quarter with a cramped and marginal atmosphere, its tiny inter-linked squares quiet and isolated from the noisy centre. Only the Maestranza bullring built between 1761 and 1881 raised the area up and integrated it into the rest of the city. The neighbourhood, as the local historian Antonio Zoido told me as he took me round these silent crooked lanes, was *el barrio de malvivir*—the lowlife quarter. Famed throughout Spain, this was the area of *pícaros*, blacks, mulattoes, galley slaves, gypsies and orphans, all of whom are celebrated in the art and literature of the time.

The great Golden Age playwright Lope de Vega set the entire action of his 1603 play *El Arenal de Sevilla* in the city's bustling portside. The lighthearted piece, which is not, according to the expert on Golden Age theatre David Castillejo, one of Lope's finest works, tells the story of Don Lope, who has abandoned his sweetheart Lucinda and seeks to enlist for the Indies. But along the portside in the Arenal, Don

Lope meets another woman, Laura. Lucinda meanwhile arrives in Seville dressed as a gypsy, and starts spreading lies in an effort to break up the new love affair. Don Lope ends up spurning her and marries Laura. "The work depends upon its intense portside atmosphere," comments Castillejo in his comprehensive guide to Golden Age comedies. The play opens with the following scene-setting dialogue between the lady Laura and her aunt Urbana.

> *L: It's famous, this Arenal!*
> *U: No one would deny it.*
> *L: There is not in my opinion*
> *such a spectacle anywhere in the world.*
> *So many galleons and ships*
> *greatly ennoble the Betis.*
> *U: This seems a different Seville*
> *founded upon the river…*
> *I've never seen it with so many people…*
> *It would be better if we head*
> *towards the Torre del Oro*
> *and we will see all that great treasure*
> *that goes to the Indies.*

Lope de Vega takes us through various picaresque dockside episodes: in one an unwary visitor from Castile who is identified only as *un forastero* (a stranger) is cheated by fettered Moorish galley slaves, who are then carted off by soldiers to be punished. The stranger, none the less, is astonished by the grandeur and bustle of the port. One soldier says: "You think this is a marvel?/Wait till the fleet arrives/and you'll see all this sand/full of carts of silver,/you can imagine the hubbub." His comrade backs him up: "This is the Indies gate/that sends off so many millions/ port of several nations,/gateway for everyone. All Spain, Italy and France/live from this Arenal,/because it's the market square/for all trade and profit." Don Lope is later challenged and knifed by four caped and masked attackers. "Arenal and a dark night", says Don Lope, as if he expected nothing less in such circumstances. But he recovers from his wound to win his new love.

The Indies Archive: A Propaganda Exercise

In 1785 the Lonja took on its present role: to house the General Archive of the Indies, the vast body of documents generated since the sixteenth century by the Spanish Crown in its dealings with its American colonies. The aim was outlined by Carlos III's son in the founding document:

> *My revered father and master, God rest his soul, seeing that the records of the Indies were dispersed widely and kept without the order and distinction befitting their importance, commanded that a General Archive be created for them in the Casa Lonja de Mercaderes in the city of Seville, where, duly ordered and kept under the charge of the Archivist and Officers, they should be of the greatest possible use.*

This was an admirable reflection of the spirit of the Enlightenment, but there was a deeper, more urgent, reason for undertaking this noble task: namely to write a favourable history of Spanish colonization and rebut a number of derogatory works written in the 1770s by European critics. Both the French historian Abbé Raynal in 1770 and William Robertson in 1777 had cast the Spanish colonial experience in a distinctly negative light, displeasing King Carlos III who refused to allow their works to be translated into Spanish. The king was accordingly convinced of the need to commission a "well-informed" in-house history to counter these undesirable and harmful accounts. "In order to achieve such a worthy end, to silence those slanderers and imitators once and for all, to make their ignorance inexcusable, the matter had to be approached seriously, referring back to the original sources and carrying out an examination of refutable documents, as if nothing had ever been written or published on the subject, and in this way, set the record straight, in a manner of speaking". So ran the introduction of the official version, quoted in a brochure produced by the Indies Archive.

A clearer argument for turning to primary source material to write history could hardly be made. The king duly commissioned Juan Bautista Muñoz in 1779 to write the definitive history of the New World, with the intention of countering the works of Raynal and Robertson in a well-documented work that would correct falsehoods and errors. Unsurprisingly, given the magnitude of the task, Bautista Muñoz produced only the first volume of his great history, but in the course of his research and gathering of documents and books he had the idea of creating an archive solely for documents dealing with the Indies. These records were until then dispersed among the various organizations that had generated them, in Madrid, Cadiz and Seville, which were groaning under the accumulated mass of books, letters, maps, orders, accounts, insurance policies, diaries, records of trials, bills of lading, contracts and the rest. The scheme to unite them in one spot was enthusiastically promoted by Muñoz's patron José de Gálvez, Marquis of Sonora, who was Minister for the Indies—possibly the most powerful post in Spain, after the monarch. Madrid was far from the scene; Cadiz was under constant threat from the English. The king, moreover, had close links with Seville, and so the city was settled upon as the seat of this new archive, and the marquis chose the Lonja, which was at that moment all but empty, to house it.

The building needed some structural alterations. The large inner square with its surrounded arcades was glassed in, and all but two outer doors were sealed off. (The entire building was recently closed for extensive refurbishment set to finish in late 2004.) As part of that first renovation, a handsome marble staircase was installed; walls were torn down upstairs, converting thirteen rooms into a single U-shaped gallery, which was then lined with handsome bookcases of Cuban mahogany and Guatemalan cedar. These cases today house more than 40,000 documents, including Columbus' diary, which are consulted by scholars from throughout the world. Among those who pore over the documents and maps of the Archive are treasure hunters seeking to discover the maritime routes of sunken galleons.

A local politician, Manuel Pimentel, formerly a member of Spain's conservative cabinet, gave up his ministerial job in 2001 to write an entertaining novel that begins in the Indies Archive. The story is of a mysterious Mexican who arrives in Seville and befriends a young archivist. He uses her expertise in penetrating the archives to try to discover the solution to an ancient Maya riddle that he thinks will reveal hidden riches in his homeland. *La Puerta de Indias* is not great literature, but it gives a fascinating inside look at this great Sevillian institution and its records on Spanish America, and the pre-Columbian civilizations that the Spaniards discovered and then mostly destroyed.

Pimentel's novel also takes us into a lesser-known but equally historic library, housed in the cathedral.

The *Columbina*: Library in a Cathedral

The Biblioteca Columbina contains what remains of a vast international collection of 15,000 books assembled by Christopher Columbus' illegitimate son, Hernando. Entrance to his library is by an unmarked side door on the north face of the cathedral that leads into a tall narrow gallery overlooking the Orange Tree Patio. At the end of the passage is the precious collection housed in gorgeous carved mahogany bookcases reaching to the vaulted ceiling.

Hernando Colón, mapmaker and lawyer, had an interesting life. He travelled to the Americas with his father, spent years in legal battles with the court over money owed, endlessly sketched maps and drew up itineraries, and criss-crossed Europe in a constant and insatiable pursuit of books. Perhaps he inherited his bibliophile tendencies from his father who, years before he embarked upon his historic voyages, sold books and nautical charts to make a living. Christopher spent time kicking his heels in Córdoba, where the Catholic monarchs Fernando and Isabella held court after 1483, trying to obtain an audience so that he could explain his plans to explore a sea route to India. There he met 20-year-old Beatriz de Arana, of peasant stock. Hernando was born in 1489, just as Columbus was about to embark upon his historic voyage. When the Admiral returned, he had no desire to marry his humble former companion, so he took the child and left her, installing Hernando, aged five, as a page at the court of Prince Juan in Barcelona.

When his father died, ill, worn out by voyages and disputes, Hernando was just 17. His father's will ordered him to fight for the honours and riches promised to him before the Discovery. Christopher claimed a part of those American riches that had surpassed everyone's wildest imaginings, and in pursuing his father's legal battles, Hernando became a hard-nosed lawyer. He was said to have been intelligent but abrupt and undiplomatic, and was eventually pushed out of Columbus' lawsuits because he was so inflexible with the agents of the Crown. He turned to other things: the Emperor Carlos V appointed him official cosmographer and he started work on an enormous mapamundi that he never finished. In 1517 he started editing a huge study on the geography of Spain, but that too was never completed; the Council of

State—the king's private cabinet—put a stop to it, fearing the revelation of dangerous information.

Hernando was a brilliant bibliophile. He built a mansion in Seville near the Puerta de Goles, in the area now around the footbridge leading across the river to La Cartuja monastery, to house his library. At the heart of the collection were 238 books that he inherited from his father and uncles in 1509. Then he travelled across Europe, to Frankfurt, Nuremberg, Cologne, Rome and Venice, buying books just as the first products of the new technology of printing were becoming widely available. Hernando's tastes covered Greek and Latin classics, philosophy, history, nautical science, travel, poetry, music and languages. He assembled 15,000 volumes and invented a system for classifying them, which the library still follows. When money ran short he asked King Carlos V for sponsorship, but the request was refused. Fearful that his precious collection might be dispersed, he bequeathed them to his nephew Luis, on condition that he spend 100,000 *maravedís* a year to look after them. If not, he said, they would go to Seville's cathedral—which is where the collection ended up, albeit much depleted. Clerics helped themselves to volumes they fancied; part of the collection went to the royal palace of El Escorial to boost the library of Felipe II. And in the seventeenth century the Inquisition destroyed or mutilated 600 books. Finally, in 1986, the ceiling of the cathedral collapsed over the library, and 1,000 books were damaged.

Just 3,200 volumes of the original collection survive, including 587 manuscripts, mostly medieval, and some 1,250 bound and printed volumes. Treasures include Columbus's Book of Prophecies, the only book that we know was written by the Admiral (apart from his diary), in which he sought Biblical precedents predicting his discoveries; a book of the voyages of Marco Polo, with Columbus' handwritten marginal notes; a map by Ptolemy; and a map of the Mexican town of Tenochtitlán of such exactitude that historians believe the Spanish cartographer must have received cooperation from indigenous locals. Others include a Catalan book on caring for horses, and a pioneering Spanish grammar by Antonio de Lebrija, a distinguished scholar from Salamanca. Facsimiles of these works are kept in a mahogany case and proudly shown to visitors.

Chapter Five

THE HOSPITAL OF CHARITY AND THE LEGEND OF DON JUAN

Don Juan, the legendary Sevillian nobleman who has become the universal embodiment of the cruel seducer—a timeless Latin lover—is based on a real person, so they say. Sevillians mention the city's seventeenth-century aristocrat Miguel de Mañara and the fictional Don Juan in the same breath, only to add that of course there is no proof that the real man inspired the unscrupulous literary legend. Locals, in other words, hail this callous libertine, this "Don Juan", as a real compatriot, then feel ashamed of the admission. Others distance the two men in an effort to show that Don Miguel had nothing to do with Don Juan. They point out, for example, that Mañara was a boy in short trousers when *El burlador de Sevilla* (The Trickster of Seville), the play attributed to the great Golden Age playwright Tirso de Molina, introduced the character of Don Juan on to the Spanish stage. The Spanish historian and doctor Gregorio Marañón even goes so far as to deny that Don Juan's personality has anything to do with Seville and is, if anything, *Madrileño*—from Madrid—a cynical and manipulative figure typical of the royal court at a moment of national moral decadence. But the legend persists, to the point that Don Juan is probably the world's best known Sevillian.

The real Miguel de Mañara, born in 1627, was the kind of well-born layabout of whom Cervantes, who knew the city well, had the measure: "There is in Seville a class of useless idle people usually known as men about town; these are the richer young men from every parish, sauntering, showy, plausible people, always finding means to make themselves welcome at rich men's feasts." Cervantes made this astute observation in his 1613 novella *El celoso extremeño* (The Jealous Extremaduran). Such men still exist in Andalusia, where they are called *señoritos*. Don Miguel was, it seems, a perfect specimen. "Money was his key, the sword his guarantee, the deceptive music of his words the magic potion that perturbed hearts. There was no convent cloister whose austere seclusion was not penetrated by his worldly and determined presence; no palace he did not assault, nor poor dwelling that did not suffer his breaking and entering if within lived some woman who spoke to his senses with the ardent language of desires." So wrote the Sevillian journalist Rogelio Pérez Olivares in 1929, in a book lauding his home city and aimed at visitors to the Iberian-American exhibition that year. Pérez Olivares was describing, with a typically Sevillian flourish, the real Miguel Mañara, not the fictional Don Juan. His words indicate the extent to which locals in reality longed to identify one man with the other.

Mañara's parents came originally from Italy, perhaps Corsica, and made their fortune in Spain as traders with the Indies. Mañara *padre*, through the copious distribution of influence and money, obtained entry to the noble Order of Santiago, and succeeded in inscribing his son into the equally illustrious military-religious Order of Calatrava while still an infant. As a young man Don Miguel is supposed to have been a dissolute drinker and philanderer. One of his friends later wrote: "There was no folly which he did not commit, no youthful indulgence into which he did not plunge… until what occurred to him in the street of the coffin." The story goes that early one morning, Mañara was rolling home after a night of wild revelry—some versions say a drunken brawl—through the crooked alleys of Seville's picturesque heart, the Barrio de Santa Cruz, which remains as it appeared then, albeit much rebuilt to conserve its traditional look. Suddenly, in the Calle del Ataúd (Coffin Street), he stumbled across a passing funeral cortege, a procession accompanied by chanting priests and guttering candles that brought him up short. He asked who the deceased was and, leaning over the coffin, was dumbstruck to come face to face with his own corpse.

The wastrel instantly repented his past life and resolved to devote the rest of his days to self-sacrifice and good works. In 1662 Mañara joined a religious order called the Very Humble Brotherhood, whose job was to care for the city's vagrants and criminals. The brotherhood undertook, among other charitable works, to bury those who had drowned in the waters of the Guadalquivir, and the victims of execution. Mañara drew up new principles for the order, stipulating that only love for his or her neighbour could save the individual from eternal damnation. He eventually left his luxurious family mansion, which still stands in the ancient Calle Levíes, in the Judería (the former Jewish quarter, abandoned when the Jews were expelled from Spain after 1492), and handed most of his wealth to the poor and sick. He died in 1679 and is buried in the church of the Hospital of Holy Charity in Calle Dos de Mayo by the riverside Arenal quarter, beneath the florid inscription: "Here lie the bones and ashes of the worst man who ever lived in the world. Pray to God for him."

The Hospital of Holy Charity

The handsome hospital is spectacularly described in an early tourist guide as "opening the door to Seville's finest period of funereal asceticism and baroque pessimism." Apart from its importance in ostensibly pinning the Don Juan legend to real-life Seville, the hospital is an architectural jewel in a city crammed with fine buildings. The white façade is decorated with blue and white tiles and elegant baroque curlicues rendered in the typical Sevillian ochre or *albero*, the colour of the alluvial sand strewn in the bullring and on the streets in the Feria. Within is a broad, serene patio containing two marble fountains crowned with groups representing Mercy and Charity. The walls are decorated with more seventeenth-century Dutch blue and white tiles, depicting biblical scenes—though not, as the inscription mistakenly says, *De tien Geboden* (the Ten Commandments). Rose trees planted in the courtyard by Mañara himself are said to survive and flower. "Roses that still display every spring the same tint of sinful flesh and the same intoxicating aroma they had when Mañara offered them to his sweethearts," rhapsodizes Marañón with some poetic licence. The patio is shaded in the summer, as are many such Sevillian suntraps, by a ruched canvas canopy or *toldo*. This patrician pile belies its humble purpose, for the building is still used as a hospice for the relief of the dying and destitute, and whenever a patient dies the chapel is closed on the day of the funeral. In the gardens across the street opposite stands a melodramatic bronze statue of Don Miguel striding out, holding in his arms an almost naked young man who seems to be expiring from hunger and exposure.

Dominating the inside of the chapel above the entrance are two dramatic, indeed frightening, canvases by the Sevillian artist Juan de Valdés Leal depicting the Triumph of Death. One portrays the fleeting nature of life, with the skeletal figure of Death carrying a coffin under

his arm, and symbols of wealth and power strewn at his feet. His bony finger points to the message *In Ictu Oculi* ("in the blink of an eye") as he extinguishes the candle-flame of life. The other work also illustrates the ephemeral nature of worldly pomp, with the life-sized figure of a decomposing bishop being eaten by worms beneath scales of justice suspended from heaven. Beside him lies a nobleman in his coffin, whose face is that of Mañara, shrouded in a cloak bearing the scarlet cross of the Order of Calatrava to which Mañara belonged. This macabre painting, suggesting that all men are equal before death, reinforces the legend that Mañara witnessed his own funeral. The penitent libertine would have contemplated this work every day when he entered the chapel to pray.

This ambiguous and intriguing interplay between fact and folktale threads through the entire Don Juan saga. Valdés Leal's work, painted in dramatic tones of red, white and black, is beautifully lit to highlight the grisly scene, which bears the label *Finis Gloriae Mundi*. The artist Murillo found it so repulsive that he declared to his fellow artist who created it: "I'm sorry, friend, but you have to hold your nose to look at this." The work's dark mood is said to owe much to the vivid memory of the 1649 plague that killed almost half the population of Seville, and cast a shadow over the city's sunny personality for generations.

Between 1660 and 1674, Don Miguel commissioned from his artist friend Bartolomé Esteban Murillo a series of eleven paintings for the chapel, seven of which remain after Maréchal Soult looted the other four during the Napoleonic occupation in the early 1800s, and never gave them back. The paintings, "made to measure" for the available light, hang in the original spaces that they were intended to fill. They include a huge *Loaves and Fishes* depicting Christ feeding the Five Thousand, a matching *Miracle of the Waters* of Moses striking water from the rock, and a fine scene of *St. Isabel of Hungary Curing the Lepers*, vividly described in 1800 by the visiting German traveller Wilhelm von Humboldt as "a very beautiful painting, although nauseating. The saint is washing the head of one of them; another is scratching what his expression suggests is a frenetic itch; a third opens his suppurating wound." The painting was returned to its original home after being exhibited for years in the Prado Museum in Madrid. The fourth work is "a *San Juan de Dios* equal to Rembrandt", in the words of the nineteenth-century British traveller and writer Richard

Ford, who was a fervent admirer of Murillo. Mañara himself posed as the saint. The paintings are a revelation for those who associate Murillo with chocolate box cherubs.

The chapel is a gloomy place with its recurring images of speared hearts, and skull and crossbones set in the floor. A dank, sour blast smacks the nostrils like a wet fish as you descend the steps to the crypt where Mañara's body now rests. The Murillos by contrast are soothing and consoling, designed for spiritual refreshment after the crude horrors of death. The overwhelming idea of death infuses the Don Juan legend, and the soul of the city.

Scenes of Seduction

Don Juan makes his fictional debut in a racy, action-packed play, *El burlador de Sevilla* attributed to Tirso de Molina some time after 1620. Tirso was the *nom de plume* of an erudite theologian, Fray Gabriel Téllez, who was born in Madrid around 1579, possibly the illegitimate son of the Duke of Osuna, and studied for the priesthood in Salamanca and Toledo. Téllez began to write plays around 1610, changing his name to Tirso de Molina in 1615. He spent three years in the Spanish Caribbean colony of Santo Domingo, where he taught theology, before returning to Spain in 1619. In all, he wrote some 400 plays of which around seventy remain. They compare well with the works of his great contemporaries Lope de Vega and Calderón de la Barca, whom Tirso greatly admired. The essayist Gregorio Marañón, in his book analysing the psyche of Don Juan, judged that Tirso even surpassed his contemporaries "in his direct knowledge of human, and especially, female passions."

In one of the several scenes of seduction in Tirso's play (the hero has just intercepted a love note handed to him anonymously through the bars of a window, and he immediately plans to trick the writer into bed) Don Juan boasts in an aside: "Seville loudly proclaims me/a seducer and the greatest/pleasure that I could have/is to seduce a woman/and leave her without honour." One might think that such a figure would be reviled, rather than feted as a hero. But the English traveller and commentator on Spain V. S. Pritchett offers this explanation for Don Juan's enduring popularity: "Don Juan is an act which, in some form or other, every Spaniard dreams of performing, and in fact in his inner life is doing all the time. He is asserting the exclusive dramatic right of the human ego, myself before all other selves, unrepentantly."

Tirso's play opens in the most dramatic way possible: a gentleman and a duchess emerge from a darkened bedroom in the royal palace of the King of Naples. In the lamplight, the lady realizes with horror that the man she has been embracing is not, as she thought, her future husband, but a stranger. He has tricked her and she is ruined. It might be thought impossible that a woman would not recognize her lover in the dark, but this apparently incredible theatrical convention gains force when it is remembered that a lady was not supposed to know her husband physically until after the marriage. For a lady to be accompanied in the bedroom by her betrothed was bad enough, but to find he was the wrong man constitutes a dramatic bombshell.

Having aroused the wrath of the king, Don Juan flees to Spain, where he is shipwrecked on the Catalan coast and saved by a lovely fisher girl who nurses him back to health and whom he seduces with promises of marriage. He moves on to the court of the Castilian king in Seville, where his father holds high rank, and where his servant observes that a public cryer should issue a proclamation: "Let all beware of a man who deceives women and is the seducer of Spain." The king has heard of the Naples adventure, but forgives him on condition that he marries the duchess. But Don Juan tricks his way into the house of a noble lady loved by one of his friends, and tries to seduce her. When her father, a commander in the noble Order of Calatrava, rushes to her protection, Don Juan kills him. He flees again, bursting into a humble country wedding where he seduces the bride-to-be with an impetuous promise of marriage. Returning to Seville, he chances upon the grave of the commander, seizes the stone statue by the beard and invites him to dine. To his astonishment, the statue appears and invites Don Juan to eat with him in the chapel the following night. Don Juan keeps the appointment, and at the end of a meal of scorpions and vipers, accompanied by wine of bile and vinegar, the statue extends his hand, which is taken, and host and guest descend into the fires of hell. Don Juan, dishonourable in every other respect, shows his bravery by facing up to his gruesome stone guest—*el convidado de piedra*, a figure that has a long tradition in Spanish romances as the personification of death—while his servant quails in fear and horror. When, at the last moment, he desires to confess and repent, the statue tells him it is too late.

The demonic force of the hero-villain of this powerful work prompted numerous reincarnations in plays, epic poems and operas that swept Europe for centuries. The play by Molière (1665), then Thomas Corneille (1677) the opera by Mozart (1787) and the poem by Lord Byron (1819-24) are among the best known. But Tirso's fleeting desire for redemption was built by later authors into a denouement quite contrary to the original, to satisfy changing moral tastes. Tirso's themes of sexual cynicism, sin and death, a faithful reflection of sixteenth-century Seville, transmute—via Molière's witty amalgam of French farce and cynical rationalism—into a moral tale of love and redemption that produces a happy end. In Molière's play Don Juan's philosophy is examined and justified in keeping with the rationalist spirit of France of the time. He is portrayed as a man who believes in nothing, not heaven, not marriage, not family, nor God. Molière's Don Juan, in the words of the servant of his victim Dona Elvira, "went as far as invading the holy calm of a convent to carry off Dona Elvira" and married her. But he is as casual about matrimony as is Tirso's hero of betrothal, and deserts her when someone else catches his eye. "Fidelity is for imbeciles," he says, echoing Tirso's boastful hero: "There is no pleasure to compare with overcoming the resistance of a beautiful woman and in this my ambition is the same as that of all great conquerors who march continually from one victory to the next and are incapable of even thinking of setting a limit to what they want."

Don Juan's servant, the long-suffering, tragi-comic Sganarelle, declares in the opening scene: "In Don Juan my master you see the greatest villain the world has ever known, a maniac, a cur, a devil, a Turk, a heretic, who doesn't believe in Heaven or Hell or things that go bump in the night... A wedding doesn't mean a thing to him. It's the only sort of trap he sets for ensnaring women: he weds them left, right and centre, ladies, their daughters, shopkeepers' wives, peasant girls, there's none too bold or shy for him... I'd rather serve the devil himself than Don Juan... But if any word of [this] ever came to his notice I'd say you were lying." Molière himself played the part of Sganarelle at the play's sensational premiere at the Palais-Royal, Paris.

Molière's *Don Juan* is set in Sicily, perhaps considered as exotically remote from Paris as Seville was from Madrid. Like Tirso's *burlador*—which in Spanish usage refers essentially to a seducer—Molière's anti-hero tries to steal a humble man's peasant fiancée and also, as the climax to the action, meets his nemesis in the form of a ghostly stone statue at the feast: "le festin de pierre". The statue's glacial handshake and final words—"Don Juan, those who persist in their wickedness shall meet a dreadful end. Those who reject the mercy of heaven call down its wrath"—consign the libertine to the flames of hell. The work makes a wider comment that a skilled, unscrupulous hypocrite can prosper in a corrupt society.

The best-known Spanish version of the Don Juan story, which is performed nationwide around All Saints' Day and All Souls' Day on 1 and 2 November, is the play *Don Juan Tenorio*, written by José Zorrilla in 1844. Zorrilla was born in the Castilian city of Valladolid in 1817, but spent most of his life in Madrid. *Don Juan Tenorio* is his most famous work, and one of the most frequently performed plays in Spain. It is set in the Seville of 1545, and Zorrilla makes accurate references to places and events in the sixteenth-century city. In this romanticized version of the legend, Don Juan falls truly in love and repents, and thus saves his soul. The twist marks an interesting shift of Spanish literary and theatrical convention. Nineteenth-century popular taste— especially in Madrid, where the play was instantly a favourite—recoiled from the brutal logic of sin and hell, favouring the more uplifting virtues of confession, forgiveness and redemption. Zorrilla's is a fine piece of theatre, with some wonderful scenes and poetic dialogue, despite the dismissive comments of James Michener, the American writer who left a magnificent chronicle of his journeys in Spain in the1960s. "It was a sloppy play filled with so many improbabilities that any critic could tear it apart, as many did," Michener wrote, unmoved by the work's overblown Romanticism.

Certainly, the implacable dramatic process of Tirso's original is much softened, the tension ebbs once you realize that the myth is being derailed, and it comes as little surprise when the villain turns out to be a good guy after all. Molière and, more than a century on, Mozart, send their man down to eternal hellfire. Don Juan's fate is considered entirely appropriate for his heartless behaviour and in tune with both Europe's seventeenth-century rationalist thinking and then with the eighteenth-century spirit of the Enlightenment. But Zorrilla's happy end expresses the ideal of forgiveness and redemption typical of the nineteenth-century Romantic age.

Zorrilla says in his memoirs that he had only twenty days to deliver his play, and he acknowledges his debt to Tirso, describing his own effort as "the greatest nonsense ever written", according to Michener. But despite such self-deprecation, he develops some original religious elements. In particular, Don Juan rises to the challenge of his friend Don Luis to add to his repertoire one more type of seduction that he has failed to achieve: that of a novice about to take her vows as a nun. Don Juan caps the challenge by adding a further category, that of winning the intended bride of his friend. To the horror of his father, Don Juan storms the convent and abducts a novice of seventeen, Doña Inés, earmarked as a potential wife for Don Luis, but whom instead he ruins. Don Juan bamboozles this innocent child without experience of the outside world, and carries her off from her convent at night. He is morally compelled to acknowledge his guilt and repent, a process eased by his falling genuinely in love with Inés, who forgives him, thus effecting his salvation.

Barrio de Santa Cruz: Innocence and Corruption

Don Juan in Zorrilla's play prowls the cobbled lanes of Seville's Barrio de Santa Cruz, home of the Laurel tavern where the gentlemen assemble in the opening scene. La Hostería del Laurel still exists, in the Plaza de los Venerables, near a spectacular seventeenth-century palace for retired priests, and the tavern boasts proudly of its Don Juan connections. Though here again, the myth and the reality intertwine. The menu perused by diners as they sit at tables grouped in the cobbled square is adorned with a sketch of the seducer, with cape and sword, doublet and hose, holding aloft a glass of wine. The exterior of the building, washed in ochre and white and decorated with wrought-iron balconies dripping with geraniums, is very atmospheric, especially at night when lit with soft lamps. But it is best to enjoy the seductive medieval atmosphere outside in the square amid the orange trees, because inside the tavern is brutally anonymous, modernized with harsh strip lighting and plastic wood. Perhaps the aged, upper floors and picturesque balconies are equally fake.

The neighbourhood's flat-faced houses offer windows directly on to the street encased in fat wrought-iron bars or *rejas*. This typical component of Andalusian architecture traditionally imprisoned the womenfolk, enforcing the fierce distinction, said to have originated

with the Moors, between indoors (women's domain) and the public street (male territory). But like any frontier zone, the *rejas* are ambiguous. They protect women from men's advances, while simultaneously providing the opportunity for them to display themselves and for clandestine—or even open—nocturnal contact. Gerald Brenan, in his 1930s memoir *South of Granada*, reflected on the importance of *rejas*, which persisted until the 1950s, in Andalusian romantic life. "Young men and women, though separated by physical barriers, were given ample opportunity for seeing and speaking to one another in privacy. Indeed, the bars of the reja were so far from being a real obstacle that it might be said that they actually increased the strength of the forces that played across them, in much the same way as a barrage increases the strength of the current in a river. Love was generated, as it always is, by difficulties, while the fact that the two novios (sweethearts) could never be together on the same side of the fence allowed them an ease and naturalness in conversation that was unknown to our Victorian ancestors..." Brenan confesses that he fell victim to the complaint of "eating iron", loitering by the *rejas* to win the favour of a young woman half-hidden within. He was disillusioned, however, when he finally met the object of his desires, to find that she was very short, and had increased her stature by standing on a box.

Scene Two of Zorrilla's play is set in such a street, and makes full dramatic use of the shadowy corners and whispered through-the-bars intrigue. This atmospheric Santa Cruz quarter contains unexpected nooks and passages, and bewitching inner patios glimpsed behind barred gates. The area is particularly enchanting after dark, with its muted lamps and its hush. The soft tread of passersby and their quiet voices produce a seductive intimacy, especially during warm nights when the air is heavy with the scent of orange blossom. You may brush your shoulders against barred doors and windows that allow outsiders to peep inside, indeed encourage them to admire the leafy patios with their tiled fountains, but not to enter. Such barriers proved powerless before Don Juan's ability to charm his way behind them by force of persuasion lubricated by money. Spanish literature is full of tales of locks, gates and iron bars that melt away when those who are supposed to guard them are seduced by a wily charmer. For men like Don Juan, who uses his talent for eloquence to advance his seduction, the stout iron *rejas* offer a provocation for dalliance, not a barrier to it.

By introducing the convent, whose walls Don Juan storms by guile, Zorrilla brilliantly develops another key figure: the scheming *duenna* or ladies' maid. This woman, perhaps a nun, but worldly and wily, is suborned by money or the prospect of an amorous adventure of her own to betray the innocent virgin in her charge. Brígida, who is guardian, governess and companion to Inés in Zorrilla's piece, is a character known in Spanish tradition as a *celestina*. At its most innocent, a *celestina* is a go-between or matchmaker, but she also carries connotations of being someone who supplies an innocent girl in exchange for money or favours: in other words a procuress, or madam. The name comes from the protagonist of the celebrated 1499 play by Fernando de Rojas in which a scheming woman brings about the misery and death of a pair of young lovers.

A related theme highlighted in the Don Juan legend is the precarious fragility of a young maiden's virtue, so easily overthrown by a determined suitor and a pliant accomplice. Cervantes' *The Jealous Extremaduran*, also set in Seville, hinges on the duplicity of a *duenna*. The old man of the title marries a beautiful young girl, Leonora, and builds a house without windows, with high walls and complicated double doors so that his young wife never goes out, nor has contact with any other man. Houses like this can still be seen throughout Santa Cruz and the Judería, the old Jewish quarter. "And the principal duty of guarding and looking after Leonora was entrusted to a wise and circumspect duenna, who was a sort of governess for Leonora, with the duty of supervising everything that went on the house," Cervantes writes, deadpan, and one realizes with a chill that here lie the seeds of tragedy. A young Sevillian "man about town", Loaysa, lays an elaborate plan to gain entry to the house, and eventually to Leonora. His success is ensured when he stirs the desire of the *duenna*, Marialonso, who addresses "loving words" to him. Loaysa resolves, in Cervantes' crisp phrase, "to use her as a hook to catch her mistress" and the *duenna* rushes off to convince the unworldly young wife to receive the adventurer. Cervantes rails: "Oh you duennas, placed by birth and custom in the world to bring to naught a thousand good honest intentions! You with your long, pleated headdresses, chosen to rule over the halls and drawing rooms of illustrious ladies, how ill you exercise your function, a function which is now more or less unavoidable! In short, the duenna said so much, the duenna was so persuasive that Leonora gave in, Leonora was deceived and Leonora was ruined."

Cervantes' Marialonso, Zorrilla's Brígida and Rojas' Celestina are, notwithstanding their social standing and the responsibility entrusted in them, light women, easily corrupted. They all share a persuasive verbal agility that, in combination with their authority, convinces the maiden in their charge to override her better judgment. One of the most moving moments in Zorrilla's *Don Juan Tenorio* is when the innocent Doña Inés half resists but is egged on by her *duenna* to accept Don Juan's scheme. These characters are vividly drawn and as vital a component of Spain's literary tradition as is Don Juan himself, Don Quijote or Sancho Panza. These formidable schemers are frighteningly credible, and the audience trembles for the fate of the frail, vulnerable females in their care.

Don Juan's Neurosis

Don Juan did not really enjoy his conquests. This is one of the most interesting contradictions of his compelling personality. Obsessed with women, he lingers over none. In none of his literary incarnations does he experience joy in an encounter, or regret its passing. His life is a mechanical series of physical conquests, each forgotten as new victims cross his path. Don Juan, confident of his sexual power, loves the thrill of pursuit, a thrill conveyed in breathless, passionate verse. His urgency fuels a stirring eloquence that dissolves the will of his victims. The famous "sofa scene" in *Don Juan Tenorio*, when he declares his (at this stage, still fabricated) love for Inés, and seduces her, is a high point of Spanish drama, and the bane of generations of schoolchildren condemned to learn the passage by heart. He begins by assuring the frightened child, whom he has effectively kidnapped, that she is "under his protection" and then captivates her with his silver words: "Ah! Isn't it true, angel of love,/that on this secluded shore/the moon shines brighter/and you breathe more freely?" He builds up to an impassioned declaration of love that Inés interrupts with a distraught "Silence, for God's sake, oh Don Juan!/I cannot resist/much longer without dying/such never experienced desire." And she concludes: "Don Juan! Don Juan! I implore you/with your noble compassion:/rip out my heart, or love me, for I adore you."

In later years the author dismissed this exchange as too flowery and prolix, dramatically absurd considering the lovers were in imminent danger of being discovered. Eloquence alone does not finally convince his victim to submit, however, until Don Juan falsely promises marriage. Once the seduction is accomplished, his pleasure is to boast of his conquests and bask in the admiration of his friends. He relishes his fame as a seducer, and scorns the grief of the women he casts off. In one cruel scene in Zorrilla's play, when Don Juan and Don Luis are comparing their conquests, Don Juan brags of a having murdered 32 men in duels and conquered 72 women in the course of the past year. He also boasts of their social range: "From a royal princess/to a fisherman's daughter,/Oh! My love has encompassed/the entire social scale". He promises to conquer his friend's intended bride, and reckons that six days will be sufficient because he does not need much time to win and dispatch his victims: "One day to fall in love with them,/another to enjoy them/another to get rid of them,/two days to replace them/and an hour to forget them."

This is not healthy behaviour. Gregorio Marañón, who in addition to being a distinguished historian was also something of a psychologist, believed that "Donjuanism" was adolescent, even pathological. He observed that Don Juan's actions revealed that far from loving women, he despised them as individuals. "Permanently loved, he was incapable of loving". Marañón suggests that Don Juan may even have been homosexual. Donjuanism, he posits, is a young man's malady. "This juvenile, transient donjuanism, which is usually the most frequent, supports my theory of Don Juan's weak virility, because adolescence is the stage when normal sexual orientation is still indeterminate. The real man, when he is mature, ceases to be Don Juan." It is a mistake, a literary mirage, to consider Don Juan as an archetype of virility, as V. S. Pritchett suggests. Marañón adds: "In reality, Don Juans who continue as such to the end of their lives, retain all the traits of this youthful indeterminacy. And that, precisely, is one of the secrets of their seductive power."

But the analyst of libido resists his own conclusion: "I don't mean to say exactly that Don Juan is an effeminate man, or homosexual. Don Juan has an immature, adolescent instinct, blocked at the stage of being attracted to women in general… He loves women but is incapable of loving *a woman*, which is the stage when a man becomes a real, perfect man." Don Juan is always on the run, always has a horse or a boat prepared to whisk him to the next conquest on a perpetual voyage of promiscuity. He leads an essentially peripatetic life, which is perhaps why, Marañón speculates in an intriguing aside, "there is such a great abundance of Don Juans in the diplomatic corps." Even the scientific Marañón has at this point taken on the myth as if it were reality. You have to keep reminding yourself that Don Juan is a literary invention. Or, if he seems real, it must be because he strikes such a deep echo in the Spanish, particularly the Sevillian, soul. An interesting detail that reveals the constant interweaving of myth and reality is that Zorrilla's Don Juan also witnesses his own midnight funeral, just as the real Miguel Mañara did, or is reputed to have done.

Mythical or not, in the centre of the Plaza de Refinadores in the Barrio de Santa Cruz is a bronze statue of Don Juan standing on an elegant, if somewhat chipped, granite plinth. He is wearing a doublet and thigh-high boots and, with his cape hanging from his arm, manages to look both arrogant and supplicating. "To Don Juan, in homage to his universal personality and the pride of his myth," the inscription reads. It is dated spring 1974, the closing months of Franco's dictatorship, a period shrouded in double standards, when male promiscuity was tolerated and glorified, while women who fell victim to male predators were persecuted and ostracized. This was a time, like the period of moral decadence in which Don Juan strode the land, when stifling sexual repression created a grotesque moral architecture of double standards, betrayals, hypocrisy and mostly silent female suffering.

Around the plinth are the lines from Zorrilla extolling the Don's swaggering prowess, taken from a notice that Don Juan posts up while on the run in Naples. "Here is Don Juan Tenorio/And there is no man his equal./ From the haughty princess/to the lowly fisherwoman/all women are fair prey;/and he will undertake anything if it involves gold or valor. Let troublemakers seek him out;/let gamblers encircle him;/let anyone who dares come forth/to see if anyone can outsmart him,/in gambling, duelling or making love." Seville's city authorities erected this monument: they must have believed that Don Juan is more than just a myth, more even than a "universal personality". For them, and for many Spanish men, he remains a local hero.

Chapter Six
CARMEN: FEMME FATALE

Students sit hunched on the stairs, loll along the corridors, pour into the canteen. They seem bright and alert, despite the studied casualness of their attire: fringed everything, and the occasional rainbow-striped crochet shoulder bag. But neat hair, corduroy trousers and cashmere jumpers are much in evidence too. These youngsters are a credit to the grandeur of their surroundings. Seville's university has some of the handsomest lecture halls, finest rose-marble staircases, courtyards and tinkling sculptured fountains of any comparable institution in Spain, if not Europe. Some vaulted ceilings have been lowered, some high and wide oak portals give on to administrative offices carved up cruelly by screens and flimsy partitions. But few of those who rush from one lecture to the next, or queue to complete some administrative task, seem conscious of their surroundings, or of the fact that this magnificent building was until 1959 Spain's—that is, Europe's—powerhouse for the manufacture of cigars. Or that this is the setting for Seville's most renowned literary heroine, the free-spirited gypsy girl who embodies the Spanish ideal of the sultry femme fatale.

Seville University makes little fuss over its present home in the historic Royal Tobacco Factory, despite a glorious main door crowned with a marble trumpeter with gilded wings who seems about to launch off into the heavens. The building, constructed between 1725 and 1766, houses the faculties of Law, Science, Philosophy and Literature, each occupying a wing of the four-square construction. With its 28 patios (some say 100, which sounds excessive) this is said to be Spain's biggest building after the gigantic El Escorial palace and monastery north of Madrid. At the time of its completion it was possibly the biggest industrial structure in Europe. Those responsible for the university's external relations provide information only about academic courses. They know little about their building's illustrious and romantic past. An elderly concierge huddled in a smoky cubbyhole confides some tantalizing snippets about the factory's original purpose, perhaps embroidered for a curious foreign visitor, that none the less fizzle out with a shrug and a "that's all I know".

The present tobacco factory, situated since 1959 in the city's Los Remedios suburb across the Guadalquivir, seems equally indifferent to the cultural and literary legacy of its original site, where Carmen, the seductive cigar-girl or *cigarrera*, captured the heart of the noble-minded if weak-willed soldier Don José. Carmen persuades Don José to desert his regiment and join her band of smugglers and, when her fickle passion cools, he becomes so tormented with jealousy that he kills her rather lose her to a rival.

This quintessentially Spanish—or, more properly, Andalusian—heroine was created by the Frenchman Prosper Mérimée in 1845, apparently after hearing a story from a friend, the Countess Montijo, in 1830, on one of his visits to Spain. During the 15-year gestation of his short story—a genre Mérimée is considered to have pioneered in its modern form—he added impressions from his Spanish travels, gatherings from his wide reading of Spanish literature, and especially material about gypsies, including numerous pungent proverbs.

Yet Carmen's claim to world immortality is really due to the opera by another Frenchman, Georges Bizet, premiered in 1875, the year the composer died at only 37. Bizet's *Carmen* initially left the critics cold, but the composer was apparently confident that he had produced something special. Mérimée and Bizet were both driven by Romantic notions blossoming around this time that had more basis in fantasy than fact. Mérimée was a knowledgeable Hispanist, but Bizet, whose rousing music stirs up vivid impressions of Seville's coarse, shrieking factory girls, lowlife taverns, bandits' mountain lair and the death and glory of the bullfight, never crossed the Pyrenees. He was, however, deeply influenced by painters such as Edouard Manet, and by other travellers who visited Spain. These included the poet and art critic Théophile Gautier, Mérimée of course, and one Baron Charles de Davillier, who wrote a chronicle of Spain illustrated by his travelling companion, the artist Gustave Doré, which was said to be Bizet's prime source of inspiration during his composition of the opera. *Carmen*, story and opera, is steeped in what became Romantic clichés of Spain: dramatic mountain landscapes frequented by gypsies, *bandoleros* and bullfighters, whose dances and fiestas celebrated the allure of freedom, eroticism and death.

A creature of nineteenth-century French Romanticism, then, Carmen was long scorned and rejected by Spaniards as a misleading pseudo-exotic caricature created by and for outsiders who knew nothing of the real Andalusia. The American writer James Michener wrote in his classic *Iberia*: "Say the Spanish intellectuals with resignation, 'Carmen is the cross each Spaniard has to bear.' But others confess, 'We're just bitter that it took two Frenchmen to invent her.'" Belatedly, in recent years, the personality of Carmen is being re-appropriated within Spain. Carlos Saura's flamenco version of the story became an international hit film in 1983. A year later, Francesco Rosi's big-screen opera, filmed in Seville, catapulted the Spanish-American opera singer Julia Migénes Johnson to world fame in the title role, eventually stabbed by none other than Plácido Domingo. The Spanish director Vicente Aranda recently filmed in the Tobacco Factory as backdrop to yet another blockbuster cinema version of the steamy tale. A planned open-air version of the opera, set in Seville's bullring, the tobacco factory and the streets of the city seeks to celebrate the heroine and attract international opera lovers. A historian of science, who occupies a cosy office in the factory's former private prison, now a department of the university, insists—without offering evidence—that Carmen is just the legendary face of a person who really did exist.

The libretto adapted by Henri Meilhac and Ludovic Halévy for Bizet's opera is lighter and simpler than Mérimée's story. But both contain the inexorable drive towards tragedy prefigured in Carmen's first seductive promise to Don José, which includes the warning: "If I love you, watch out!" In Mérimée's story, after their first glorious romp in Calle Candilejo, Don José asks when he will see her again, and Carmen taunts: "You've had a brush with the devil… Think no more of Carmencita, or else she may wed you to a widow with wooden legs" (i.e. the gallows, widow of the last man hanged). The drama moves inevitably to the gates of the bullring where Don José stabs his tempestuous lover, and Carmen's dying cry mingles with the cheers inside the arena where her new love is savouring his taurine triumph.

The Royal Tobacco Factory
Built by order of King Fernando VI, the Real Fábrica de Tabacos, the Royal Tobacco Factory, was conceived as a self-contained mini-city, a semi-fortress. A company of soldiers had its barracks inside the factory. The building is still surrounded on three sides by a deep ditch or moat,

whose damp floor is smothered in greenery. And it still has its little guardhouses at each corner, though these days they contain nothing more military than plant pots, ladders and gardening tools. There even remains a little drawbridge on the side facing the neighbouring Alfonso XIII Hotel. The concierge in his cubbyhole told me there was a hidden *embarcadero*, a mooring point for boats that could travel via an underground river to and from the Torre del Oro just a few yards down the road towards the banks of the Guadalquivir. He said the secret waterway was once used to bring tobacco in from galleons moored in the river, to prevent the precious cargo being seized by pirates before it reached its destination. He added that the entrance to this underground rivulet was "in the gardens" and "infested by cockroaches". I could not find it, but perhaps it exists, clogged by undergrowth. However, a couple of prints of the sixteenth-century city that I bought nearby clearly show a rivulet winding inland beside the Torre del Oro. It was the Tagarete, a tributary that meandered into the Guadalquivir in this marshy city. The waterway disappears from the maps in the early 1700s, when the factory was built. Did it silt up, as did the Guadalquivir itself, eventually bringing this great imperial seaport to its knees? Or was the little waterway covered over, as buildings and parklands spread beyond the ancient walls?

The main door is crowned by the female trumpeter with gilded copper wings who represents Fame, the back of her left hand turned against her hip in true Sevillian style. Also adorning the portal are busts of Christopher Columbus—"discoverer" of the lands of tobacco who brought the precious leaves home to the city in triumph—and of the conquistador Hernán Cortés, the first European said to adopt the custom of smoking it. (Anglo-Saxon tradition, bolstered some decades ago by a hilarious comic monologue by the American comedian Bob Lockhart, attributes this pioneering achievement to Sir Walter Raleigh.)

Flanking the imposing main entrance, two modest but elegant brick buildings face each other across a broad open courtyard dotted with motorcycles, stray cats and crowds of bright youngsters. On the left is the chapel, of refreshingly non-imposing human dimensions by Sevillian standards, containing a weeping Virgin draped in white lace and black velvet. She holds a rosary in her left hand, a lace handkerchief in her right, and has a jewelled dagger plunged through her heart.

The matching building on the right of the courtyard, painted in Seville's traditional bullring colours of blood red and sand yellow, was constructed in 1757 as the factory's private prison. Within the heavy studded door is a pretty patio, and a ceramic plaque on the wall explains that the prison originally contained 16 cells, graded by comfort according to the professional category of the employees who were disciplined under the factory's autonomous justice system. The brick-lined cells with their low vaulted ceilings were converted in 1974 into offices for the university's History of Science department. With roof grilles and circular barred portholes, the cells upstairs on the second floor were more spacious and luxurious, and offered natural light. These upper cells were for "distinguished prisoners", the plaque says, quoting the words of a historian of the 1950s, E. González de León. But it adds that even the downstairs cells for ordinary workers who transgressed factory rules were "very comfortable". The factory had its own military anti-disturbance guard and disciplinary tribunals so that theft, fights and other misdemeanours could all be punished within the factory gates. Such an apparatus of control suggests that the factory, with its thousands of workers, plus its stables for horses and for mules that worked the mills, was as much a fortress-cum-barracks as workplace. An autonomous legal and penal system made sense in what was, after all, not just the production centre of a hugely lucrative royal monopoly of one of the world's most expensive stimulants, but also the custodian of the vast revenues it generated.

Early in Mérimée's story, and Bizet's opera, the gypsy girl Carmen gets into a fight inside the factory and slashes the face of one of her workmates with a knife. The conscientious soldier Don José rushes to investigate, handcuffs her and takes her to prison. But she exerts her seductive charms upon him, promises him further favours, and he frees her. He is then himself jailed for his dereliction of duty, and months pass before he can meet her in the tavern of gypsies and smugglers where she has promised to surrender to him. In the meantime, a dashing young bullfighter, Lucas in Mérimée's tale, Escamillo in Bizet's opera, has caught her eye. After a night of dancing, Don José has to return to barracks, but Carmen challenges him to desert and join her band of gypsy robbers, which he does, and burns his boats by raising his sword to a superior officer.

The scene moves to the gypsies' encampment in the mountains, and finally to the bullring for the tragic climax. In Mérimée's story it is clear that the prison in which Carmen, then Don José, is confined is in the heart of town, down Calle Sierpes (Serpent Street), the site of the prison where Cervantes was held. The name Serpent is also, supposedly, Mérimée's reference to the serpent in the Garden of Eden that led Adam to his downfall. How much more claustrophobic and intimate, however, how much more stifling the emotional turmoil of the poor hero if one imagines that the prison in which Don José first detains Carmen, and where he then languishes, is within the factory gates, and that he is held captive at the scene of his first fatal lapse.

The Cigarreras

The outer passages and rooms of the main building contained offices and residential quarters, while the inner core around the central patio housed enormous galleries and vaults supported by pillars where the various processes of tobacco production were carried out. Some 5,000 women are said to have been employed there in 1800, although one estimate puts the figure at 12,000. They prepared and rolled the tobacco leaf into cigars or chopped rolled and ground it for pipe tobacco or snuff. The leaves were dried in special ovens that demanded a constant temperature and humidity apparently secured by a system of subterranean waterways (that underground river again) punctured by ten wells.

An atmospheric—if romanticized—painting *Las Cigarreras* by Gonzalo Bilbao y Martínez of 1915, hangs in Seville's Museo de Bellas Artes just across town, a gallery reputed to be surpassed in Spain only by the Prado in Madrid. The painting shows crowds of artfully posed, smiling, beautiful young women working at their tobacco-related tasks in a long arched gallery lit by shafts of sunlight flooding the scene from high circular windows. At the heart of the picture is a mother nursing her baby, with a cradle beside her, surrounded by admiring companions. That image is brilliantly recalled in the opening sequence of Aranda's recent film version of Carmen. The *cigarreras* were particularly fond of this painting and took a vast procession of decorated horse-drawn carriages to the railway station to greet "their painter" with full honours when Bilbao y Martínez returned in triumph from the National Exhibition in Madrid.

The right to bring babies into the factory was one of the important early victories of the *cigarreras'* labour struggles. These feisty, mostly gypsy women were pioneers of European trade union rights. The factory even provided high-sided, wooden cradles that their mothers could rock with their foot without having to interrupt their work. Other victories achieved as early as the eighteenth century were the eight-hour day, retirement pensions, working clothes and the custom of respecting the preferences of workers nearing retirement. An engraving by Gustave Doré of the tobacco workers in 1862, sketched on a visit to the factory with Baron Davillier, shows a mother glancing from her workbench to her baby asleep in a cradle, and a toddler squatting on the floor. Workers could even come and go as they please, if we are to believe a snatch of dialogue in a fin-de-siècle tale by the French novelist, Pierre Louÿs.

> *"Do you come every day?"*
> *"Practically."*
> *"You mean...?"*
> *"I mean, if it doesn't rain, if I'm not tired or if I don't fancy taking a stroll. Here you come and go as you like. Ask the other girls. But you have to be here by midday; otherwise they won't let you in."*

The only inflexible rule was the absolute prohibition on stealing tobacco. This prompted the much remarked-upon personal searches that each operative had to undergo individually. The practice prompted ribald nineteenth-century popular couplets: "The cigarreras carry in their chignon/a little Havana cigar for their José." Carmen herself may have enjoyed more fame in the rest of Europe than among Spaniards, but the spirited cigar-workers were celebrated in their home city for their grace and wit, even for their special way of tapping their feet. A popular *sevillana* sung at the Feria in May includes the line: "Cigarreras have in their shoes/a lyric that says 'Viva tobacco!'"

This social hothouse (although the composer never actually saw the real thing) inspires the scene that opens Bizet's opera. It was apparently customary for young men to gather at the factory gate to watch the women going to and from their work. The courtyard of the Tobacco Factory is where Mérimée's doomed hero makes his dramatic and fateful first encounter with Carmen.

She was wearing a very short red skirt, beneath which you could see her white silk stockings with holes in them and dainty red morocco-leather shoes fastened with flame-coloured ribbons. Her mantilla was parted so as to reveal her shoulders and a big bunch of acacia flowers which she had in the front of her blouse. She had another acacia bloom in one corner of her mouth, and she moved forward swaying her hips like some filly out of the Córdoba stud. In my part of the world everyone would have crossed themselves at the sight of a woman dressed like that; but here in Seville everyone paid her some risqué compliment on her appearance. She replied to them all, eyeing them archly, with her fist on her hip, brazen like the true Gypsy she was.

Carmen taunts the soldier with some flirtatious repartee and "taking the acacia flower from her mouth, she flicked it at me with her thumb, right between the eyes. Señor, it was like a bullet hitting me. I didn't know where to hide myself. I stood there like a block of wood. When she had gone into the factory, I saw the acacia flower had fallen to the ground at my feet. I don't know what came over me, but I picked it up without my companions noticing and tucked it away in my tunic for safe keeping. That was my first piece of folly!"

It is hardly surprising that this exotic stuff fired the feverish imaginings of Romantic travellers throughout the nineteenth century. The Tobacco Factory became a destination on the European Grand Tour for well-bred and inhibited northern boys in search of sexual titillation. "By Mérimée's day the interest of foreigners was concentrated on four connected rooms at the heart of the immense complex of the factory, for here were gathered a reputed three thousand female cigar makers, chattering away, their colourful street clothes hanging around the walls," observes the English travel writer Michael Jacobs. "One of Andalusia's great attractions was its beautiful women. And these four rooms, with their steamy, hothouse atmosphere, seemed to offer travellers unlimited possibilities for studying these women in a suitably sensual environment."

The nineteenth-century traveller and writer on Spain, Richard Ford, enhanced the women's racy reputation by commenting that they were known to be "more impertinent than chaste" and that they sometimes smuggled out "the weed in a manner her most Catholic majesty never dreamt of." The French Romantic writer and traveller

Théophile Gautier was enchanted. He wrote in *Voyage en Espagne* (1845): "We were taken to the workrooms where the leaves are rolled into cigars. From five to six hundred women are employed in preparing them. As soon as we set foot in the room we were assailed by a hurricane of noise: they were all talking, singing and quarrelling at the same time. I have never heard such an uproar. They were for the most part young, and some of them were very pretty. The extreme simplicity of their dress and the carelessness with which they wore it enabled one to appreciate their charms with complete freedom. Some of them had a cigar stump stuck resolutely in the corner of their mouths, with all the aplomb of a cavalry officer; others—O Muse come to my aid!—chewed away like old sea dogs, for they are allowed to take as much tobacco as they can consume at the workplace."

Yet the reality of these women, famed as sensual, impertinent beauties, often fell short of their eager visitors' inflated expectations. "I have never beheld such an assemblage of uglinesses," wrote one, George Dennis in his travel book *A Summer in Andalucia* (1839). The writer Willis Bexley remarked in 1875 that Spanish women did not have a good complexion and that "in the Tobacco Factory it is absolutely repulsive... in this pest-house the women smell as if they had breathed the deadly malaria of the Pontine marshes and were becoming prematurely mummified. Sallow, shrunken, shrivelled specimens of humanity, life seems to have but little hold upon the older of the operatives."

These male writers, whether adulatory or contemptuous, observed the *cigarerras* as alien, exotic objects, with a voyeuristic prurience. It is a pity no female traveller recorded her impressions of the scene. But the distinguished Galician novelist Emilia Pardo Bazán did visit the cigar factory in her native La Coruña for her 1882 novel *La Tribuna*, and noted that the cigarette workshop was a more agreeable place than the rooms devoted to cigar-making. The work was cleaner and more delicate, and done mostly by city girls, she said. The cigar-makers were mostly village women, and mothers of large families overwhelmed with work and bundled up in their shawls, indifferent about how they looked.

The account by Edmondo de Amicis, the Italian self-styled writer-tourist, in 1872 describes his astonishment at the spectacle of the factory in full swing:

The first impression is stupendous: some 800 young women appear before you, divided into groups of five or six, crowded together, seated round work tables, fading confusedly into the distance until the far ones are barely visible; all young, some just girls. Eight hundred heads of deep black hair, dark faces from all the provinces of Andalusia. You hear a buzzing like a town square full of people. The walls, from the entrance to the exit, in the three halls, are covered with clothes, skirts, shawls, handkerchiefs and scarves. And curiously, all that mountain of clothes that would fill a hundred shops present two dominant colours one on top of the other, like the colours of a huge flag: black of the shawls and the pink of the dresses, mixed with red, white, purple and yellow. It seems like an immense fancy-dress shop or an immense dance hall where the dancers, to be freer, had hung on the walls all that was not strictly necessary to guard their modesty... Since the heat was unbearable, all had taken off as much as possible, and among the 5,000 workers, there were scarcely 50 whose arms and shoulders could not be glimpsed by a visitor. To say nothing of the extraordinary examples who flitted from one room to the next, behind doors and columns, in far corners. There are beautiful faces, and even those not beautiful have something that catches the attention and imprints itself on the memory: the colour, the eyes, the eyebrows, the smile... All have a rose, some violets or a sprig of wild flowers plaited in their hair. Mothers work while moving a leg that's tied to a little cord that makes the cradle rock.

None of the contemporary accounts, however overheated, recounts the legend that the tawny beauties hoisted their skirts to roll the cigars against their thigh. Bexley even showed some interest in working conditions: he said that the women worked twelve hours a day, with an hour's break for lunch, which was provided on the premises to reduce the opportunity for smuggling. He considered the stifling, nicotine-laden atmosphere a health risk, nicotine "being among the deadliest of poisons." One Dr. Hauser, who spent many years in Seville, published a report on conditions in the Tobacco Factory in 1882, when some 5,000 workers were employed there. He observed that the workshops were spacious and seemed hygienic, but insisted that the nature of the work demanded a better ventilation system to cut down the inhalation of tobacco powder, which damaged not only the lungs and skin but also the eyes. The Romantic visitors were most struck by the *cigarreras'* eyes: "Leaving the factory, you seem to see for a moment on all sides black pupils that watch you with a thousand different expressions of curiosity, boredom, sympathy, joy, sadness, sleepiness," concludes Amicis. But there is intriguing evidence to suggest that the *cigarreras'* famed black eyes were actually symptoms of a disease caused by their work. Two doctors from Marseilles, Richaud and Morin, wrote that the handling of tobacco produces a particular eye complaint, what they called "a sort of ophthalmia" characterized by the dilation of the pupil and the congestion of the iris and the retina. The wide, brilliant, jet-black eyes peculiar to the *cigarreras*, which inspired poets and fluttered the hearts of young travellers who intercepted their bold glances, could have been simply an occupational hazard caused by nicotine poisoning.

Holy Smoke

Tobacco continues to play a central part in Spanish social and cultural life, as anyone who has suffered from Spain's seemingly obligatory custom of smoking can testify. The allure of the aromatic, addictive leaf has its origins in the conquest of America. The Sevillian friar Bartolomé de Las Casas, in his unfinished *History of the Indies* chronicling Christopher Columbus' first voyages, describes how two Spaniards walking through a village in the New World observed how men carried in their hands a lighted firebrand and "certain herbs whose fumes they savoured." The scene is thought to have been witnessed towards the end of 1492 on the eastern coast of Cuba, when Columbus sent two of his companions to explore the interior of the island. The two men discovered the plant, which locals called *cohiba* or *cojiba*, and one of the Spaniards, Rodrigo de Jerez, brought some back home to the port of Ayamonte, west of Seville, in what was probably Spain's first case of tobacco smuggling. "Dried herbs placed in a certain dry leaf, in the form of a musket barrel… and one end is lit and through the other the smoke is drawn or sucked or taken in with inhaled breath. This has the effect of sending the flesh to sleep, almost causing drunkenness, and they say that they do not then feel fatigue. These muskets, or whatever we should call them, they call tobaccos," wrote Las Casas.

Spaniards still call cigarettes "tobacco", as in the phrase "I'm going to buy tobacco." Tobacco was officially introduced into Spain—that is, into Seville—in the early sixteenth century. "The seamen brought back the habit of chewing a brownish plant, which stained their saliva yellow and gave their beards a strong smell of licorice, vinegar, spices and many other things, none of them pleasant," wrote one contemporary chronicler. But tobacco's calming effects were noticed from the first moment of the conquest, and Sevillian doctors and pharmacists began to study the plant's therapeutic qualities. One medic, Nicolás Monardes, catalogued 65 diseases that could be cured by tobacco. He cultivated a small tobacco plantation of his own in the garden of his house in Calle Sierpes, to study the plant's possible uses. Dr. Monardes found that chewing the leaf and root of the plant cured his toothache.

The Portuguese, the English and the French did much to spread tobacco throughout Europe, but the world's best tobacco was said to come from the Spanish colony of Cuba. From 1659 onwards, the objections of Cuban (i.e. occupying Spanish) cattle farmers, plus the moral warnings of the danger of addiction, and of the perils of contraband, were all swept away. Tobacco was planted extensively in Cuba and great cargoes were soon being unloaded on to the harbours of Cadiz and Seville. Until the early seventeenth century, tobacco was usually smoked in a pipe, but Spanish sailors returning from America in the early sixteenth century introduced the custom of smoking what they called *cigarros*—because they looked like *cigarras* or cicadas— wrapping the dried leaves within other leaves in the form of a tube or *canuto*, as they had seen the Caribbean indigenous people do. (*Canuto* is today a popular Spanish term for a marijuana joint.) In the seventeenth century tobacco became popular among all social classes in Spain, either the dried leaf for smoking, or more usually, as powder for snuff. In 1632 the Crown declared the selling of Spanish tobacco a state monopoly and in 1684, Seville became the only city where it could be produced.

Seville's (and Spain's) first tobacco factory, devoted essentially to producing snuff, was in the Plaza de San Pedro in the heart of the medieval city. Snuff was originally produced by grinding the tobacco using a pestle and mortar, and later by mills, which were at first hand-driven, later worked by mules. Milling was heavy and skilled work, and the operatives were men. The factory was expanded in 1687 and 1714, taking over part of Calle Morería, then occupying a floor of the Church of San Ildefonso, even a property belonging to the Inquisition. Finally, in 1725, it was decided to build a new, bigger factory to meet booming demand throughout Europe. A prime site was chosen on the banks of the Tagarete rivulet, between the Palace of San Telmo and the Alcázar palace, along the Calle San Fernando, with the Puerta de Jeréz on one side and the Prado de San Sebastián on the other. The factory took 33 years to complete. The first tobacco entered in 1758, and production continued there until 1959.

France produced its own snuff—*râpé* (grated)—which became an important fashion accessory up to the 1789 Revolution. The exquisite aristocrat, twirling his rococo snuffbox and elaborately sniffing sneezing powder from his frilly cuffs, symbolized the decadent opulence of the ancien régime. But Seville's own fine, golden dust known as *polvo sevillano* (Sevillian powder) was held to be superior, and came to be prized even in French salons. Gautier praises, albeit with some irony, *polvo sevillano*, which he watched being made at Seville's Tobacco Factory: "that pungent, impalpable golden-yellow powder with which the marquises of the Regency loved to sprinkle their lace ruffles: this snuff is so strong and volatile that one sneezes as soon as one enters the rooms in which it is prepared." Frenchified Spaniards, by contrast, preferred the thicker, darker Parisian *râpé*. As a result, the two countries banned the consumption of the rival nation's product, and thus fuelled flourishing cross-border contraband.

In response, the factory in Seville decided to grate its own home-produced *râpé*, and in 1786 it imported the requisite machinery, plus three young Frenchwomen to teach the workers the new skills: for French snuff was produced overwhelmingly by female workers. The French Revolution, followed by the Peninsular War, in which Spain defeated Napoleon's occupying forces in the 1810s, and the independence movements in the Spanish American colonies, transformed the political and social face of Europe, and its tobacco customs changed too.

Smoking, hitherto a plebeian practice, became a popular social custom in the early 1800s. It became smart to smoke cigars and, later, cigarettes. The tobacco factory swung into cigar production in the 1820s, and thousands of Sevillian women flocked through the gates for decades to carry out the new tasks of rolling cigars, chopping tobacco for *cigarillos*, and making cigarettes rolled in paper. Cigarettes were initially considered a humble byproduct, improvised by the factory girls to enable them to smoke discarded scraps from cigar production. The women's principal tool was the pair of scissors, to finish off the completed cigar. The scissors became the symbol of their trade, according to the verse of a popular song of around 1888, when the numbers of women employees reached their peak: "God said: Man, the bread you will eat,/you will win by the sweat of your brow./Cigarrera, He added, you'll earn your living/making your scissors go snip, snip, snip."

The workforce was organized in a sophisticated hierarchy ranging from apprentices who started work aged thirteen, peeling the stalks from the leaves, until—under the watchful eye of a veteran—they perfected the art of "making the baby", rolling a cigar with the delicacy and precision of a midwife wrapping a new-born child. The aristocrat of this noble profession was the *purera* or maker of *puros* (cigars), who received top wages. Spaniards still call cigars *puros* from the original expression: *Havanas puros*, or "pure Havanas". The Galician novelist Pardo Bazán described work in La Coruña's cigar factory in detail, without the prurience of male observers.

> *It didn't do to hurry. First you had to spread the outer wrapping, the epidermis of the cigar, very carefully over the rolling block, then cut it with a semicircular knife, tracing a 15-millimetre curve around the centre of the leaf so it fits tightly round the cigar. This layer must be a dry, wide and fine leaf of the best quality. The next layer, the dermis, can be of lesser quality, as can the filling. But the most essential and difficult art was to finish off the cigar, taper it to a point with a skilful twist of the thumb and a spatula soaked in liquid rubber, then to clip the end with a rapid snip of the scissors. The tapered point, the oblong body, the outer skin wound in an elegant spiral, the filling not so tightly pressed as to block the passage of smoke, nor so loose as to cause the cigar to wrinkle as it dried, these are the signs of a good cigar.*

By far the majority of the women workers were employed in the humbler, poorer-paid, tasks of making cigarettes and pipe tobacco. We may assume this would have been Carmen's work, since she says, in Mérimée's tale, that she had entered the factory only to earn enough money to return home to Echalar, her village in Navarra, to help her mother cultivate her twenty cider-apple trees. (The idea that this quintessentially Andalusian heroine hailed from Spain's far north and spoke Basque does not perhaps admit detailed scrutiny, although her professed affinity with the Navarran José first prompted the smitten soldier to drop his guard.) When Davillier visited the factory with Doré in 1862, he noticed that far more women were occupied making cigarettes than cigars, and that these women were overwhelmingly gypsies.

With the advent of mechanical improvements in the twentieth century to meet mounting demand for cigarettes, the number of workers decreased, leaving the teeming mass of young women a spectacle of folk memory. Yet despite the idealistic exaggerations of the Romantic writers, the myth and the reality of the tobacco workers often did coincide. The *cigarreras'* special air of fiesta, their boldness and libertarianism was no invention. Historically, their extraordinary social importance and impact upon Seville reached its peak as the Romantic movement was in full flood. Observers testify how the progress of the *cigarreras* through the city's streets always aroused excitement and comment. They actively participated in all the important festivals of Seville, including Semana Santa and the Feria. Their provocative, colourful dress, their flounces, fringed shawls and elaborate hair are a matter of historic record conserved in grainy early photographs. And their salty wit, plus their propensity to break into a *bronca* or shouting match, is perhaps the most durable of their attributes. "I want a pretty girl/even if she's not ladylike./I'd like a cigarrera/ more than eighty señoritas./Has anyone on earth more brio/than the cigarreras?" asked a nineteenth-century popular song. Carmen, an idealized fictional heroine invented by an outsider, came to personify a real social phenomenon. But by 1918, it was all over. The United States seized control of the world's tobacco trade, and both the economic reality and mythic reputation of Seville's Tobacco Factory entered into decline.

Cliché or Essence?

For the Spanish filmmaker Vicente Aranda, Carmen's most distinctive trait was her love of freedom and her contempt for authority and convention. She warns Don José: "What I want is to be free and to do as I please. Take care not to overstep the mark." Aranda directed the young Sevillian actress Paz Vega in the central role, and she plays Carmen with an uninhibited boldness reflected in several steamy sex scenes. Aranda claims that his latest of a string of screen Carmens is the first to have nothing to do with Bizet—whom he says he detests—and is based entirely on Mérimée. Aranda's Carmen is a wild and disturbing character, unredeemed by a Bizetesque heart of gold. The film portrays the chaotic social inequalities and freewheeling bandit life of the Andalusian mountains sketched by Mérimée. These scenes are drenched in gorgeous sunshine or flickering candlelight, full of flouncing girls, snarling bandits and plunging horses. Critics say that the film perpetuates the clichés of "folkloric" Andalusia, to which Aranda responds that he is only showing the reality of Carmen's world: "I filmed it all in Andalusia... what can I do if what has come out is this, if the cliché exists in Andalusia?" He added that filmmakers should not always flee from clichés. The same response was made by the popular author Arturo Pérez Reverte, whose hugely successful thriller *The Seville Communion,* which appeared in English in 1998, was also criticized for characters who embodied every Sevillian cliché from the drunken gypsy crooner to the cynical moneyed *señorito.* But that is what you find in Seville, he responded. That is what they are like.

An imposing, if curiously matronly, statue of Carmen stands across the road from Seville's Maestranza bullring, considered the finest in Spain. She is watching the main entrance, with her back turned to the Guadalquivir. Shaded by orange trees, she is given no particular prominence: you have to seek her out, which goes totally against the grain of her legendary magnetism. The statue pales in comparison with the site it occupies, and with the powerful influence that Carmen, myth or reality, continues to wield in the culture of her city.

Chapter Seven

LA MAESTRANZA AND LA FERIA:
BULLS, SHAWLS AND FLOUNCES

La Maestranza bullring, a white and ochre shrine to the art of tauromachy, is not the largest in Spain but it is, together with that of nearby Ronda, among the oldest and the most beautiful. "The bullring in Seville, by the wide slow river is one of the prettiest in Spain. Seville is the city of the bull," wrote the British author V. S. Pritchett in his chronicle *The Spanish Temper*, published in 1954 but based on his travels in Spain in the 1920s and 1930s. Bullfighting is not a sport and is therefore not a cruel sport, Pritchett claims, prefiguring Ernest Hemingway who insisted that the bullfight—"a Spanish institution"— was an art. Bullfighting reports duly appear in the culture section of Spanish newspapers, not on the sports pages. Pritchett goes further: "It is a ritual and a ceremony. It is primitive, barbarous, possibly religious in its remote origin, a descendent of the gladiatorial contest and the mediaeval tournament. There are ugly moments in the bullfight, for there are good and bad fights; but since it is conducted in hot blood and in an atmosphere where the swell of great emotion is natural, the killing of the bull is not a sadistic performance; nor does it awaken, I think, cold sadistic emotions in the audience."

Bullfighting began in Andalusia, brought, Pritchett believes, by the Moors, and Spain's best fighting bulls are bred on the region's big estates. There used to be some debate over whether bullfighting was of Roman or Moorish origin, but during the twentieth century it came to be thought that the roots went further back still, to Minoan sports, ancient agrarian rites and the cult of the ancient bull-god Mithras. No one seems to know. There is certainly a tension between bullfighting's popular roots, in collective bull festivals still favoured in northern Spain, most famously at the San Fermines or bull-running in Pamplona, and its southern counterpart. The elitist, aristocratic, individualist refinement of the taurine art launched by the matador Francisco Romero, an eighteenth-century shoemaker from the *Andaluz* town of Ronda, evolved into the *corrida* as we know it.

Aficionados consider love for *los toros* a dominant trait of Seville's personality: it makes the city, for them, centre of the universe. The obsessive self-absorption for which *Sevillanos* are renowned is summed up by the celebrated utterance of the gypsy matador Rafael Gómez y Ortega, "El Gallo", one of the heroes of Hemingway's classic study on bullfighting *Death in the Afternoon* (1932). On his return from a gruelling bullfighting tour of Colombia, El Gallo finally landed in Spain's north-eastern Galician port of La Coruña. The crossing had been terrible and left him weakened by seasickness, but the matador told his attendant he wanted to return immediately home to Seville. The attendant advised the weary bullfighter to rest before taking such a long journey, stressing that they were very far from Seville. To which El Gallo replied with the immortal words: "Seville is exactly where it should be. It is this place that is far away." And they set off forthwith.

El Gallo's younger brother José "Joselito" was one of Seville's best-loved matadors who died in the ring in Talavera de la Reina in Castile in 1920. His neighbourhood of Macarena went into deep mourning and honoured him in an elaborate mausoleum in the city's San Fernando cemetery. Mariano Benlliure's sensationally overwrought monument depicts the hero's coffin borne to his grave by life-sized figures of men, women and children in an ecstasy of grief.

The other great bullfighter who achieved glory in La Maestranza is Juan Belmonte, the poor boy from the slums of Triana who died in 1962. Belmonte tells in his autobiography (written with the help of the Sevillian journalist Chaves Nogales) how he used to row down the Guadalquivir to the flatlands near the aerodrome of La Tablada to fight bulls in the fields at moonlight, harrying them with his shirt while they were at pasture.

When we reached Tablada, a clear moon bathed the meadow in blue milk. As we reached the corral we fell silent; the oars worked dumbly with slow strokes until the boat ran aground in the mud. One of us jumped ashore first to explore the terrain. Nobody. We all disembarked and advanced through the corral avoiding the barbed wire fencing. Thistles and thorn bushes concealed us. We walked cautiously through the pasture, when suddenly an ox's baritone lowing scandalised the night. "Bulls!" we cried triumphantly. Then came the

*hard task of running through the meadow bristling with thorns to
separate the animal we wanted to fight, tire it out and surround it.*

This adventure amounted to poaching, and was illegal. Further, if these
were truly fighting bulls, and not oxen, the practice was more than
illegal; it was murderous. The *corrida* is based on the amount of time it
takes for the bull to realize that it is the man, not the cape that is the
target. A bull that has been fought before has that crucial piece of
experience, and is hence potentially more deadly.

"The urchins often played the bulls naked. Small, stunted by early
poverty, often very ill, and without great physical strength, Belmonte
developed a terrible, almost suicidal intensity, working so close to the
bull that after one corrida he found his clothes covered with the hairs
of the animal," Pritchett writes. Belmonte's intellectual temperament
attracted writers and artists, and his passion for excellence turned him
to education: "He was a distinctive figure in that intellectual movement
which arose in Spain in the generation before the Civil War and which
went to pieces when that war was lost," Pritchett concludes. Belmonte
is commemorated with a statue in Plaza del Altozano at the entrance to
Triana, near where the Inquisition's Castle of St. George used to stand.
The statue emphasizes the matador's proud bearing and the angular
determination of his jaw.

Seville is still today linked to Spain's greatest bullfighters. True
Sevillanos see their city as the hub around which the world revolves; and
the city's beating heart, the hub of the hub, so to speak, is the elegant,
late baroque bullring, renowned nationwide. La Maestranza is
identified more closely than any other Spanish bullring with the
neighbourhood that enfolds it: the populous, once deeply insalubrious,
Baratillo area of the Arenal riverside district. The illustrious bullring
lifted up Seville's marginal shantytown and endowed the area with a
pride and dignity it has sustained for more than two centuries.

Michael Jacobs opens his lively account of bullfighting in Seville
with the following astute—if for most of us impracticable—advice:
"The very attending of a bullfight demands a certain amount of ritual.
Ideally you should arrive at the Maestranza in a horse and carriage, and
enjoy a glass or two of aguardiente in one of the animated bars beside
the building before the fight. Do not get too carried away, however, as
bullfights are renowned as one of the few Andalusian activities that

always begin exactly on time." The *fiesta nacional*, as it is still called in Seville, and throughout Spain, has its most sophisticated and deeply rooted expression in the city. Many of the finest bulls that are killed in the afternoon are bred on *fincas* or estates nearby, owned by grand old *Sevillano* families, which enables enthusiasts to participate in the beasts' complete life cycle from birth to death. But there are constant complaints, best expressed by the late great *corrida* chronicler Joaquín Vidal, that bulls' current quality is hopelessly compromised by unscrupulous breeding techniques, drugging and horn-shaving. They frequently fall over at the quiver of a cape, putting the long-term future of the fiesta in doubt.

Seville's bullring was begun in 1760 by Vicente San Martin, rebuilt in 1777 and completed in 1880 by Juan de Talavera. It is owned by the Royal Equestrian School, an institution founded by Sevillian nobles in the sixteenth century. The façade recalls the sprawling rural splendour of an eighteenth-century *hacienda* or country estate. The main entrance, facing the river across the Paseo de Colón, is the Prince's Gate, decorated with marble slabs and a seventeenth-century portal taken from a convent long demolished. The life's ambition of any matador is to be carried shoulder high through this main door, borne aloft by his supporters in homage to a triumphant afternoon. *Salir por la puerta grande* ("to leave through the main gate") is a common Spanish expression applied to a person who has triumphed in any profession or line of activity.

The inside of the bullring is a great circle in which the upper tiers are covered by a gallery of rounded arches linking marble columns. The regularity of the curve is interrupted by an imposing late eighteenth-century presidential box, from which the master of ceremonies decides with a flick of his white handkerchief whether a matador's performance merits the award of, in mounting order, one ear, two ears, or two ears and a tail of his vanquished beast. The upper gallery is tiled with curved russet tiles behind which landmarks like the Giralda soar into what you hope will be a clear blue sky, although a rare cloudy one might be preferable. This is one of the most uncomfortable as well as hottest rings in the world. Most spectators must squeeze into a numbered square about a foot wide, with the knees of the person in the row behind hugging your ears, and the head of the person in front and below nestled in your lap. The ring is open to the public when bullfights are not taking place, enabling visitors to explore the handsome corridors and passageways behind the scenes. And adjoining the Maestranza is a museum containing posters, paintings, statues of past heroes, the matadors' spangled "suits of lights", and other examples of paraphernalia celebrating the transcendental importance of *los toros* in the city.

Outside are the traditional rustic wooden stands from whose upended cartwheel-like structures dangle plain earthenware water pots or *botijos* that you tilt to shoot a jet of cold water between your lips— or down your freshly pressed shirt if you are unpractised at this Andalusian art. (A similar experience can befall those who try to drink from the leather *bota* of wine, which visitors may be more familiar with.) *Botijos* date from an age before water came from the tap and are still the ideal way of keeping water cool in baking temperatures. Cheap to buy and widely available, they make good souvenirs. Just be sure to rest it on a waterproof tile, or Andalusia's fierce dry heat will produce evaporation of such power as to strip the polish from your floor.

Death in the Afternoon
Any decent guidebook will give a good account of what the bullfight entails. Hemingway's encyclopedic *Death in the Afternoon* describes in spare, passionate detail everything you may ever wish to know, including the moral dilemma facing anyone who gains pleasure from the death of an animal. He writes that it is a good idea to know what to expect before attending a bullfight. "As in all arts the enjoyment increases with the knowledge of the art, but people will know the first time they go, if they go open-mindedly and only feel those things they actually feel and not the things they think they should feel, whether they will care for the bullfight or not. They may not care for them at all, no matter whether the fight should be good or bad, and all explanation will be meaningless beside the obvious moral wrongness of the bullfight, just as people could refuse to drink wine which they might enjoy because they did not believe it was right to do so." Hemingway resolved his own moral dilemma in a characteristically pragmatic way: "I know only that what is moral is what you feel good after and what is immoral is what you feel bad after and judged by these moral standards, which I do not defend, the bullfight is very moral to me because I feel very fine while it is going on and have a feeling of life

and death and mortality and immortality, and after it is over I feel very sad but very fine." This is a sentiment which most Sevillians would endorse, except perhaps the part about feeling sad.

Tradition dictates that the men wear a smart tight-fitting jacket with a *clavel* or carnation in the buttonhole, a flat, broad brimmed hat and a cigar tucked in the top pocket. The flourishing of a cigar—which would traditionally have most likely been rolled just down the road—was an important part of the bullfight ritual. The women's duty is to dress as vividly and flamboyantly as possible, whilst taking care to avoid the colour yellow, which is considered bad luck. Some superstitious bullfighters went to the trouble of lining their traditional pink-and-gold cape in blue, to avoid handling the cursed yellow, said to recall the jaundiced hue of a corpse. Women are clad in the traditional flounced and frilled dresses, plus a lace mantilla and their finest *mantón de Manila* or huge square fringed and embroidered silk shawl. Those who sit in the front row, especially during the April spring fair, may drape their magnificent shawl over the *barrera* or barrier in a dramatic gesture of celebration, in vibrant counterpoint to the spangled suits and bright capes below.

Galleons and Silk

Like the *botijo* but much more glamorous, the eye-catching Spanish shawl is considered a symbol of Spain as a whole. But it actually belongs specifically to Andalusia and Seville, in whose rural suburbs to the west seamstresses still bend over sewing frames in shaded patios, tracing traditional patterns, embroidering with bright silks, and plaiting sumptuous fringes. The history of this unique garment is an astonishing tale of transoceanic enterprise and adventure that reveals much about the renaissance of this port city in the early nineteenth-century Romantic age. "The embroidered silk Manila shawl, as majestic as it is common, worn by great ladies and gypsies alike… suits their beauty so well," wrote Spain's great nineteenth-century novelist Benito Pérez Galdós in his best-known epic *Fortunata y Jacinta*:

> *Wrapping one around you is like dressing in a painting. Modern industry will never invent anything to equal the ingenuous poetry of the shawl, splashed with flowers, undulating and clinging, with the silken fringe that recalls the tangles of a dream. Its brilliant colours*

*once made entire crowds shimmer when it was in style. This beauti-
ful garment is gradually being exiled. Only the common people, with
their admirable instinct, have saved it, taking it out of trunks for life's
big occasions, baptisms and weddings... Such shawls would be
vulgar garments if they contained only the science of design; they are
not, because they preserve something of primitive and folk art, like
legends or stories from childhood, candid and richly coloured, easily
understood and resistant to the whims of fashion.*

Galdós wrote these words in 1887 when, as he says, the shawl was in
decline as a popular fashion item, becoming something of an heirloom,
a fusty curiosity. But today more than a century on, Sevillian women
still flaunt their shawls for fiestas, just as they did in the days when the
bright fragile silks were first unpacked from the galleons bringing
treasures from Spain's far eastern colony.

The Manila shawl is made from fine silk with bright embroidery of
flowers and animals, each of elaborate symbolic significance, and
bordered with an astoundingly long and swirly fringe. Some say the
fringe was a Spanish adaptation of Moorish taste. The shawl was
originally Chinese and started to become a popular female fashion
accessory in Spain and Spanish America after 1821. That was the year
trade with the colony of the Philippines was centralized in Seville. In
the second half of the nineteenth century, anything Chinese or
Japanese—silk, porcelain, fans and tea—became hugely fashionable
throughout Europe. The Philippines' capital, Manila, became a key city
for Spanish and Latin American trade and the so-called Manila shawl,
the *mantón de Manila*, a much-prized commodity. But the origins of
how this Chinese product became identified with Spanish ladies go
back nearly three centuries before.

In 1559 King Felipe II ordered a new voyage to Spain's far eastern
island possessions and instructed those he contracted for this adventure
"to know the way home, because the way out is already certain." After
long preparations the expedition set sail from Puerto de Navidad on the
west coast of Mexico in November 1564, and landed in the Philippine
island of Cebu in April 1565. Months later, on 8 October, the *nao*
(sailing ship) San Pedro crossed the Pacific from Asia to Mexico, and
entered the port of Acapulco. This was the first successful Pacific round
trip, a historic moment in the consolidation of the Spanish empire. The

voyage established a route that was to be plied by the so-called Galleon of Acapulco, or Galleon of Manila, for 250 years, the longest route in the history of navigation. From 1565 to 1815 cargo ships set out from Manila to Acapulco in late June or early July to take advantage of favourable monsoon winds for a voyage that lasted about six months. The journey from Acapulco to Manila was easier, the waters calmer. Ships set sail in February or March and entered port after just three months.

The German traveller and writer Alexander von Humboldt observed in the early 1800s that in Mexico it was said that the ships heading east "went laden with silver and priests." Passengers were mostly missionaries, royal emissaries, merchants and soldiers. They brought Christianity and Hispanic customs, including the penitents of Holy Week and religious paintings and sculptures. The principal cargo was silver, in bars or coins struck in Mexico and Peru, to pay the upkeep of colonial administrators and building works. Cows and horses were taken to Asia, and American plants like maize, cocoa, sugarcane, peanuts, tomatoes, pumpkins, papayas, peppers and avocados. On the way home, the ship brought spices, silk, ivory, porcelain, carpets, cotton cloth, mother of pearl, and cigarettes from India and Ceylon, China and Japan, whose merchants brought their goods to Manila to trade. Manila thus became one of the world's leading entrepôt ports, and its merchants made vast fortunes. The ships then returned to Acapulco to be greeted with what Humboldt called "the most renowned trade fair in the whole world". Part of the cargo remained in Mexico, some went to Peru, and the rest was carried overland to Veracruz on Mexico's eastern shore to be loaded on to the Indies Fleet and shipped across the Atlantic to Spain, to Seville.

The most important cargo transported from Manila to Acapulco was silk. The galleons, also known as silk ships, carried silk of all kinds in every stage of manufacture. They brought delicate gauze, crepe, embroidery, velvet, taffeta, damask, brocades with gold and silver thread, tens of thousands of stockings per trip, skirts and velvet bodices, capes, suits and kimonos. The hold was packed with silk counterpanes and tapestries, scarves, tablecloths, napkins, elaborate vestments for churches and convents throughout the Americas. All this came from China. At first the quality was mediocre. When the first consignments landed in Mexico the Viceroy Enriques considered them poor stuff. "I think all this business is a wasted effort, and the commerce is damaging rather than profitable, because all they bring are some miserable silks, mostly with a bad weave, and some false brocades," he scoffed. But the Chinese traders learned fast to meet the demands of their new Spanish and Mexican clients who wanted top quality and were ready to pay for it in precious metal—the only commodity offered them by Europeans in which they showed the slightest interest. And they began to copy with great skill the Spaniards' favourite designs, which soon equalled the coloured silks of Andalusia. They surpassed Europe in producing the coveted white silk: "snow is no whiter than this—there is no silk in Europe that can compare with this," wrote the seventeenth-century aristocrat Diego de Bobadilla.

By the end of the sixteenth century the quality of Chinese silk had so improved and the price dropped so much that it competed fiercely with the silks of Andalusia in the American colonies. Spanish manufacturers called in alarm for Chinese silk imports to be banned. Some early colonial governors wrote to the king warning him that the Spanish empire was handing over huge quantities of silver to Chinese merchants, who used it to buy opium—although it was the depletion of Spanish silver rather than the use to which it was put that worried the colonial authorities. Mexican pieces of silver circulated freely in China, where they constituted a form of savings. In 1535 trade was restricted, and in 1718 the silk trade with China was banned, but, following protests from the mighty middlemen of Manila, a further decree in 1734 allowed Manilans to continue their lucrative traffic with the Chinese.

They used to call the range of religious vestments, shawls, counterpanes and other hangings that reached Spain from Manila "Manila embroidery", even though it was worked in south-east China. The Philippines tried several times to establish its own silk industry, but locals did not take to planting mulberry trees or caring for silkworms, and the attempts failed. So the Philippines remained dependent on Chinese silk, and built its riches on the export trade. Packers in Manila became renowned for the skill with which they wrapped and protected their precious cargo, and packed every corner of the ship's hold to the best advantage. China became a major exporter of silk religious vestments, either painted or embroidered, which were loaded in Manila on to ships bound for Acapulco then brought to Seville and Cadiz, gateways to Europe. Similar objects of beauty and luxury reached London and Paris on ships from Britain's East India Company. The diarist John Evelyn wrote in 1664 that among a collection of rarities sent by Jesuits in China and Japan to their order in Paris were "sumptuous vestments embroidered with flowers, trees, animals and birds... the vivacity of the colours stands out... since we have nothing in Europe that can compare with this vividness and splendour."

And in its closing years, the Acapulco galleon brought the so-called "Manila shawls", which actually came from China. The square shawl is not, however, a part of traditional Chinese dress. The form was imposed by the demands of European fashion that dictated that shawls were both a garment and a decoration piece, to spread across tables and pianos or hang on walls. China began to produce *mantones* tailor-made for Europeans in the eighteenth century, and for large-scale export around 1820. Around the 1840s, a shawl manufacturing industry grew up around Canton, with the silk brought from outside the region. Shawls and china, lacquerware and ivory were later brought directly from Manila to Spain on the steam ships of the Royal Philippines Company from 1769, when the Suez Canal was opened, until 1834.

The Sevillian Cover-up

Developments in Spain shaped changing fashion and demand. In 1492 the Crown forbade Moorish women to wear the veil; bishops railed against it, and it was banned. So Muslim women living in Spain adapted the traditional shawl or wrap, which had long been an important item of women's dress throughout Castile, and put it over their head and face, leaving only their eyes visible. The fashion was immediately adopted by Christian women in the Andalusian cities of Seville, Córdoba and Granada, giving rise to the so-called *tapadas* (covered-up women). The Vatican condemned this form of covering up, and the Church warned women that if they disobeyed the order they risked being condemned as prostitutes and even excommunicated.

From Seville the veil crossed to the New World, first to Peru, where *las tapadas*, their identity protected by the enveloping cloth, embarked upon what was considered a scandalous lifestyle. The garment, far from guaranteeing a lady's modesty, enabled her to engage incognito in acts that neither the Church nor the viceroys could control. In Spain the shawl was initially simple, mostly black, decorated with a fringe, lace or stripes of ribbon, in common with the *mantas* or *mantillas* common to traditional costumes throughout Spain. The Peruvian authorities launched a ferocious campaign against the *tapadas*: police condemned any woman who covered her face to ten days jail, fined her sixty pesos and confiscated the offending shawl. For black, indigenous or mixed race women, the penalty was still harsher, and could even include corporal punishment. So, a bizarre form of entertainment arose among Lima's society women, who played cat and mouse with the police, covering and uncovering their faces whenever they spotted a patrol in the street. They defiantly made their shawls brighter and more sumptuous, which meant that the women were reluctant to lose them, so raising the stakes still higher.

By the early nineteenth century the woman in a bright enveloping shawl became a cutting-edge fashion figure in both the New World and in Spain. And the image of a woman in a shawl—from gypsy girl to fine lady—became a favourite subject for artists. The British naturalist and scientist Charles Darwin, in his exploratory voyage around South America in HMS *Beagle* in 1833, was much struck by the ladies of Lima, and wrote in his diary:

> *The close elastic gown fits the figure closely and obliges the ladies to walk with very small steps, which they do very elegantly, and display very white stockings and very pretty feet. They wear a black silk veil which is fixed round the waist behind and brought over the head and held by the hands before the face, allowing only one eye to remain uncovered. But then that one is so black and brilliant and has such powers of motion and expression, that its effect is very powerful. Altogether the ladies are so metamorphosed that I at first felt as much surprised as if I had been introduced amongst a number of nice round mermaids. I could not keep my eyes away from them.*

Later, in the Argentine capital of Buenos Aires, Darwin noticed a surprising informality among the congregation of the ornate churches: "The Spanish lady with her brilliant shawl kneels by the side of her black servant in the open aisle."

The Chinese embroideries that reached Spain from Central America were unloaded at the Casa de Contratación in Seville, and subsequently in Cadiz. In 1795, with the founding of the Royal

Philippines Company, Spain was able to negotiate directly with its far eastern colony, and no longer needed to operate through the intermediary of Mexico. In 1821 the port of Seville was reopened to ships chartered directly from Manila, which is the moment when *mantones de Manila* started to become an indispensable accessory for Spanish women, and an exotic item sought after throughout Europe. Flora Tristan, the Parisian but half-Peruvian grandmother of the painter Paul Gauguin, who later became a trailblazing feminist and campaigner for women's suffrage, arrived in 1833 in Lima in search of her paternal family. Flora Tristan's story is told in the recent novel by the Peruvian author Mario Vargas Llosa, *The Way to Paradise*. Vargas Llosa tells of how Flora, escaping a brutal husband, asks her father's Peruvian family for her inheritance. She finds in Peru revolution and her own passion for justice. In her journal "Peregrinations of a Pariah" she wrote of a lady she met there: "Señora Watrin wore a dress of cherry-coloured Florence cloth. It was very short, very low cut and with short sleeves. An immense shawl of blue crepe de Chine, on which pretty white embroidered flowers stood out, served her at one moment as a shawl, another as a mantilla. With this huge shawl, which covered up the back of her head, her dress was very extravagant... The other ladies could not approach the luxury of Señora Watrin: their dress was of blue, red or white cotton, but the form of the shawls and dresses was the same." Flora Tristan added: "Recently it has become fashionable to wear great square shawls of crepe de Chine embroidered in all colours. The adoption of this garment makes the costume more decent, hiding in its bulk the wearer's nakedness and her excessive curves."

Shawls first started to become fashionable in Europe in the late eighteenth century, worn over the simple, gauzy Empire style frocks, to complement the outfit and protect the wearer's chilly shoulders from northern draughts. These were not *mantones*; they were mostly long and narrow, often of cashmere. This fashion was reportedly introduced by Napoleon, who brought a magnificent shawl back from Egypt for Josephine. Square shawls arrived after 1820, when wide skirts had replaced the slender Empire line. They were embroidered on fine silk, and the embroiderers were said to be mostly men, even in Seville, where male embroiderers were until the end of the century masters of the elaborate vestments of the figures taken round the city during Holy Week.

Trade declined towards the end of the nineteenth century as Spain's command of the seas was challenged by other European powers, and collapsed totally with the catastrophic loss of the colonies of the Philippines and Cuba in 1898 in a foolish war against the United States that is known in Spanish history simply as The Disaster. Yet Seville's popular aesthetic in art and fashion, rooted in the early nineteenth-century Romantic age, remains strongly marked by the shawl. It simultaneously reveals and conceals; it embodies the twin spirits of wild abandon and innocent modesty, and its vibrant, exotic beauty enhances that of the wearer. No wonder Sevillian women still love it, and popular songs still celebrate it. Here are some:

> *Across the Triana bridge, Ay, passed the queen*
> *The queen passed, she wore no crown*
> *Catch up the skirt you are trailing*
> *She wore no crown, Ay, she wore a comb*
>
> *But she wore a Manila shawl*
> *Catch up your skirt that is trailing*
> *A Manila shawl, ay, that she trailed behind her.*

> *Blessed land of Cadiz/made of salt and foam*
> *you are a Manila shawl/made of sea foam.*

> *On the feast of Virgin of the dove*
> *A shawl from China, from China*
> *I'm going to give you, going to give you.*

> *Where are you going with your Manila shawl?*
> *Where are you going with your Chinese dress?*
> *I'm going to enjoy the fiesta*
> *And then I'm going home to bed.*

✻

With a Manila shawl tinted in a thousands colours
Another count passed and tried to swear love to me...

✻

If you were a true gypsy girl
With hot blood in your veins,
You'd grab your shawl
And come away with me.

Feria de Abril: High Society

You may hear songs like these, and see smaller, but equally colourful shawls at the Feria de Abril, the spring fair that Seville celebrates about a month after Semana Santa. The two festivities could not be more different. Apparently open and easygoing, the Feria is in reality a ritual even more rigidly orchestrated than the supposedly rigorous religious festival that precedes it.

It is a colourful, week-long revelry; but unless you are invited to join in, you will remain an outsider, never a participant. At the Feria, Sevillian high society and those aspiring to join it hold open house for their friends in little marquees called *casetas*, which operate as a surrogate home—a Wendy house for grownups—for the week. *Sevillanos* almost always prefer to meet friends outside the home, since a bar or restaurant is thought to be more entertaining than the front room. But the Feria is a rare opportunity to repay hospitality "at home". The event occupies an undistinguished dusty site south of the district of Los Remedios across the river. The zone, deserted for the rest of the year, forms a mini-city of criss-crossed streets named after bullfighters, strewn with Seville's characteristic fine ochre bullring sand known as *albero* and lined with rows of scarlet and green striped canvas huts. The fun, the dancing, the round the clock partying, eating and drinking, take place inside the *caseta*, and entry is checked by guards on the door, so unless you are invited—forget it. Everything about this ostensibly sociable fiesta is about exclusion. If you are not in, you are out.

The Feria originated as a cattle and horse market in 1846, invented—as non-Sevillians gleefully point out—by a Basque, Narciso

Bonaplata, and a Catalan, José María Ybarra, two local councillors in their adopted city. All the references, the costumes and the customs, are to do with the countryside and particularly the aristocratic landowners' style of country life. At the first Feria, in April 1847, in the Prado de San Sebastián where the Inquisition once burned people for heresy and which now surrounds a bus station, there was bullfighting and as much singing, dancing and drinking as horse-trading. For the opening fair 19 *casetas* were installed—simple canvas shelters where dealers could conduct their business in the shade beside the corrals of their livestock. As the years progressed, the fiesta vastly outstripped the market. In 1850 the town hall granted licences for coffee and fritter stalls, taverns, sellers of blocks of *turrón* (the almond paste much enjoyed in these parts) and of toys and water. In the 1860s gas lighting was installed, replaced in 1873 by electric bulbs. *Casetas* gradually invaded the surrounding streets. In 1877, when Queen Isabel II visited for the first time on the arm of Mayor José María Ybarra, the now traditional ruched paper lanterns bouncing overhead made their appearance, a much admired Italian import that became a Feria trademark.

Suspended during the Civil War between 1936 and 1939, the Feria made a timid reappearance in the "hungry Forties", then consolidated itself as a society event in the 1960s when Orson Welles, Prince Rainier and Princess Grace of Monaco, and Jacqueline Kennedy attended. The American president's wife wowed snobbish Sevillian society with her elegance and accomplished horsewomanship. "Oh she's just like one of us," gushed the Duchess of Alba. In 1972 the Feria moved to its present bigger site across the river, but this is now too small for the ever-increasing crowds and *casetas*, which these days number more than a thousand. The search is on for another site, but one that does not remove the festivities too far from the city centre. After all, the whole point is to be able to walk or ride to and from your Sevillian home to the Feria, and to and from the bullring, so that everyone can admire your horses, your carriages, your finery and your beautiful young women, for whom the Feria functions as a "coming-out" ceremony.

Woman's World
If Semana Santa is a man's world, the Feria is designed to show off the woman, who frequently dresses *de flamenca* or, more colloquially, *de gitana* (like a gypsy) or *de faralaes* (in ruffles). This means flaunting a

long, bright, polka-dot, flounced frock, with a flower and a tall comb (or several) in her hair, dangling earrings, and a colourful fringed shawl clasped at the waist. Handbags are not part of the costume. Essentials like purses, fans and mobile phones must be invisibly stowed in a flap-like pocket concealed behind the ruffles. Or the woman can dress *de amazona*, as a horsewoman, with tightly fitting riding jacket, high necked shirt and long hacking skirt scooped up when she rides side-saddle. Once mounted—and only then—she may wear the flat wide-brimmed Cordoban hat tilted over one eyebrow. This costume is restrained and monochrome, unlikely to frighten the horses. The men dress sombrely and discreetly, to fade into the background.

The flamenco frock, widely regarded abroad as Spain's national dress, is purely Andalusian, inspired apparently by the gaudy, frilly working overalls of gypsies and humble peasant women of the late nineteenth century who accompanied their cattle-dealing menfolk to the fair. The costume flatters the slender-torsoed but stumpy-legged Mediterranean female, and was enthusiastically taken up and refined by aristocratic local ladies eager for lively, seductive and practical party wear. The flamenco frock is Spain's—perhaps the world's—only traditional costume that is influenced by annual vagaries of fashion. You must be careful how you choose your frock for the Feria (outsiders are warned not to bother, unless in a spirit of ironical self-mockery). You have to make sure you have the right number of flounces, of the right width, with sufficiently dropped waistline or cutaway sleeve, and that you do not make the mistake of setting forth in last year's model, or colours. Most women "dress" for just one day.

Lorna Scott Fox, an English writer who lives in Seville, described in the Spanish paper *El País* how, when she put on a flamenco dress to go to the Feria she found she "wore a different body." Encasing yourself in this tight-fitting costume "is a disturbing experience," she wrote. "The tight fit and the swaying weight of so much fabric fluttering to the floor forces you into a majestic rhythmic movement quite unlike my usual gait; I wanted to twirl round, ruffle my petticoats, sit this way and that. I felt I had an entirely different body, created for the garment itself." One has a sense, when observing the women who have, as they say, "dressed", that the head and shoulders lift more proudly, their gait sways more seductively and their arms move more elegantly amid the flounces.

A Day at the Feria

A day at the Feria goes like this: arrive around midday, after a good breakfast to provide stamina for hours of walking, standing, drinking and dancing; meet friends at their *caseta* for the *aperitivo*, manzanilla or sherry—or a nauseating mixture of sherry and fizzy lemonade known as *rebujito*—or beer. This will be served with tapas of sliced chorizo or fried fish. Watch the parade of horses and carriages, being careful to avoid causing an equine traffic jam, which will produce a fierce jangling of bells, hauling back of foaming steeds, angry prancing of haughty profiles as young women perched behind their young man's saddle, clinging to his waist or to the horse's tail, crane their lovely necks to see the idiot who has shattered the austere harmony of the spectacle.

At 5pm those with tickets head groggily to the bullring and then home to sleep until nightfall. The rest may congregate at the rear of their *caseta* at a long trestle table to eat plates of hearty country fare: stewed sausage with chickpeas, gazpacho, tomato salad, slices of ham and cheese, veal sandwiches, scrambled egg with mushrooms. When I was invited to the *caseta* of my friend Isabel and her family, much of the enjoyment was in trying to restrain the ecstatic bursts of energy of a favourite three-year-old niece, "dressed" for the first time and determined to dance the whole time, her little arms permanently aloft, fingers stretched like starfish as she twirled and stamped, her face ablaze with an expression of unremitting bliss. Then it is time for a stroll, a *paseo* along the sandy streets to friends' *casetas* (the niece by now slumped exhausted in a buggy, her ruffles trailing in the dust) or just to enjoy the spectacle with the dusk descending and the lanterns twinkling.

With nightfall things become more animated, and those with sufficient energy dance *sevillanas* until dawn. These lively twirling dances look spontaneous and freeform, but have their own complex internal discipline and are not to be attempted unless the dancer knows what he/she is doing, unless of course one wants to flaunt one's status as an outsider for all to see. Standard unhelpful beginners' advice is to act as though you were plucking an apple from the tree then casting it angrily behind you. Youngsters head for the vast, seedy funfair in what is known as the Calle del Infierno, Hell Street, whose tombola stalls, scary rides and circus shows have a long tradition dating from the Feria's earliest years. Here you can buy *calentitos*, hot curly *churros* or strips of batter dipped in plastic beakers of chocolate, essential fuel in the unexpected chill of the early hours. You can watch *churros* being made in their huge vats of oil, as the *churreros* with their long pole turn and prod the coil of batter spluttering in the boiling fat, then pull it out and chop the crisp batter into manageable lengths, bundling them up rough paper parcels for customers to eat while still steaming hot. (From which comes the expressive saying *está mas caliente que el palo de un churrero*, "she's hotter than the pole of a churro-maker", usually applied to an over-eager woman.)

The rhythms of the Feria rise and fall during the day and night. You become bored and jaded, then a new group of friends arrive and you are lifted on an inebriated cloud of fun, conversation and music for hours more. You think you cannot bear another rendering of the same relentless *sevillana* songs, as people mindlessly reinsert the tape. The barman manning the 24-hour bar in the *caseta* of my friend's family confesses that he cannot bear to listen to them for the rest of the year. Before cassette machines, some people used to bring a barrel organ into their *caseta* to provide music to accompany their dancing. One year, recounts the Sevillian writer Antonio Burgos, the Polish-born classical pianist Artur Rubinstein visited the Feria and was fascinated by the *pianillo*, spending hours and hours happily turning the handle.

The Sevillian poet Manuel Machado wrote of this celebration of the Feria in 1920:

> *A caseta in the Feria is the traditional luxury of many Sevillian families. It's a luxury of the finest quality, far superior to a box at the Opera or a season ticket for the bullfight; it may be notably more expensive, but it's infinitely more enjoyable. At the same time the caseta is an extension of the home, a continuation of family life, both intimate and personal... the caseta is the home itself, conjugal, paternal, fraternal—which for a few days conveys all the pleasure and charm of the Feria, whether in the morning with the neighing of the horses from Jerez, in the afternoon, basking in a gentle breeze, or in the fantasy of the evening, full of enchanted songs and dances.*

The Feria is always the same, but constantly different, monotonous but endlessly stimulating. You do not think you can endure another hour of tedium and fatigue, but you feel regret when a huge firework display lights up the city on Sunday night to announce that it is all over for another year. The authorities thoughtfully permit an additional day's holiday—"hangover Monday"—to help revellers adjust to reality. But after a week inhabiting a flimsy stage-set, a never-never land of make-believe houses, overriding the usual conventions for eating and sleeping usually imposed day and night, you wonder how you can return to work and readjust to the real world. You may wonder, indeed, what the real world is.

Chapter Eight
FRANCO'S FIRST FOOTHOLD

Seville was Spain's first big town to fall to Franco. The city surrendered to Franco's nationalist troops on their initial assault upon the Spanish mainland from rebel bases across the Gibraltar Strait in Tangiers, in Morocco, and in the Canary Islands. Seville produced its own idiosyncratic Francoist hero, a ranting general who dominated the first days of the Civil War in the summer of 1936, and later commanded Franco's southern flank. The street now called Avenida de la Constitución was named in honour of Gonzalo Queipo de Llano until after the end of the forty-year dictatorship. Some of the earliest film footage of the Civil War shows General Queipo de Llano and his forces swaggering though the streets of Seville, with the Giralda and the cathedral—forming one of Spain's most distinctive urban profiles— prominently in the background. This demonstrated to the nation and the world that Franco's forces had landed and were advancing north in their quest to take over the country.

Queipo de Llano was commander of the frontier guards in Seville on the day of the uprising, 18 July 1936. He was not a native of the city, having arrived only the day before in his official Hispano-Suiza limousine. He had been cruising round the country in this spectacular vehicle ostensibly to inspect customs posts, but in reality, as he later confessed, mounting conspiracies against the Republic. Accompanied by just three officers and an aide-de-camp, Queipo installed himself in an office in the headquarters that had been abandoned because of the heat. Then he went along the passage to General Fernández Villa-Abrille, commander of Andalusia's armed forces. "I have to tell you," announced Queipo, "that the time has come to take a decision: either you are with me and my other comrades, or you are with this government which is leading Spain to ruin." Villa-Abrille and his staff dithered, afraid perhaps that the rising would fail, as had a conspiracy against the Republic four years earlier, and that they would be packed off to a steamy jail in the colonies. So Queipo arrested them, pushed them in a room and stationed a corporal at the door with orders to shoot anyone who came out.

Then he went to the infantry barracks where he was surprised to see the troops drawn up under arms on the square. Addressing the colonel, whom he had never met before, Queipo said. "I shake your hand, my dear colonel, and congratulate you on your decision to put yourself on the side of your brothers in arms in these hours when the fate of our country is being decided." The colonel replied "I have decided to support the government," whereupon Queipo stripped him of his command, and replaced him—after some casting about—with a captain. Then he locked up all the other officers.

With the infantry subdued, the commander of the artillery barracks and his officers also rallied to Queipo, but he found he had only 130 troops at his command: a puny force to quell a city of a quarter of a million. Summer leave had depleted the army's effective strength in Seville, as in the rest of Spain. But he sent a captain to march into the city at the head of his men to proclaim a State of War.

A heavy field gun was wheeled into the Plaza San Fernando—what is today the handsome and tranquil Plaza Nueva—and trained upon the civil government building, behind which stood the Hotel Inglaterra. Some assault guards had gathered in the hotel and in the nearby telephone exchange. The assault guards were a force created by the republican government to operate as loyal urban police, a counterweight to the paramilitary civil guard that had existed for nearly a century. (The Hotel Inglaterra remains a popular meeting place today, because of its central location, and it is renowned as Seville's oldest hotel. But it is a bit stuffy in style, despite offering good breakfasts.) It was shelled that morning. One shell hit the civil government building, and the civil governor telephoned Queipo offering to surrender if the assault guards' lives were spared. Queipo agreed, but in an early demonstration of his merciless style shot them anyway. Just before the police chief was executed, he was told his wife would receive a full salary if he handed over secret files on workers' organizations. He explained where they had been hidden, but his widow is thought to have received nothing.

Seville's paramilitary civil guard then joined the rebels when the assault troops gave in, and the city centre was in Queipo's hands by lunchtime. Radio Seville tried to rally those loyal to the republican government. The radio issued a call for a general strike and urged villagers to come in from the surrounding countryside to defend the city. But differences between feuding communists and anarchists fatally weakened the attempted counter-attack. Eleven churches and a silk factory belonging to a leading conspirator, the Marquis Luca de Tena (a powerful name in Seville still), were set on fire, and barricades built throughout the suburbs. But when workers rushed to the centre and rallied in the Plaza Nueva, they were met by groups who urged them to go back to their neighbourhoods, to defend their "strongholds".

That evening, in a decisive *coup de main*, Queipo captured the radio station. Half an hour later, he was making his first broadcast. "From time to time I had to rub my eyes to convince myself I wasn't dreaming," Queipo wrote later. Within a matter of hours, he had taken the centre of Spain's fourth largest city—"red" Seville—in a coup that had the support of two majors and a handful of captains to whom he had not even spoken. His ensuing broadcast was the first of what the British historian Hugh Thomas called "a notorious series of harangues". Thomas writes: "In a voice seasoned by many years' consumption of sherry, he declared that Spain was saved and that the rabble who resisted the rising would be shot like dogs."

The broadcast went as follows:

> *Sevillanos: To arms! The fatherland is in danger and in order to save it some men of spirit, some generals, have assumed the responsibility of placing themselves at the forefront of a movement of salvation that is triumphant everywhere.*
>
> *The Army of Africa is preparing to cross to Spain to take part in the task of crushing this unworthy government that has resolved to destroy Spain in order to convert the country into a colony of Moscow.*
>
> *Sevillanos: The die is cast, it is useless for the scum to resist. Legionaries and Moroccan troops are en route for Seville, and when they arrive they will hunt down these troublemakers like wild animals. Viva España! Viva la república!*

By nightfall, Seville was divided in two. Queipo's rousing speech, spread by the technological innovation of wireless, did much to rally Andalusia to the nationalist uprising. Most importantly, he was able to deny government claims that the revolt had been crushed in mainland Spain. "The rising of 18 July, 1936 was the first modern coup in which radio stations, telephone exchanges and aerodromes were of major importance," writes the historian Anthony Beevor in *The Spanish Civil War* (2001). The civil guard commander in Madrid ordered the local detachment in nearby Huelva, which remained under left-wing control for the first few days, to attack Seville but it went over to Queipo's forces immediately on its arrival in the city. Even so, Queipo's grotesque nightly rants from Seville were said to have provoked reprisals from republicans, and later prompted revulsion even among other Francoist commanders in Spain. His bloodthirsty harangues possibly hindered the ascent to senior positions under Franco's rule that his decisive action in Seville that first crucial day might have led him to expect.

Two days later, on 20 July, two Fokker bombers from Morocco landed in the military aerodrome of La Tablada south of the city carrying 20 legionaries. That afternoon a further 24 legionaries and 20 Moroccan troops were ferried across. Thus started the first major airlift in history. As soon as the troops arrived, Queipo de Llano had them driven round and round Seville to make everybody think far greater numbers had reached the city, Rafael Medina, a pro-Franco businessman, recalled, adding: "The Moorish troops arrived feeling very airsick." The next day Medina—later to become the Duke of Medinaceli, another influential aristocrat whose descendents are today among the most fervent defenders of Seville's architectural heritage—took part with a group of legionaries in the attack on the working-class district of San Julián.

> *I quickly saw their combative spirit. After a couple of cannon rounds from a field piece emplaced by the famous Macarena arch, we advanced. The revolutionaries started firing. We suffered casualties. A legionary was killed. The man behind jumped over his body shout-ing "Long live death!" and advanced down the street. We reached our objective, but as night was coming on the order came to withdraw. Shouting their battle cries, the legionaries led out withdrawal to safety. They were magnificent. The next day the red "barrio" fell.*

Church artefacts had been swiftly carried to safety ahead of the attack, but you can still see the scars left by bullets and cannon fire on the little Church of San Gil, inside the Roman walls behind the Macarena arch. That was the beginning and end of workers' resistance in Seville.

Reign of Terror

In the following days, Queipo's incendiary broadcasts on Seville radio included the following brutal messages: "I order and command that anyone caught inciting others to strike, or striking himself, shall be shot immediately. Don't be frightened. If someone tries to compel you, I authorize you to kill him like a dog and you will be free of all responsibility." (22 July 1936) "In various villages of which I have heard, right-wing people are being held prisoner and threatened with barbarous fates. I want to make known my system with regard to this. For every person killed I shall kill 10 and perhaps even exceed this proportion. The leaders of these village movements may believe that they can flee; they are wrong. Even if they hide beneath the earth, I shall dig them out; even if they're already dead, I shall kill them again" (25 July 1936).

The Seville-based national newspaper *ABC* swiftly got the message: "Let us repeat the phrase so often pronounced by our illustrious general, Queipo de Llano: the words 'pardon' and 'amnesty' must disappear from the Spanish dictionary," it wrote on 1 September 1936. In March 1937 Queipo summed up his social philosophy in a speech to inaugurate the building site for a cheap working-class housing project in the city: "Social equality is nonsense. Equality among men is impossible… I ask you, workers, do disorder, anarchy and gangsterism suit you better than a government that imposed freedom from above? The real freedom, which ends where that of your neighbour begins?"

Gamel Woolsey, the American wife of the English writer Gerald Brenan who settled near Granada as a young man and stayed there most of his life, wrote a lively portrait of Queipo de Llano and his despotic rule of Seville in her classic civil war memoir *Death's Other Kingdom* (1939). The couple had by 1936 moved to Churriana, near Malaga, and Woolsey describes how, on a trip to what was then the tiny fishing village of Torremolinos, they bought "a horrid-looking little radio… a wretched little thing." But she adds: "Yet, bad as it was, it became one of the greatest interests of our lives… Radio in time of war becomes absolutely fascinating. The pronouncements, denials, alarms, rumours, propaganda, speeches of national leaders, make it enthralling to the listener who is at all emotionally involved, especially if he can follow the news in several languages."

But the thing we waited for most eagerly was not the foreign stations nor the government's but the insurgent broadcasts from Seville. During the day Seville played music and made personal announcements, in the evening the news began, and I might as well mention at this point that this news was far more accurate than news from the government side, having indeed some relation to fact which government news then never did, being simply a recital of triumphs and victories, almost all entirely imaginary, so that we listened anxiously to Seville hoping to get at least some faint idea of what was really going on in Spain. The BBC news at that time appeared to be obtained by adding together news from Madrid and Seville and dividing by three; it was always unlikely and generally fascinating sounding.

What made the broadcasts so eagerly anticipated were the speeches of "that amazing radio personality General Queipo de Llano". It was hard, Woolsey writes, to describe him. "He has to be heard. Nothing at all like him can ever have been heard on the air before, and never will be again… He creates a character that seems combined of ferocity and a sort of boisterous, ferocious good humour. I am told that he does not drink at all, but he has the mellow loose voice and the cheerful wandering manner of the habitual drinker. He talks on for hours always perfectly at ease, sometimes he stumbles over a word and corrects himself with a complete lack of embarrassment, speaks of 'these villainous fascists' and an agonised voice can be heard behind him correcting him 'No, no mi general, *Marxistas*.' 'What difference does it make?' says the general and sweeps grandly on. 'Yes, you *canalla* (scum) you anarchists of Malaga, you wait until I get there in ten days' time! You just wait! I'll be sitting in a café in the Calle Larios sipping my beer, and for every sip I take ten of you will fall. I shall shoot ten of you for every one of ours! (he bellows) If I have to drag them out of their graves to shoot them!"

Gamel Woolsey was told by an Italian journalist that Queipo de Llano always broadcast in full dress uniform with all his medals on, and that his staff, similarly dressed, lined up behind him. These were the ones who corrected him when he made a slip. "He had a tremendous fascination for us, we could never resist him. He was like a tyrant in an old melodrama… But unfortunately it was real," she writes.

Brenan lifted his wife's account and put it in his own memoirs, his "Personal Record 1920-1975". But Brenan added some details. "Queipo was always natural and at ease. Sometimes, for instance, he couldn't decipher his notes. So he turned to his companions and said 'I can't see what this says. Have we killed five hundred or five thousand reds?' 'Five hundred, *mi general.*' 'Well, it doesn't matter. It's all the same if this time it was only five hundred. Because we are going to kill five thousand, five hundred thousand. Then we'll see'…

"His broadcasts were full of vulgar anecdotes, jokes, insults, absurdities, all extraordinarily vivid but excruciating when you realised that mass executions were taking place all round, so fugitives told us, in a city [Seville] where all the workers were anarchists or communists… Most of his programmes ended in the same way. 'Marxist scum! Marxist scum!' he repeated, 'when we catch you we'll know how to treat you. We'll skin you alive. Scum! Rabble!'" Brenan concedes that Queipo felt he had to rule by terror to hold down a uniformly hostile working class. "But he didn't mind doing so because he was a sadist by nature and the executions continued for months without interruption even when his position was secured."

The Central European writer Arthur Koestler, who had arrived in Malaga in January 1937 to work as a journalist, had the opportunity to see the general ranting at the microphone in the decrepit, makeshift studio. He quotes the following examples of Queipo's broadcasts: "The Marxists are ravening beasts, but we are gentlemen. Señor [Lluis] Companys [Naval Minister of the Republic] deserves to be stuck like a pig." "I have given orders for three members of the families of each of the sailors of the loyalist cruisers that bombarded La Linea to be shot… To conclude my talk I should like to tell my daughter in Paris that we are all in excellent health and that we should like to hear from her." Koestler was later arrested and spent many months in prison, narrowly escaping execution. His experiences formed the basis for his novel *Darkness at Noon* (1940).

Prisoners' Canal

With civil war raging across Spain, General Queipo de Llano set in train a number of ambitious projects, including a plan to drain and cultivate the marshlands along the Guadalquivir from Seville to the sea to provide homes and work for thousands of families. The landowners were asked to contribute funds in proportion to the size of their holdings. They consented to the plan only when told that costs could be cut to one third by "the use of personnel whom the general will put at the scheme's disposal", in the words of *ABC* in June 1937. The "personnel" were battalions of vanquished republican prisoners marshalled by force to carry out backbreaking toil amidst conditions of sickness, malnutrition and humiliation. The great Guadalquivir Canal, which came to be known as "the prisoners' canal", is the most ambitious infrastructure project that Franco undertook in his forty-year rule, according to the journalist Leslie Crawford, who made a study of the project for the *Financial Times* newspaper. "The canal is 180km long, construction lasted 22 years and it was built by slave labour," Crawford wrote.

The canal starts from the village of Peñaflor north-east of Seville upriver towards Córdoba, and bisects Andalusia to the port of Sanlúcar de Barrameda. Sanlúcar is best known today for its distinctive manzanilla, a sherry-like wine that aficionados say carries a salty tang of the sea. The port became the gateway to Seville after the Guadalquivir silted up in the eighteenth century, preventing big ships from advancing further upstream.

The Guadalquivir Canal was the first militarized penal colony to be created shortly after Franco's victory in 1939. It was opened on 20 January 1940, and was the last to close, twenty years later. It was the most ambitious hydraulic project in Andalusia: by rechannelling the river, the canal drained marshlands to transform them into cultivable land, and brought some 80,000 hectares under irrigation, turning swampy wasteland into a rich and fertile farming region. It made fortunes for the owners of land that had formerly been used only for the grazing of goats. Throughout the 1940s, thousands of prisoners dug the canal. They hacked out a daily quota of earth and rocks with picks and shovels, then carried it away on their backs. Then, in the early 1950s, they began to build new villages in the land irrigated by the canal. Among them was Villa Franco del Guadalquivir, today known as Villafranco, to veil the name of the man who inspired it. (South-east of Villafranco is the settlement of Queipo de Llano, named to remember the strongman from Seville who masterminded the project.) A hundred prisoners worked at Villa Franco between 1952 and 1953, laying out the settlement and constructing the water and sewage system. They then built or rehabilitated more than a hundred houses intended for agricultural labourers who later colonized the reclaimed lands which were turned over to the cultivation of rice.

So it was that the area became an important rice producer. Local landowners became rich, and so did the construction companies who helped rebuild a war-shattered, economically ruined Spain on the backs of forced labour. When the workers had finished at Villa Franco, they were sent to Guillena, a town north of Seville, to construct a similar new settlement at Torre de la Reina, between Guillena and Seville, just north of the historic Roman remains of Itálica.

When the war ended in 1939 the outcome was not peace—which was never formally declared—but "victory". For Franco's vanquished opponents, the war went on. "The Spanish civil war did not end in 1939," the historian José Luis Gutierrez told Leslie Crawford. "The regime never talked about peace; it talked about 'the first year of victory, the second year of victory' and so on. Spain became an immense jail, in which the vanquished were put at the service of the victors," he said. Political prisoners, that is Spaniards who had supported the elected republican government, were organized into military battalions and put to work in iron foundries, mines, the construction of dams and canals, and the recovery of railways, barracks, churches and other buildings destroyed during the war. After the republican army surrendered, Franco eagerly tracked down those who had fought with the "reds". Laws were passed, with retroactive effect, to persecute those who had sympathized with the republican government.

Some 280,000 Spaniards were locked up as political prisoners, so many that they had to build their own prisons to house such huge numbers. The authorities started to catalogue the professional qualifications of this vast captive labour force. Then they mobilized them for work, on public projects or for private companies who could not find skilled workers on the open market, and they had to build their own labour camps where they lived while carrying out their toil. Merinales camp served the Guadalquivir project, though scarcely a trace remains of it now. The Guadalquivir Canal absorbed 5,000 prisoners a month, supplied by the regime's Trust for the Redemption of Jail Sentences. This body functioned as a huge labour exchange for political prisoners—and the Trust was very satisfied with the results of prison labour. "In all the professional categories employed, prison labour has greatly exceeded the productivity of free labour," the organization boasted in a report to Franco in 1948. The records of the harsh early years of Franco's victory still remain, and are only now starting to be examined by a new generation of young Spanish historians keen to recover these forgotten episodes. Survivors of those years are at last starting to overcome fears that dogged them for decades, and to recount their experiences before they die. Since Seville and its surrounding region fell so swiftly to the fascists in the early days of the Civil War, and suffered so cruelly in the forty years that followed, it is hardly surprising that fears still lie dormant and stories remain untold.

Rafael Alberti: Poet of the Sea

Rafael Alberti's was a rare voice that spoke for the other Andalusia—the land that rang with passion and clamoured for liberty—in the years before and after the Civil War. Alberti was born in 1902 at Puerto de Santa María, a little town at the mouth of the Guadalete, a tributary of the great Guadalquivir downstream from Seville. Though not strictly a Sevillian, Alberti was proudly *Andaluz*. "This is the Andalusian people./Serious, pure and torn apart,/in the lands of light." He was the longest surviving member of that great literary flowering known as the

Generation of '27, a group of poets and writers so-called after a commemoration they organized in Seville in 1927 of the death of the Cordoban author Luis de Góngora. Among these artists, said to represent a new golden age brutally annihilated by the outbreak of civil war, was Alberti's Andalusian contemporary and friend Federico García Lorca, shot by fascists in July 1936. Alberti's poetry expresses the grief and shock felt by half the nation at Franco's successful rebellion, a shock that traumatized Alberti's native region, the frontline of Franco's first assault upon Spain's republic.

Rafael Alberti

The poet was born within sight of Cadiz's vast naval dockyards and the love of the sea impregnated his life and work. His father, son of Genoese immigrants, worked for a wine-producer, and as a boy Rafael spent hours in bodegas and among wine vats under the whitewashed vaults of cellars and storehouses. Wine, music, song and poetry formed part of his daily life, and he recalled in his memoirs "violent alcoholic twilights in which the scent of basil and night-scenting jasmine mingled with the sharp, acrid smell of vomit." Alberti was a master of the pithy Andalusian short verse, the *copla*, which fuses pain and poetry: "Love makes you mad./I speak from experience,/For that is how I/Lost my mind for love." His work was filled with images of life, love and death, of workers and, especially, sailors and the sea, in the city whose salty tang wafts upriver and reminds *Sevillanos* of their maritime heritage.

In May 1917, when Rafael was 15, the Albertis moved to Madrid, a wrench that prompted one of his best-loved poems, "El Mar. La Mar" (The Sea. The Sea): "The sea. The sea./The sea. Only the sea!/Why did you bring me, father,/to the city?/Why did you uproot me/from the sea?/In dreams, the tide/pulls my heart./It would like to carry it away./Father, why did you bring me/here?" Alberti became politically active against the dictatorship of Primo de Rivera in the 1920s, and in 1924 produced the collection of poems that made his name, *Marinero en Tierra* (Earth Sailor). The collection, which included "El Mar", won a national literature prize in 1925, and remains the work for which he is best remembered. He joined student demonstrations in 1930, and in 1934, after a visit to the Soviet Union, founded the left-wing periodical *Octubre*, pouring out poetry all the while. The monarchist *ABC* newspaper hailed his work as "a return to the primitive, the fundamental, the spontaneous... to the people".

A communist supporter, Alberti campaigned for the Popular Front government in Spain's Republic of 1936, but was aware of the menace of fascism that was sweeping through Europe. Former friends cold-shouldered him because of his sympathy with communism, and he wrote: "I returned,/I came back here,/and I saw corpses indolently/seated at café tables with their money and their bodies putrefying on their chairs,/my friends prepared to receive without giving anything in return/the salary that was the death of the others."

Alberti was fighting for the republicans in Valencia when their side finally surrendered. He was in Ibiza when paramilitary civil guardsmen surrounded the island and he took refuge in a cave, emerging only when fishermen helped him to safety. This was in March 1939, and he escaped on a light plane to Oran in Algeria, on the first leg of an itinerant exile that lasted 38 years. He moved to Paris, Buenos Aires, Rome... As the decades passed, he became afflicted with nostalgia for his lost youth and his homeland, and his work became suffused with themes of searching, longing and perpetual motion. Such feelings possibly come naturally to someone from a port, with its constant atmosphere of farewells and departures, but were heightened by exile and wandering.

Alberti did not come back to Spain until 1977, two years after Franco's death. Even after his return he still carried in his pocket a little transistor radio to listen to the news, in case fascism returned and he had to make a swift departure. He was elected Communist Deputy for Cadiz in Spain's new democratic parliament, and settled in Puerto de Santa María. Towards the end of his life he wrote: "Poetry should be understood by everyone, even if it says things that are often difficult and mysterious. It is an art that puts men in contact with each other, which makes them communicate. Poetry is the greatest thing in the world. If it disappears, man too will disappear." He had spent most of his life exiled from his hometown, but clung to it in his later years. In 1998 King Juan Carlos and Queen Sofía visited him in Puerto de Santa María and inaugurated the Rafael Alberti Foundation, with a permanent exhibition of his work. The institution seeks to embody Andalusia's artistic and political resistance to tyranny, a voice all but silenced for forty years.

Rafael Alberti and Queipo de Llano were contemporaries, but two more polar opposites could not be imagined. They represent in the starkest terms the ideological divide that rent Seville and the surrounding area during the Civil War and the dictatorship. In a poem criticized by some as crudely pro-communist, Alberti wrote the following *coplas* of praise to the Virgin of La Macarena:

> *Let me this dawn*
> *wash your tears in my sorrow,*
> *Virgin of the Macarena,*
> *by calling you comrade.*
>
> *Flower of the Sevillian orchard,*
> *Blood of your holy land,*
> *of peace, not of war,*
> *never of Queipo de Llano.*

After the war, Alberti, and countless others were subjected to a vicious smear campaign, and *ABC*, which had hailed the poet before the war, wrote in May 1939: "Sender, Alberti, Cernuda... are the sad Homers of an Iliad of the vanquished. The verses of Alberti, of Cernuda... are laboratory poems, with neither force nor beauty, they are mistaken, cowardly cry-babies." Alberti's passion for freedom, silenced for decades, triumphed in the end over the cruel bombast of Queipo de Llano. The general was adopted into the *cofradía* of La Macarena, an extraordinary honour for a non-Sevillian, and is buried in the Macarena church beneath an imposing marble slab set in the floor. The two men are remembered, and by their supporters honoured, on their common turf.

Luis Cernuda: Poet of the Air

Timid, sensitive, homosexual Luis Cernuda was born in Seville in 1902, the same year as Alberti. Cernuda was another poet of the Generation of '27 forced into exile, less by Franco—although he too headed for the US and Mexico when Franco won—than by the social constraints of his time. Cernuda is not well known outside Spain, although he produced fine writing while he lived in London and New York in the 1940s and 1950s. But like Alberti, Cernuda produced his defining work when he was young, and under the impact of his hometown. He lived with his parents and two sisters in Calle del Aire (Air Street) in Seville's Barrio de Santa Cruz. The family was prosperous, but strict. His father was a military engineer and subjected his son to a severe Jesuit education. In Air Street Cernuda composed his first collection of poems *Perfil del Aire* (Profile of Air), published in 1927. There followed *Forbidden Pleasures* in 1931, *Where Oblivion Dwells* (1934), and *Reality and Desire* (1936). These translated titles indicate his preoccupations, and reveal his sense of emotional isolation. He defined himself as "maladjusted", and at odds with the world.

> *My land?*
> *My land is you.*
> *My people?*
> *My people are you.*
> *Exile and death*
> *Are for me where*
> *You are not.*
> *And my life?*
> *Tell me, my life,*
> *What is it, if it is not you?*

He identified strongly with Federico García Lorca, for whom he wrote "To a Dead Poet":

> *Just as on the rock we never see*
> *the bright flower bloom,*
> *amidst a hard and sullen people*
> *there never beautifully shines*
> *the fresh uplifting decoration of life.*

That is why they killed you, because you were
verdure in our arid land
and blue in our darkened air.

Light is the part of life
that like gods the poets scavenge.
Hatred and destruction endure for ever
deaf and buried within
the everlasting ice of the terrible Spaniard,
Who lurks upon the hillside
With a stone in his hand...

You were the salt of our world,
Alive like a ray of sun...

And in *Forbidden Pleasures*, he wrote:

I'll tell how you were born, forbidden pleasures,
As a desire grows from towers of dread.

It is hardly surprising that this troubled soul, an admirer of the
Romantic Bécquer, never practised the profession of law in which he
obtained his degree at Seville's university. He fled to Madrid on the
death of his mother in 1928, and formed part of that circle of gifted
young men that included his compatriots Alberti and Lorca, as well as
Dalí and Buñuel at the free-thinking Students' Residence. Such a man
would have been eaten alive by Queipo de Llano.

Valverde: "Father of the Coto Doñana"

The French Romantic writer Théophile Gautier made the trip down
the Guadalquivir from Seville by paddle steamer, an excursion you can
still take, and he—along with Richard Ford—was one of the first
travellers to comment on the wild marshy estuary land known as the
Coto Doñana. The steamship, Gautier observed in his memoir,
"convenient though it may be, seems hideous beside a sailing vessel.
The one is like swan spreading its white winds to catch the breath of the
breeze, the other a stove perched upon mill-wheels, and riding off as fast
as its legs will carry it." Using, none the less, this convenient mode of

transport, Gautier remarked on the magic optical effect created as Seville receded: "as the roofs of the town appeared to shrink into the earth and melt into the horizontal distance, the cathedral grew larger."

Along the banks of the Guadalquivir, he resumed, "one sees nothing but low-lying, sandy, ochre-coloured banks and yellow, turbid waters, whose earthy hue cannot be attributed to the rain, which is so rare in this country... The hard blue of the sky has something to do with it, for its extreme intensity dulls by comparison the tone of the water, which is always less vivid." As the steamer pursued its languid course to the sea, "the river grew broader and broader, the banks dwindled and grew flat," and reminded Gautier of northern Belgium.

> There was, moreover, little traffic on the river, and what one could see of the country beyond it seemed uncultivated and deserted; it is true that it was in the height of the dog-days, a season at which Spain is hardly more than a vast heap of ashes without verdure or vegetation. The only living creatures were the herons and storks, with one leg folded under them, the other half-plunged into the water, waiting in such complete immobility for a fish to go by, that they might have been taken for wooden birds stuck on the end of stick.

Towards evening they passed the port of Sanlúcar de Barrameda. "From San Lucar onwards, the Guadalquivir widens out considerably, and assumes the proportions of an arm of the sea. The banks are now no more than a gradually shrinking line between sky and sea. It is grand, but with rather a cold, monotonous grandeur, and we should have been bored if it had not been for the games, dances, castanets and tambourines of the soldiers [on board]."

More than a century after Gautier wrote this, one man pioneered a campaign that turned these wild estuary marshlands into Europe's most important wetlands reserve. José Antonio Valverde was a naturalist from the northern city of Valladolid who first visited the Coto Doñana as a young man in the 1950s, and resolved to challenge Francoist plans to drain the Guadalquivir. Valverde recognized the site as a haunt of unique natural beauty, and devoted his career as a biological scientist to building an unlikely alliance between big landowners and international scientists to preserve it. Local aristocrats had for centuries used the vast wetlands as private hunting grounds, pursuing what have become endangered species like the elusive Iberian Lynx. Part belonged to the Dukes of Medina Sidonia, part to the house of Alba and other grandees. But Valverde turned the area into Europe's first biological reservation.

If Gautier considered these marshy wastes monotonous and deserted, and Franco saw them as unexploited land crying out for profitable cultivation, Valverde wanted to protect them from human predation of any kind. The young man from Spain's arid north was fascinated by these strange and beautiful southern marshes. At this spot the meeting of river and sea, and of crosswinds from Europe and Africa, created a unique ecosystem that he spent his life investigating. Through his determination to save this fragile natural paradise Valverde became known as "Father of the Doñana". He saw that proposals to drain the area for farming would destroy the rich wildlife it supported. So at a time when nature conservation was in its infancy, and almost unknown in Spain, Valverde conducted a study of the Doñana and proposed that it should be declared a national park. In 1950 he requested the equivalent of £200 from the Spanish government to fund his research. With Queipo de Llano's drainage operation in full swing, it is hardly surprising that the authorities found his idea preposterous and turned him down. He sought support from abroad, and appealed to international scientists to recognise the importance of the estuary. He led the first scientific expedition to the Doñana in 1957, Joining him on that pioneering trip were the British scientific naturalists Guy Mountfort, Roger Peterson and Sir Julian Huxley. It marked the start of decades of campaigning.

Valverde linked up with the British Nature Conservancy to form an international organization that bought up 7,000 hectares of the Doñana in 1963. He was helped by the scientists Luc Hoffman, Max Nicholson and his friend Mauricio González Gordon, who owned much of the erstwhile hunting ground. He even drafted letters that Prince Bernhard of the Netherlands sent to Franco, urging him to save the Doñana, and a few weeks later wrote at the Generalísimo's request a reply to the Prince. Neither party ever discovered Valverde's role as "double agent". The correspondence cleared the way for the creation of the Doñana Reservation, embryo of the National Park declared in 1969, of which Valverde became curator. He installed in Seville a Doñana Biological Station, as a branch of the state scientific research institute, CSIC, which employs more than 150 scientists, and was director from 1964 to 1975. Valverde co-founded with the ornithologist Francisco Bernis the Spanish Ornithological Society in 1954, and was its president for many years. The two men visited the Doñana in 1952 and carried out Spain's first bird-ringing operation.

The Doñana is today Europe's most important wetland reserve. Shortly before Valverde died in Seville in 2003, I visited the observation station that bears his name in the protected marshlands at the heart of the Doñana. The spot is reached by a long drive in a four-wheel vehicle along a dusty track where herons and storks still perch motionless, as Gautier described. The area is not far from the towns of Queipo de Llano and Villafranco, where local landowners—who spend most of their time in Seville—are rehabilitating the slave-built settlements on their estates that once housed labourers who worked the reclaimed cotton and rice fields. These humble dwellings are being transforming into pretty, and profitable, holiday apartments for weekend visitors, tourists and wedding parties.

The Valverde observation post lies at the hub of an intercontinental crossroads for migrating birds. The spring morning I visited, bee-eaters, egrets, fish eagles, purple herons, storks, avocets, spoonbills, coots and flamingos flapped and squabbled, swooped and preened amidst the rushes and reeds. A crowd of youngsters, enthralled, peered through telescopes while a young guide explained and identified the teeming spectacle before us, his words tumbling over themselves in enthusiasm.

Chapter Nine
FLAMENCO: GYPSY MUSIC

La Carbonería, a former coal merchants' store is not easy to find, tucked away in Seville's labyrinthine Judería quarter off the Calle Levíes. It is a smoky, cavernous bar and music spot whose two interconnected chambers open on to a broad patio. Way after midnight you are likely to hear impromptu flamenco sessions of variable quality, but whose hoarse, improvised immediacy catches in your chest. Locals can be rather dismissive of La Carbonería, saying it has become too touristy. But outsiders find it a lot more authentic than the stuff served up on leaflets in hotel lobbies. None the less, the raucous buzz from prosperous youngsters of all nationalities is a world apart from the solemn reverence that envelopes true flamenco. That closed gypsy world is far less easy to penetrate, but aficionados have spent centuries trying to get close and to understand its mysteries.

Farruquito is in his twenties, a slope-shouldered waif from Seville's gypsy suburbs who carries himself like a prince. He is grandson and heir of the flamenco star Antonio Montoya "Farruco" who is hailed as the greatest gypsy dancer of the twentieth century. The old man Farruco came from an itinerant family of gypsy basket-makers who travelled the country with their cart, and sought shelter under bridges to sleep. Some saw in the steps of Farruco the trotting movements of restless horses, the hasty steps of the animals amidst which he lived. He was married at 14, a father at 15, widowed at 16, a grandfather at 33. Farruco died in 1997, aged 64, after a lifetime of drinking and smoking when Farruquito, who adored his grandfather, was just 14. Farruquito's father Juan Fernando Flores, the *cantaor* El Moreno, died in 2001 at the age of 38 in his son's arms after a heart attack on stage while the family was touring Argentina. Farruquito's mother, the dancer La Farruca—Farruco's daughter—has not performed since her husband's death. She mourns not just her husband and her father, but also her brother, Farruquito, Farruco's only son, who died in a car accident when he was 18 and already a huge star in the image of his father. Farruco senior quit

the stage for years in grief for the death of his son, saying life had lost its meaning for him. Juan Manuel Fernández Montoya, Farruquito, whom his family call Mani, is now the young patriarch of his clan, and fully conscious of the responsibility he bears. This almost saintly image of a gypsy hero received a terrible blow early in 2004 when tragedy hit Farruquito and threatened to blight his dancing career, indeed his whole life.

This slender, serious young man is unlikely to frequent La Carbonería, but he offers aficionados the nearest thing they are likely to see of authentic flamenco music and dance at its purest and least self-conscious. Farruquito devised, choreographed and stars in his stage show *Alma Vieja* (Ancient Soul), accompanied by his gypsy clan: his aunt Pilar Montoya, "La Faraona"; his younger brother Antonio ("Farruco"); his young cousins Juan, "Barullo" and Antonio, "Polito"; and his childhood friend El Perla, the guitarist. Farruquito describes *Alma Vieja* as a tribute to his ancestors, to ancient songs, the purest form of gypsy dance, the sum of experiences and the legacy to be handed on. The performers, the *cantaores* (singers), *bailaores* (dancers) and *tocaores* (guitarists) range from the bearded patriarch Manuel Molina, whose voice stops the show minutes after the curtain rises, to the child Polito who lashes his long hair and flying elbows into a frenzy with precise, demonic energy. They have all imbibed flamenco from birth. "Mani learned flamenco before he could speak," said his fond aunt La Faraona. "He watched his mother dance and marked time in the cradle waving his elbows forward and back. He danced before he walked: one day we put his basket on a heater, and we marked the rhythm and he started kicking the stove with his feet!"

Farruquito hung up his boots for a year after his father died, "I still miss him every day," he said recently. Then gradually he started dancing again, teaching, then performing. He took over the school his grandfather founded in Seville, in Calle Salteras in the old gypsy quarter of Triana, across the river, dedicated to the old man's style. Devotees gasp at seeing Farruco's movements and spirit echoed by Farruquito, repository of his elders' dreams and ambitions, guardian and inspiration to his younger kin. "When he was five he seemed to be ten, when he was ten he seemed like twenty, and now he seems like an old man," his aunt La Faraona remarked. He made his debut on Broadway at five, danced his first season in Madrid at eight, at 12 appeared with his grandfather in Carlos Saura's film *Flamenco*, and all but stole the movie. After a tour of the United States the dance critic of *The New York Times* named him visiting artist of the year. In 2003 *People* magazine voted him one the world's fifty most beautiful people, alongside George Clooney and Halle Berry.

Alma Vieja opened in Seville in 2003, took Madrid then Barcelona by storm, toured Britain, France and the Far East. It is defiant and elegant, furious and tender, terrifying and beautiful. Filling theatres worldwide, the show remains basically a gypsy song and dance party or *juerga* of the kind improvised for centuries in Andalusian patios, low dives and hillside encampments. A gathering of family and friends to sing, stamp and strum the guitar, to impress each other and develop the proficiency and emotional expressiveness of their unique, spectacular art. "It's just us, with dancing at its most savage," says Farruquito.

Forget the clichés for a moment. The hammering heels, the tossed heads, the clawing back of raven's-wing curls, the arched bodies. Farruquito does all that—as do grinning showgirls and boys in gaudy flamenco costumes throughout Spain every night to the delight of visitors. Of course he is good at what he does. He has talent, dedication and pedigree. But what has the gypsy grandees sobbing at his performances, moaning *ole* while he stands on stage before he has made a single move, what makes them fall upon his neck after the show and invoke upon him the blessing of God is something more. What prompts admirers to such extremes of emotion is what they call *duende*. *Duende*, which translates as devil, or spirit, is that elusive moment of ecstasy, when the hairs rise on your neck, that fleeting instant you will never forget, a stab to the heart that writers and bar-room Spaniards pursue for a lifetime, and have spent centuries trying to define. In *Alma Vieja*, there is a moment when Farruquito and his young brother Farruco face each other after a few moments of frenetic stamping and suddenly jump in the air, their arms rippling a tattoo on their knees and chests, their trousers leaping so far up their legs to reveal a flash of white shin above the boots. It is a blur, like a puff of smoke left after the explosion of a firecracker that prompts a shudder through the audience like a collective sigh. Is this *duende*? It is over too soon. You want to call the moment back for another look.

Duende

Duende is the heart of flamenco, that Andalusian gypsy music centred around Seville. Heroes like Farruquito emerge here every generation or so, possessed of a mercurial outsider fierceness that seems unique to gypsy performers. You have to be careful not to drift into romantic or racial stereotypes, but Farruquito himself invokes his gypsy heritage as something that defines his life and his work, including the famed machismo of his grandfather: "It's true," he admitted. "He was like that. But you must understand that gypsies have a form of life in which the man is always above the woman. Although we like them to have their place: the home is their domain. Farruco lived in a time when it needed a lot of effort to get bread and boots. And it's normal that people like that have a very distinctive personality. He was closed, but for good reason. Now we are more open. I don't consider myself machista or authoritarian, but that's for others to say."

Joaquín Cortés, the charismatic *bailaor* from Córdoba, is another flamenco dancer proud of his gypsy origins. Cortés became a world star in the 1990s by devising gigantic flamenco spectacles modelled on stadium rock concerts. He sought to modernize the ancient art with concepts of "fusion", linking flamenco to rock and blues. Swathed in dramatic Armani costumes and naked from the waist up, he conquered the stages of Europe and the US with his hammering heels and flying beads of sweat. Cortés strove to escape from the cliché of donkeys and campsites and show that gypsies, too, could be worldly and cultivated, and that flamenco did not have to be kitsch to win mass appeal. His shows have impact, but critics say that in his pursuit of world stardom the young Cordoban lost *duende*.

Farruquito upholds an older, more austere style: "mixing flamenco with other things is to lose respect for it," he believes. He performs in three-piece suits, in black, gold, white or scarlet. "Dancing fast and furious, macho like the man I am, that's what I like, and what comes naturally." In moments of climax he may fling aside his jacket, but he makes no conscious display of sex appeal, despite his fragile beauty. He is covered up, self-absorbed, his passion focused on the footwork, the song, the guitar, and the emotional impact, the *duende*. The most overtly sexy performer in *Alma Vieja* is Farruquito's portly aunt, Pilar La Faraona, Farruco's daughter. Encased in a stridently spotted costume, La Faraona leans perilously backwards as she steers herself on stage. She glares mockingly at the audience, shrugs, hoists her frills, sketches some flirtatious steps in a manner simultaneously off-hand and menacing. Whatever it is she does, and it does not seem to amount to much, the force of her personality slaps you between the eyes and makes you gasp.

Farruquito casts a quieter spell. When he teaches a group, he speaks quietly, as if to himself, he clicks his fingers, marks the rhythm with his feet, claps his hands, makes curious noises: *taca taca tun tran trin.* He does not rap instructions, just murmurs advice as he moves amidst his students, straightening shoulders. His words seem to have less to do with the steps than with the underlying philosophy of his world. "Quieter," he says at one point. "it's no better for being louder. Take the step without running, recreate it with each accent. Don't forget. Just because you know the step doesn't mean you have to rush it, you must listen to it from the inside, not just the stamp. There must be air between the steps." His upper body never moves as he grasps his black T-shirt above his mahogany midriff to demonstrate a move. "Don't weave to and fro. If you step firmly you don't need to move your upper body. Take your time," he adds, before casually swinging into a few steps that sound like a round of artillery fire. "Leave the force till the end. Pim, pum, pah! Yes?" The floorboards leap and judder beneath his feet. "However loud your steps, you must always listen to the guitar. And at the end don't move a thing, not a hair." Words drop like pearls, while his students listen, ears and bodies straining, lungs heaving. "Keep your gestures gentle, to give them more flavour."

Farruquito exemplifies what we imagine to be the typical Sevillian gypsy artist: elegant, enigmatic, intriguing, defined by his clan loyalty, mature beyond his years. The journalist and aficionado Miguel Mora spent time with him on his home ground and wrote in *El País*: "The world may fall, but to see this young stripling walk through Triana on a cloudy spring morning serves to keep your faith alive. He is a prince. He wears black corduroy trousers, a black shiny overcoat in imitation Astrakhan, his greased black hair falls in curls upon his shoulders. A chain of gold at his neck, two bracelets, four or five rings, also in *sonakay* (Romany for gold). One carries the number 13 engraved in diamonds. 'You know that gypsies are very superstitious. "Twelve plus one," they say. But I don't care. I love thirteen.'" Farruquito drives Mora to the family's home, a small apartment in Seville's humble San Pablo district: "Farruquito drives listening to a fandango of Antonio el Rubio, saying 'oles' and chatting with this brother Farruco, a blond and cheeky gypsy who dances at his brother's side without being upstaged…"

Outsiders have long tried to get close to this alien but compulsively fascinating culture. George Borrow, the eccentric Englishman who travelled all over Spain trying to sell Protestant bibles in the 1830s— something of a challenge in a fiercely Catholic country where the Inquisition still ruled peoples' consciences and reading matter—learned their language and wrote a book about them, *The Zincali*, in 1841. But the Sevillian author and local historian Antonio Zoido believes that even Borrow, champion of the gypsies who did much to promote tolerance and understanding of them, used guesswork to translate words and expressions that escaped him, and often missed the point completely.

Up the Giralda on Horseback

Raúl Sender in his classic 1960s satire *La tesis de Nancy* (Nancy's Thesis) tries to capture Seville's elusive gypsy world by describing the contrasts and misunderstandings that multiply between his heroine, the naïve but curious Californian Nancy, who is studying in the city, and her part-gypsy boyfriend Curro. The difficulties the two have in communicating, despite their romantic attachment, constitute the core of the book, which takes the form of Nancy's letters to her cousin Betsy in Philadelphia. The misunderstandings, in particular Nancy's hilarious misinterpretations of *Andaluz* slang, are only partly to do with words. Unfamiliar with Seville's macho world, she is impervious to the sexual innuendo half-hidden in every ambiguous phrase. The gulf is in reality between two alien worlds: that of the liberated 1960s young American female and the inhibited, hidebound machismo of Seville in the Franco years. Curro and Nancy gaze in fascinated wonder upon the exotic world of the other. Romance blossoms in the thrill of mutual discovery, then inevitably withers and dies. But despite the chasms of incomprehension of clashing sexual customs and expectations, Sender's elegant tale allows each, occasionally, to glimpse something of the other. Nancy says, at one point. "These gypsies are not uncultured, they just have their own, different, forms of culture." Then later: "Nobody considers it necessary in Seville to believe what people tell them, and if they listen with interest it is only because of the wit or lack of it of the person speaking. Neither does anyone try to be believed, only to be heard."

An early scene has Nancy enchanted with the tale of the guardsmen of the twelfth-century Moorish ruler Abderraman who ascended the spiral ramp inside the Giralda tower on horseback. With typical impulsiveness, she hires a horse from gypsies and rides to the top of the tower, while Curro watches fearfully from below. On the way down, fearing she will fall over the horse's head, she turns in the saddle to complete the descent facing its rear. Such an ignominious posture recalls the punishments meted out by the Inquisitors to heretics, pimps and adulterers. Curro's companions turn and flee in terror when they see her thus mounted. The young man is filled with admiration for her daring, and simultaneously convinced she is mad. Curro invites her for lunch, and while he fetches the wine, drops a notebook in which Nancy reads "I love you" written in eight languages, each with its Spanish phonetic pronunciation. "My horseman returned and I said to him with surprise and pleasure: 'That's great! I didn't know that you too were interested in modern languages. It seems that we are companions'. He saw the notebook in my hands and turned the colour of a boiled crab. I tell you I'll never understand these Spaniards." At that moment, Nancy decides to write her thesis on gypsies.

Nancy and Curro engage in a series of "typical" Sevillian encounters: with youngsters in the bar, with clumsy British spinsters who are convinced they are assimilated into local society, the elaborate intrigue and flirtatious power-play of the patio get-together or *tertulia*, and finally the arcane and bizarre world of the *señorito*, the aristocrat in his country seat. A turning point comes when Nancy overhears Curro telling a friend that although he loves Nancy he will never marry her because "she was without her flower" when he met her. "I froze," Nancy writes to Betsy, "Curro won't marry me because when we met I didn't have my flower. Imagine such a thing in the US! I cut a carnation from a pot nearby and put it in my hair. Since then I always wear a flower in my hair… You see the importance that flowers have for these Iberians."

Each party gains some enlightenment from the other, but eventually the worlds are just too distant to be reconciled. Countless Anglo-Saxon female visitors on a similar educational quest as Nancy's have struggled to come to terms with Seville, and many claim to have found their experiences reflected with excruciating accuracy in Sender's tale. Many jump the cultural chasm, and never return home. Sender— an exile from Spain during Franco's dictatorship—taught in American universities, and must have encountered numerous Nancys. He is rare in doing justice to the young woman's point of view, although he frequently mocks her—as in the flower episode—as a total idiot. He describes how the female outsider sees the Sevillian male. Armed with her robust American belief in sexual equality, political democracy and freedom of action and speech, Nancy collides with a buttoned-up society dominated by men who conceal their insecurity, poverty and ignorance beneath a veneer of swank.

Sender's 1960s heroine is the mirror opposite of the French and English Romantic gentlemen travellers of the nineteenth century, but each comes laden with the baggage of their time and their homeland. Ford and Gautier portray Andalusian women as exotic, entertaining playthings, prone to emotional trickery. Nancy's perception of the Sevillian male is not very different. For both the Romantic travellers and Sender's sharper, more modern but equally naïve feminist heroine, the gypsies were especially exotic, entertaining and tricky, albeit often admirable. Gautier writes of gypsy women in Granada: "The *gitanas* sell amulets, tell fortunes, and practise the shady trades customary among the women of their race: I have seen very few pretty ones, though… their swarthy skin sets off the clearness of their Eastern eyes whose fire is tempered by a sort of mysterious melancholy, the memory, as it were, of an absent fatherland and a fallen greatness… Almost all the women possess a natural majesty of port and a supple carriage, and hold themselves so erect from the hips that in spite of their rags, dirt and poverty, they seem conscious of the antiquity and purity of their unmixed descent, for gypsies only marry among themselves."

But the outsider, real or fictional, barely penetrates the surface, despite efforts driven by intellectual and sexual curiosity. Each remains convinced of his or her cultural superiority, a conviction founded essentially upon ignorance: Nancy remarks, *en passant*, "Yesterday there was no class so we spent the morning walking round the barrio de Santa Cruz in Seville. Charming, although so much imitation of the Californian style, with its wrought iron railings and patios, becomes tiresome after a while." This sly dig forms part of Sender's withering critique of Anglo-American culture. He is kinder to the Sevillians, whom he portrays as worldlier, smarter and cynically aware.

Ford is particularly scornful of gypsies and their music (the word "flamenco" did not emerge until late in the nineteenth century, according to Zoido).Yet, like Nancy and Borrow, Ford took the trouble to investigate the phenomenon. Ford notes that Andalusian gypsy dancers had their origins in "those dancing girls of profligate Gades (the Roman form of Cadiz), which were exported to ancient Rome, with pickled tunnies, to the delight of wicked epicures and the horrors of the good fathers of the early church... Seville is now in these matters what Gades was; never was their wanting some venerable gypsy hag, who will get up a *función* as these pretty proceedings are called, a word taken from the pontifical ceremonies; for Italy set the fashion to Spain once, as France does now. These festivals must be paid for, since the gitanesque race, according to Cervantes, were only sent into this world as "fishhooks for purses". The *callees* [gypsies] when young are very pretty—then they have such wheedling ways and traffic on such sure wants and wishes, since to Spanish men they prophesy gold, to women, husbands."

Having encapsulated the prejudices of his age, Ford continues: "The scene of the ball is generally placed in the suburb of Triana, which is the Trastevere of the town, and the home of bullfighters, smugglers, picturesque rogues, and Egyptians... The house selected is usually one of those semi-Moorish abodes and perfect pictures, where rags, poverty and ruin are mixed up with marble columns, figs, fountains and grapes; the party assembles in some stately saloon, whose gilded Arab roof hangs over whitewashed walls, and the few wooden benches on which the chaperones and invited are seated, among whom quantity is rather preferred to quality... The ladies, who seem to have no bones, resolve the problem of perpetual motion, their feet having comparatively a sinecure, as the whole person performs a pantomime, and trembles like an aspen leaf; the flexible form and Terpischore figure of a young Andalucian girl—be she gipsy or not—is said by the learned to have been designed by nature as the fit frame for her voluptuous imagination."

The spectator

beholds the unchanging balance of hands, raised as if to catch showers of roses, the tapping of the feet and the serpentine quivering movements. A contagious excitement seizes the spectators who, like Orientals, beat time with their hands in measured cadence, and at every pause applaud with cries and clappings. The damsels, thus

*encouraged, continue in violent action until nature is all but
exhausted; then aniseed brandy, wine and alpisteras are handed
about. And the fete, carried on to early dawn, often concludes in
broken heads, which here are called "gypsy's fare". These dances
appear to a stranger from the chilly north to be more marked by
energy than by grace, nor have the legs less to do than the body, hips
and arms. The sight of this unchanged pastime of antiquity, which
excites the Spaniards to frenzy, rather disgusts the English spectator…
However indecent these dances may be, yet the performers are invi-
olably chaste, and as far at least as ungypsy guests are concerned may
be compared to iced punch at a rout; young girls go through them
before the applauding eyes of their parents and brothers, who would
resent to the death any attempt on their sisters' virtue. During the
lucid intervals between the ballet and the brandy, the song is admin-
istered as a soother by some hirsute artiste, without frills, studs,
diamonds, or kid gloves, whose staves, sad and melancholy, always
begin and end with an ay! a high-pitched sigh, or cry… Let the
Spaniards enjoy what they call music, although fastidious foreigners
condemn it as Iberian and Oriental.*

Interpreting the Gypsy World

Triana, where Ford witnessed this wild scene, is traditionally Seville's
gypsy quarter, the haunt of flamenco singers and dancers, and
bullfighters. Triana was also the mariners' quarter, the home of Seville's
seamen, fishermen and dockers since before the days of Columbus. The
neighbourhood's favourite Virgin, Esperanza de Triana, sits in the tiny,
meticulously tended Sailors' Chapel on Calle Pureza, which blazes with
light and is heavy with the clove-like scent of scarlet carnations. This
one of Seville's most cherished images—a fierce rival of Esperanza de
Macarena—and enthusiasts carry her across the Triana bridge ever year
before dawn on Good Friday in a moment of high emotion at the
culmination of Holy Week. Triana's bars and narrow streets are still
lively and atmospheric, and the flamenco and bullfighting tradition
deeply rooted, but floods and high property prices have driven many
gypsies out of their ancestral quarter to dreary suburbs on the city's
outer fringes.

Spain's gypsies are thought to have come originally from Egypt in
the fifteenth century. But their fame goes way back: "Perhaps you may

be expecting a troupe of Spanish dancers/Gipsy girls with their wanton songs and routines" wrote the Roman poet Juvenal in his Tenth Satire. The gypsies have retained their cultural identity despite various official attempts to obliterate their individuality. Cervantes had a gypsy uncle, and one of his best *Novelas Ejemplares* that he wrote around 1613, is "La Gitanilla" (The Little Gypsy Girl). This idealization of gypsy life threaded with homespun wisdom and shrewd observation of human frailties could have been written yesterday. His opening lines seem damning, but Cervantes, unlike Ford, is not scornful. His language, when portraying an underworld he knew, is straightforward, even admiring, possibly ironic. After all, Cervantes and his contemporaries who invented picaresque literature were pioneers of satire.

"Gypsies seem to have been born into the world for the sole purpose of being thieves: they are born of thieving parents, they are brought up with thieves, they study in order to be thieves, and they end up as past masters in the art of thieving. Thieving, and the taste for thieving are inseparable from their existence, and they never abandon them until they reach the grave..." Cervantes describes the young Preciosa, an enchanting gypsy girl who has learnt all the "gypsy arts and frauds and thieving tricks" from her grandmother. But Preciosa, in addition to being beautiful and intelligent, "gave every sign of having been born of better stock than gypsies, for she was extremely polite and could talk well." And so we are already prepared for the denouement: a handsome nobleman falls in love with her, a common fate—apparently both literary and real—of rich young men bored and frustrated with rigid social conventions, and she insists he joins their travelling, thieving life to prove his devotion. He does so, and they share adventures as they head south, until it emerges that she is actually a changeling. Her "grandmother" robbed her at birth from a noble family. So the apparently impossible match between two lovers from incompatible social worlds becomes entirely suitable. The gulf between them not so much bridged as shown never to have existed.

At one point, after Preciosa's noble lover joins the company disguised as a gypsy, they discuss whether to press on to Seville. The grandmother vetoes the plan: "...because in years gone by she had played a trick in Seville on a cap-maker called Triguillos, very well known in the city, whom she had had put in a pitcher of water up to his neck, stripped to the buff and with a garland of cypress on his head, waiting for the stroke of midnight to get out of the pitcher and dig up a great treasure which she had led him to believe was somewhere in his house. She said that as soon as the good cap-maker heard the bell ring for matins, he got out of the pitcher so quickly, so as not to miss the right moment, that he landed with it on the floor, and with the force of the blow and with the fragments of the pitcher he hurt himself, upset the water and was swimming about in it shouting that he was drowning.

> *She went on: "His wife and his neighbours rushed up with lights and found him going through the motions of swimming, puffing, and dragging his stomach along the ground, waving his arms and legs for all he was worth and shouting out at the top of his voice, 'Help, gentlemen, I'm drowning.' He was so frightened he really did think he was drowning. They got hold of him, and rescued him, whereupon he recovered, related my trick and in spite of that, started to dig down a couple of yards in the same spot, even though everyone told him that it was a trick of mine. If a neighbour hadn't stopped him by telling him that he had got to the foundations of his house, and let him dig as much has he wanted to, he'd have had the whole house down. This story was known throughout the whole city and even the children pointed their fingers at him and told the story of his credulity and my trick."*
>
> *This is the story the old gypsy told, and she gave this as her excuse for not going to Seville.*

The company heads instead for Murcia, where Preciosa's true identity becomes known. But amidst slapstick and Romanticism, with skilful plotting and sharp dialogue, Cervantes sketches a truth: that gypsy dancers and musicians were received into aristocratic houses, and achieved fame in polite society. The two worlds interacted for centuries, each seeking to exploit the other. The gypsies wanted money or gold, and the nobles sought to take advantage of young talent and beauty. Preciosa, aware of the peril, tells the young nobleman who declares himself her slave: "Only one jewel I possess… that jewel is my integrity and virginity, and I shall not sell it in exchange for promises or gifts, precisely because then it will be something you can get for money; and if it can be purchased it will be of very little value." She continues, acutely conscious of what poor Nancy never grasped: "The flower of virginity is one which should not allow itself to be offended even by the imagination. Once the rose has been cut from the bush, how quickly and easily it fades! One touches it, another sniffs it, another strips it of its leaves, and it finally breaks in pieces in clumsy hands."

The *Andaluz* poet Federico García Lorca was one of the few *payos*—the gypsy word for non-gypsies meaning "peasant" or "serf"— to interpret the gypsy world with conviction. He encouraged his readers to look at Andalusia through gypsy eyes. Lorca grew up knowing gypsies and took guitar lessons from two gypsy musicians. He became an accomplished guitarist and loved the instrument, which figures in many of his poems. Contrast Ford's description quoted above of a gypsy *juerga* with Lorca's poem *La Guitarra*:

> *The weeping of the guitar begins.*
> *Wineglasses break at dawn.*
> *The guitar begins to weep.*
> *It's useless to silence it.*
> *Impossible to silence it.*
> *It weeps monotonously*
> *like water weeps,*
> *like wind weeps*
> *over the snowfall.*
> *Impossible to silence it.*
> *It weeps for distant things.*
> *Hot sand of the south*
> *which begs for white camellias.*
> *The arrow weeps without target,*
> *the afternoon without morning,*
> *and the first dead bird*
> *upon the branch.*
> *Oh guitar! Heart stabbed*
> *by five swords.*

Lorca believed flamenco music expressed the innate sadness of the Andalusian soul that was barely disguised by superficial merrymaking. His best-known works, perhaps the most celebrated verses in Spanish literature, are his twin series of poems: *Romancero gitano* (Gypsy Ballads) and *Poema de canto jondo* (Poem of Deep Song), written when the poet was in his early twenties. "In these compositions," Ian Gibson writes in his biography of the poet, "Lorca makes no attempt to imitate the words of the often illiterate cante jondo singers, as so many poets had done in the nineteenth century and even well into the twentieth. Nor does he write in the ubiquitous first person of the songs. What he attempts to do, rather, is to create in the mind of the reader—or the listener, for Lorca is a minstrel and conceives of poetry principally as oral communication—the sensation that he can 'see' the primitive sources (those 'remote lands of sorrow') from which wells up the anguish of cante jondo and to follow the song imaginatively from its first note until the voice of the cantaor dies away." As early as 1922, when the poet was only 24, Lorca saw the gypsy as symbolizing "the deepest elements in the Andalusian psyche," writes Gibson. Lorca himself described his book *Romancero gitano* as "a book in which the visible Andalusia is barely mentioned but in which palpitates the invisible one. And now I am going to be explicit. It is an anti-picturesque, anti-folkoric, anti-flamenco book, with not a single short jacket, bullfighter's suit of lights, wide-brimmed sombrero or tambourine; there the figures move against primeval backdrops and there is just one protagonist, Anguish, great and dark as a summer's sky, which filters into the marrow of the bones and the sap of the trees and has nothing in common with melancholy, or with nostalgia or any other affliction or distress of the soul."

Death, unhappy love, erotic frustration and despair are the themes of Lorca's poems, which follow the rhythms and structures of the different forms of flamenco music. Images of the moon, the guitar, the road, the night and the threatening presence of the paramilitary Civil Guard evoke feelings of doom and foreboding from every page. And several of his poems tragically prefigure his own death at the hands of fascist death squads.

> *The cry of leaves in the wind*
> *a shadow of cypress.*
> *(Leave me in this field weeping)*
> *Everything has broken in the world.*
> *Nothing remains but silence.*

(Leave me in this field weeping.)
The horizon without light
Is bitten by bonfires.
I've told you to leave me
in this field
weeping.

And here is his "Memento":

When I die
bury me with my guitar
beneath the sand.
When I die
amidst the orange trees
and the mint.
When I die
bury me if you will
in a weather vane.

To the Edge

The young English writer Jason Webster went in pursuit of this fatalistic spirit, the *duende*, which Lorca called "that mysterious power that everyone senses and no philosopher explains." Webster narrates his experience in a book published in 2003, entitled *Duende: a Journey in Search of Flamenco*. Webster plunges through Spain's seedy gypsy underworld of crime, drugs, partying and music to the point of self-destruction. He seeks out gypsy musicians, learns flamenco guitar and achieves a remarkable degree of integration into this marginal, violent and arbitrary world. But he becomes aware that despite all his efforts, he remains an outsider. Suddenly, after the death of his gypsy companion on his last manic joyride in a stolen car, Webster realizes that he is leaning into the abyss, and backs off just in time. The tale is a twenty-first-century urban romp, a high-octane road movie, streaked with painfully won knowledge and an undertow of tragedy. He writes: "There is an instinctive feel for flamenco, making it easy to recognise, if difficult to pin down. Part of it is to do with being away from the mainstream, or on the outside. For the past two hundred years at least, flamenco has been the music and dance of the outcasts, people on the margins of Spanish, and particularly Andalusian society. From which, perhaps, stems the natural affinity with gypsies, and accounts for the large number of songs about injustice or going to jail… the only certainty about flamenco is that it began in Andalusia and remains to this day Andalusian, despite spreading across Spain and around the world."

Amidst the chaos of improvised performances, hyped by alcohol and cocaine, the young Englishman finishes a hectic night of singing, playing and arguing with his gypsy companions: "The sun was already high in the sky when I knocked back the last of my drink and went to find sanctuary in the darkness of my bedroom. 'This is flamenco, *churumbel* [gypsy for kid].' Carlos grabbed my arm as I passed him. His breath smelt like a distillery. 'This, this life. Not all that shit you were up to in Alicante. You want to experience real flamenco? You want to know what duende is really about? It's about this. It's about living on the edge—*a tope*. It's about singing so hard you can't speak any more. Or playing until your fingers bleed. It's about taking yourself as far as you can go, and then going one step further.' At that point I believed him."

The dancer Farruquito may have taken that one step further and driven over the edge. Early in 2004 a man was run over at a pedestrian crossing in Seville by a fast car whose driver accelerated away from the scene. The man died. Police traced the car to Farruquito's family. His underage brother confessed to the crime, apparently in the belief that the penalty would be less. Months later Farruquito himself was nailed for it. We learned from press reports that gypsies rarely undertake the administrative chore of registering a vehicle, insuring it or even taking a driving test. To these offences, Farruquito had added the far worse crime of fleeing in panic the scene of a fatal accident. He said a police contact advised him to implicate his younger brother, although that practice too was said to be common among gypsies. He was freed on bail of tens of thousands of euros, to face trial for reckless homicide and years in jail if found guilty. The real life tragedy matches any literary imaginings of the dark edge of the gypsy world. It certainly makes him less godlike: he is just a kid doing stupid things. But his reputation and moral stature took a terminal hit. He continued touring and performing pending trial, but public opinion was fiercely divided: his supporters lamented the crime as a cruel blow to a young man's brilliant career, and turned up in force to applaud him on stage. But the victim's family believed he was a common killer who should be locked up instead of lauded for his status as a celebrity.

The young man is said to be smitten with remorse for the single reckless gesture that brought ruin upon him and his extensive clan. The tale perhaps reinforces the deep strain of self-destructiveness and knife-edge balancing act between glory and disgrace that characterizes the gypsy world. A product of his origins in Seville's marginal slums, not even high-flying, pure-living Farruquito could escape the curse.

Seville Southside

Where in Seville can you glimpse this elusive frontier world? Few visitors are likely to obtain access to Las Tres Mil Viviendas—Three Thousand Dwellings. The vast high-rise housing project on the city's southern outskirts has all the appeal its unimaginative name suggests. The first language of Spanish gypsies is not Romany, that of most other gypsies in Europe—although they speak it—and they are no longer nomadic. Some still inhabit makeshift shanty towns but the overwhelming majority of them have been moved into modest homes, often on high rise estates on the fringes of the main cities. Sevillian gypsies who lived in their traditional Triana neighbourhood for centuries were decanted into Las Tres Mil during the Franco years, after floods washed away their shanties. Since then, officialdom's neglect and disinvestment bear much of the responsibility for the no-go area the neighbourhood has become. Legend has it that when the local flamenco guitarist Rafael Amador and the rest of his gypsy family moved into the newly built apartments some thirty years ago, they found a donkey looking out of a ninth-floor window. The donkey had been brought there by another gypsy who was unaccustomed to high-rise living. He had been surprised to find no room for stables in the brand-new and charmless neighbourhood. So the gypsy took a bundle of straw up in the lift and gave his donkey the spare bedroom. The animal was eventually photographed and the story was repeated to such an extent that, wherever Spain's gypsies have been stuffed into high rises, someone claims to have seen a donkey. But gypsy musicians who still call this depressed estate home, swear that no one houses a donkey these days.

The disclaimer did not stop the French film director Dominique Abel from opening her 2002 drama-documentary *Polígono Sur* (Seville

Southside) with a shot of a donkey peering from a high-rise window. Abel, a former catwalk model with a long association with flamenco and who lives in Spain, says: "It shows the surrealist side of reality in Las Tres Mil." The film is a sort of flamenco version of Cuba's *Buena Vista Social Club*, revealing the stream of talent that has flowed from the squalor and poverty of this rubbish-strewn estate. "You discover not just the music but a world apart, one that you did not know existed. This is flamenco not just as music but as a way of life." In this tough neighbourhood, a bar, a street corner, a stretch of pavement can become an impromptu stage for artists who create flamenco spontaneously and irrepressibly for their own pleasure. The film captures some remarkable moments of *alegría*—joy—encouraged by payments to every performer who appeared before the camera. But it also shows the dark backdrop to the music, the harsh realities of drugs, marginalization and poverty that give it an urgent intensity. One of the artists, the singer Pelayo, is back in the barrio for the first time for nearly twenty years, after serving a prison sentence for what other gypsies in Las Tres Mil call "a blood crime." Alcohol and cocaine, the latter easily obtained from the dealers who haunt the most run-down corner of the estate, fuel some of the scenes. The film also reveals the decline of the once magnificent Rafael Amador (the more brilliant brother, some say, of the hugely successful Raimundo Amador) who has been struggling for years to get his act back together and whose talent momentarily awakens when his fingers touch the strings. It drives home flamenco's dangerous flirtation with the *juerga*, the world of the all-night, drug-based partying.

The semi-documentary assembles more than twenty artists from the barrio, bringing together the traditional singing of Juana la de Revuelo, the dance of José Bobote and the lyrical guitar playing of Emilio "Coffeeface" Caracafé, and mixing in street rap and the many fusions of "new flamenco". As one reviewer commented, it may not be the best flamenco in Spain, but it is authentic.

❋ ❋ ❋

Take the flamenco shows advertised in Seville's bright tourist leaflets in the spirit in which they are intended. They are mostly professional operations designed to provide honest entertainment and to dispel flamenco's crudely kitsch, frilly-gilt postcard image. With luck you will come out feeling elated, but do not expect an emotional charge you will treasure for years to come. You might find that defining moment in a bar in the early hours, or from a haunting song echoing from a courtyard that sounds like the soul being wrenched from the body. Some say the best place to see authentic flamenco is in a touring stage show, or in Madrid where many of the top artists have moved. This might seem paradoxical, but the finest performers now achieve wide recognition and are hoisted from their humble origins to national or international stardom. Their plunge to earth may be equally meteoric. An American might be similarly perplexed if a visiting Briton were to ask "where can I hear true blues?" For flamenco is Spain's blues, or soul, and Seville the Spanish Mississippi Delta or Detroit. Flamenco's legend is doubtless stronger than the reality, but with effort and luck, you might just brush up against the real thing.

Chapter Ten
CÓRDOBA

The Hammam

Take a bath. Córdoba once boasted 600 public bathhouses or *hammam*, if we are to believe the seventeenth-century Muslim chronicler al-Maqqari. For a brief span of two generations, Córdoba was the finest, most cultured, most glittering metropolis of Europe, a wonder of the world, home of poets, philosophers, doctors and scientists centuries ahead of their time. Perhaps with some exaggeration, al-Maqqari claimed that tenth-century Córdoba had a population of around a million (compared with 800,000 today), 3,000 mosques, 1,600 inns, 50 hospitals, 25 schools, 60,300 houses for the wealthy and officials, 213,077 ordinary homes and 4,000 shops. Córdoba was also the book centre of the world; sixty thousand were published every year. In one part of town alone 170 women copied manuscripts that were sent to mosques throughout Spain. Love poems composed and published in the city were circulated to all parts of the Islamic world.

If you find it difficult to imagine an epoch so highly cultured, so historically remote from our own, step inside the Arab Baths on Corregidor Luis de la Cerda just to the east of the great mosque. The Medina Califal baths, said to be among the biggest in Europe, were built recently within an ancient Moorish house to recreate the luxurious sensuality that the citizens of Córdoba once briefly enjoyed.

First impressions are of a hushed, arched entrance to an enchanted realm, gently illuminated by glimmering pools of light filtering through fretted vents in the walls and vaulted ceiling. Soft Andalusian music, the subdued murmur of fountains, and a damply aromatic atmosphere envelop you like a silken robe, and invite you to head to the interlocking inner chambers containing scented pools. The first bath, a long, thin stone tank, is icy, and not recommended until you have braved a cold, but not heart-stoppingly freezing, bath. This prepares you in turn for the first moment of blissful relaxation in a large, tepid bath surrounded by colonnades of arches balanced on stone columns, and walls decorated by geometric Andalusian tiles. The pool is lit by tiny circles and stars that perforate the domed ceiling, casting flickering reflections on the water. Candles gleam at floor level or from niches, and stucco walls are washed in shades of deep pink, suffusing everything with a rosy glow. Bathers pad from tepid to warm to hot pools in ever deepening twilight, and take the occasional icy plunge. Allow yourself to be soothed by a masseuse working scented oils into your back and shoulders, before sliding off the bench and sinking into warm water just two steps away. Engage in whispered conversation with your neighbours, if you want to recreate the social ambience of a Muslim baths, in whose steamy depths important matters of the day were discussed or plotted.

On leaving, with a bracing final cold plunge, you can take mint tea from an ornate silver pot in tiny gilded glasses, and browse round the bazaar, an emporium of bath oils, soaps and scented essences to enable you to create the authentic Córdoba *hammam* experience in your own bathroom.

The Mezquita and Medina Azahara: House of Prayer and a Palatial City

The creators of this sybaritic luxury were themselves only refining a sophisticated bath culture established by the Romans, though raising it to new heights. They were the Omeyas, or Umayads, a Muslim dynasty originally from Damascus in Syria who drove west and created a breakaway kingdom, or Califate, in Córdoba that ruled the Muslim kingdom of al-Andalus from around 756 to 1031. Obviously the Omeyas did not spend all their time bathing. They ruled and they prayed; and they left in Córdoba two magnificent monuments to these activities that bear witness to the city's early splendour.

One is the tenth-century mosque or Mezquita in the heart of the city, said to have been for centuries the most magnificent in the Islamic world. In the sixteenth century the Catholic monarchs built a huge cathedral in the mosque's main prayer hall, as a symbol of their conquest. Some say this ruined the mosque's austere symmetry of more than a thousand pillars, 55 of which were ripped out to make room for the cathedral. Others assert that the cathedral itself is dwarfed by the magnificence of the holy place it strove to supplant. King Carlos V, who thoughtlessly gave permission for the new work, knowing nothing of the city, came to bitterly regret his decision. When he inspected it after work began in 1523, he reproached the local clerics with one of the most crushing architectural critiques in history: "You have destroyed something unique in the world to build something that you could have put up anywhere."

The mosque is exhaustively described in any guidebook, and visitors are handed an explanatory leaflet as they enter. The complex dates from the brief rule of Abderraman III, who bore Islam's highest title of caliph, or successor to Mohamed, after he broke free from the Omeyas of Damascus to found an independent kingdom in Córdoba around 750.

The city's other dazzling legacy is the palace-fortress city of Medina Azahara, five miles north-west of Córdoba. Like the mosque, the palace-city was built by the wise and cultured Abderraman III. Here the caliph set up his palace and his court, a self-contained mini-kingdom which supposedly housed tens of thousands of people. Spread over three descending levels of broad terraces, Medina Azahara commands breathtaking views over the Guadalquivir valley and the rolling Córdoba *campiña* or countryside. You can spend a day wandering through ruined oyster-pink marble passages, gardens of aromatic trees and royal salons dominated by ornately carved stucco arches, stunning even in their semi-ruined state, and imagine the grandeur and intellectual refinement of Córdoba of the time. Ancient chronicles whose truth cannot be confirmed describe Medina Azahara in terms so extravagant they might have come from the tales of the Arabian nights.

James Michener, the American writer who visited Spain in the 1960s, describes in his classic work *Iberia* his initial disappointment at discovering Medina Azahara's "barren hillside with its unimpressive ruins". Is this, Michener asks, the glory of Islam? "Then the guide begins to speak," Michener goes on, "and if you are able to credit the greatness that once characterized Córdoba, you begin to visualize what Medinat az-Zahra must have been like in the year 960."

> *'We are five miles from Cordoba,' the guide says, 'and one day when a foreign ambassador came to see the caliph who was residing here, he found that a matting had been laid for him all the way from Cordoba. It was lined by soldiers and eunuchs and musicians who played music for him as he walked the five miles. Along the whole*

route umbrellas kept him protected from the sun and dancing girls accompanied him. When he reached this place he found a palace that covered the entire hillside. The sultan's rooms alone numbered four hundred. The roof was supported by 4,313 marble columns. The fountains were without number, for merely to feed the fish required eight hundred loaves to be baked each day. It wasn't a palace really but a sultan's city, all under one roof. More than twenty-five thousand people worked here. Slavonian eunuchs, three thousand seven hundred. Other male servants ten thousand. Female servants six thousand. Pages, at least a thousand. Musicians many score. To feed only the people living under this roof required seven tons of meat each day, not to count the chickens, partridges and fish. It was the most luxurious palace that Spain has ever seen, or the world either, perhaps.'

Michener was sceptical of the guide's claims, but recognized that she had not made them up, merely repeated them from ancient legends. It is interesting to compare Michener's guide's account with that of the contemporary Muslim historian Ibn al-Arabi, who insisted that the caliph himself lived in austere simplicity amidst the pomp. "A delegation of Christian Spaniards from the north came to negotiate with the Caliph," this account goes. "He wanted to frighten them by demonstrating the magnificence of his realm. Therefore he installed between the gate of Córdoba and the gate of Medina Azahara a row of soldiers that flanked each side of the road, who raised their flashing, long and broad swords and crossed them to resemble the beams of a roof. On the monarch's order, the delegation of Christian Spaniards was led through the ranks of soldiers as if through a covered access. The dread that gripped them before such magnificence was indescribable. The caliph ordered the space between the palace gate and the place where they were to have the audience with the monarch to be covered with brocaded cloths. At specific points he placed dignitaries who could have passed for kings, since they sat in very ornate seats and were dressed in embroidered silks. Every time the delegation members saw a dignitary they kneeled before him because they thought he was the caliph. Then they told them: 'Get up. This is just a servant of his servants.'"

Finally they reached a covered sandy patio. In the centre was the caliph. He wore a simple garment; everything he had on cost no more than four dirhams. He sat on the sand, with his head bowed. In front of him was a book of the Koran, a sword and a blazing fire. They stood still, thinking the man was perhaps a sort of hermit. 'Here is the monarch,' they told the delegation members, who threw themselves at his feet and dared not raise their heads from the floor until Abderrahman spoke. He said: 'God has ordered that we invite you to this' and he showed them the Koran. 'And if you refuse, to this'—and he indicated the sword. 'And your destiny, when we take your life, is this'—and he pointed to the fire that burned before him. They were filled with terror. He ordered them to leave without them saying a word, and they agreed peace with him under whatever conditions he should impose.

Yet another account describes a German mission to the court of Córdoba in 953. Otto I of Germany sent John, abbot of the monastery of Gorze in Lorraine, as his emissary to enlist the help of Andalusian naval power in suppressing piracy in the western Mediterranean. Diplomatic misunderstandings kept John in semi-captivity in Córdoba for three years (the letter of instruction from King Otto was couched in terms very detrimental to Islam, and an intermediary had to return to the German court to request new ones) until finally Abderraman agreed to see him. The account comes from a life of John of Gorze written shortly after the monk's death in 974:

On the day which had been agreed for John's presentation at court, all the elaborate preparations for displaying royal splendour were made. Ranks of people crowded the whole way from the lodging to the centre of the city, and from there to the palace. Here stood infantrymen with spears held erect, beside them others brandishing javelins and staging demonstrations of aiming them at each other; after them, others mounted on mules with their light armour; then horsemen urging their steeds on with spurs and shouts, to make them rear up. In this startling way the Moors hoped to put fear into our people by their various martial displays, so strange to our eyes. John and his companions were led to the palace along a very dusty road, which the very dryness of the seasons alone served to stir up (for it was the summer solstice). High officials came forward to meet them, and all the pavement of the outer area of the palace was carpeted with most costly rugs and coverings.

When John arrived at the dais where the caliph was seated alone—almost like a godhead accessible to none or to very few—he saw everything draped with rare coverings, and floor-tiles stretching evenly to the walls. The caliph himself reclined upon a richly ornate couch. They do not use thrones or chairs as other peoples do, but recline on divans or couches when conversing or eating, their legs crossed one over the other. As John came into his presence, the caliph stretched out his hand to be kissed. The hand-kissing not being customarily granted to any of his own people or to foreigners, and never to persons of low and middling mark, the caliph none the less gave John his hand to kiss.

The caliph is said to have named the city after his favourite wife—some versions say concubine—az-Zahara, the Radiant. He brought marble from all over Spain, Portugal and North Africa to build his city. Of more than 4,000 columns he ordered to be brought to the site, 140 came from the Byzantine capital, Constantinople, twelve of them gold, plus sculptures encrusted with pearls for his sleeping quarters. Abderraman entrusted the supervision of the work to his son Alhaken II, who continued to expand the city's living quarters and royal offices after his father's death. In 945, four years after the consecration of the great mosque, the entire court, including all the administrative staff, courtiers, minions and workers moved out to the new city palace. One conference room was lined with crystals, creating a rainbow when lit by the sun. Another was built round a huge shallow bowl of mercury which, when the sun's rays fell on it, was rocked by a slave, sending reflected sunbeams flashing and darting around the room, creating an effect of almost supernatural magnificence. "To the visitor it seemed that the light and the order of the natural world was broken, and that the columns and the entire room span and fragmented into prisms of momentary reflections," wrote the historian al-Maqqari. "The vertigo ceased only when the caliph made a sign and the surface of mercury was once more as immobile as that of a frozen lake. To the visitor, overwhelmed by solemnity, terror and astonishment, it seemed that a simple gesture of Abderraman could dislocate or restore the rotation of the universe."

Destruction and Resurrection

The glory that was built in a frenzied ten years was destroyed after just fifty. In 1009 Berber mercenaries from North Africa stationed in Córdoba rebelled and sacked Medina Azahara, hauled down its columns, horseshoe arches and soaring vaults, demolished its elaborate water channels, bathhouses and aqueducts, plundered the ruins, then set fire to them. The flames, it was said, could be seen from the outskirts of Córdoba and the banks of the Guadalquivir, and raged for a whole night. For centuries thereafter, what remained of the city was treated as a quarry. The splendour of Medina Azahara became a shadowy memory conserved only in ancient legends. Razed to the ground, even what remained of its floor plan was covered by meadow. "But for the testimony of historians," the Scottish traveller Dundas Murray wrote in 1849, "it would be hard to believe that Medina Azahara ever rose from the ground to cover a wide space with sumptuous edifices." Gerald Brenan paid a visit more than a hundred years later and judged that the ruins were "scarcely worth seeing, since all the stones were being carried off to build a monastery on the hill."

But in 1944 excavations unearthed remnants of an important part of the palace, the Royal House, where guests were received and ministers' meetings held. Starting from little more than the stumps at floor level, archaeologists painstakingly reconstructed the original structure. The main room, the Salon Rico, decorated with fine marble carvings, is now revealed as one of the wonders of Moorish architecture. Its walls and arches are decorated with a fretwork of delicate, flowing designs depicting the typically Syrian "tree of life". Fragments of stone salvaged from far and wide have been individually identified and returned, where possible, to their original location or laid out in small pieces on the floor. The ruins today are less desolate than when Michener saw them, and it is almost possible to believe they originally formed a city of great magnificence.

From the topmost terrace you can see laid out before you the area containing the caliph's palace and the houses of the nobles, including housing for the caliph's 1,200-strong personal guard. The level below contained splendid reception rooms and administrative and military buildings, baths, as well as a zoo, an aviary, fishponds and an arsenal. Below that on the third level—almost nothing of which survives except the outlines of a mosque—were the workers' quarters, the market place, a hunting zone, the mint, workshops, stables and an elaborate irrigation system. Each section was separated from the other by a wall punctuated by strategically positioned gates, and the whole area was enclosed by a double wall with a zigzag entry system that forced would-be intruders to double back on themselves, making them an easy target. Ten thousand workers and 1,500 beasts of burden are said to have been used in its construction, during which 6,000 carved stones were used daily. Marble was imported from Almería and Carthage, engraved basins sent from Constantinople and Syria. The roof tiles were covered in gold and silver. There was even an underground system of passageways and covered galleries reserved for the use of the caliph and his functionaries.

A dynasty from Damascus created these treasures, but most were destroyed by conquerors of various stripes down the centuries. First came the fanatical Almoravids in 1086, after them the still more fundamentalist Almohads in 1146, both from North Africa. Then a succession of wars raged throughout Andalusia among rival Muslim fiefdoms or *taifas*, until Christians drove Muslims from the city in 1236, and intensified the obliteration of "infidel" culture. Even the baths were destroyed by the unwashed Christian hordes, whose prejudice against bathing persisted until the nineteenth century when "Cathedrals of Flesh" were denounced as abhorrent and immoral. The huge site that you can see today at Medina Azahara, reveals for the first time in centuries the astonishing extent of the original complex. It amounts to barely a tenth of the city's original area. The rest remains buried beneath the tussocky meadows, the rolling vineyards and wheat fields of the *campiña*.

City Walls: Philosophers and Poets

If Caliph Abderraman's personal taste was as simple as some chroniclers make out, perhaps he was following the precepts of a previous wise son of Córdoba, the Roman philosopher Seneca. Seneca's statue outside the ancient city wall solemnly guards the Puerta de Almodovar, once known as the Jews' Gate and one of several arched gateways that allowed access to the walled city. The walls were originally built by the Romans, then rebuilt by the Moors using Roman remains. An imposing

Roman gate—the Puerta del Puente or Bridge Gate—which was restored during the Renaissance faces the city's multi-arched Roman bridge across the Guadalquivir. The bridge is the most dramatic legacy of Roman Corduba, and remains the main route out of the city to both Seville and Granada. Go to the bridge in the late afternoon and lean across the parapet for a fabulous view of the city, and of the river that glows blood-red in the sunset. Gaze upon giant *norias* or water wheels on the river bank, and four water mills, now semi-ruined, which the Moors built to catch the river's now sluggish current.

Lucius Annaeus Seneca, born around 4 BC, spent most of his life in Rome, until Emperor Nero, to whom he was tutor, accused him of involvement in a subversive plot. Nero commanded him and other real or imagined enemies to commit suicide in 65 AD, which was the usual system of imperial execution. Even in Rome, Seneca never lost his Spanish roots, and earned a substantial income from properties he owned around Córdoba. Roman occupation of Spain established the landholding system of the large estate or *latifundium*, and Seneca was an early example of that enduring Andalusian figure, the absentee landlord. Roman writers praised the *campiña* of Córdoba, or Corduba, as they called it. Pliny extolled the artichokes, Martial praised the fruit and the olive oil, and the excellence of its wool. Which adds local spice to Seneca's reflection on the importance of knowledge: "As wool imbibes certain colors and others it does not, unless it has been frequently soaked and double-dyed: so there are certain kinds of learning which, on being acquired are thoroughly mastered; but philosophy, unless she sinks deeply into the soul and has long dwelt there, and has not given a mere coloring but a deep dye, performs none of the things which she has promised."

The stone statue of Seneca by the gate portrays him bare-headed, eyes downcast, draped in his Roman toga and holding in his right hand a rolled manuscript. He faces away from the city towards the distant Andalusian hills, perhaps towards his own holdings. Seneca was a Stoic. He did not actually invent the philosophy, which was already influential in Rome during his lifetime, but he is remembered as its best-known exponent. In letters and speeches to dining companions, he coined pithy aphorisms on how to live simply and behave honourably in the face of adversity. Seneca had poor health, suffering all his life from asthma, which is something that invites stoicism, and later tuberculosis. He strove to apply his philosophy to daily life, and even his death, described by the Roman historian Tacitus, was a model of stoicism. Following Nero's orders, Seneca cut his wrists, and—because he was old and thin and his blood ran slowly—cut the veins of his legs and hams too. He then called his scribes and urged them to record his last words, hoping he would be remembered for his learning and his good friendship. As death was slow in coming, he asked for poison, but he drank it with little effect, as his limbs were already cold and his veins closed up. So he took a hot bath, whereupon the steam finally stifled his asthmatic lungs. Michener believes that the Spanish personality owes much to his principles. "I have known one politician, one novelist and one bullfighter who have assured me that the principles by which they live and practise their art derive from Seneca. His ability to see the world cynically but with wit endears him to the Spaniard," the American writes. Contemporaries, however, noted that Seneca did not always live up to his principles, especially those of questioning convention and doing without all except necessities. He amassed an impressive fortune, owned several houses and lush gardens, and had a high regard for his own importance, saying he expected his writings "to be of use to later generations."

Here are some examples of Seneca's stoic principles:

The fear of war is worse than war itself.
Life, if you know how to use it, is long enough.
Life is like a school of gladiators, where men live and fight with each other.

And here is one I found printed on the flimsy paper napkin of a café in Madrid: "Ask only for the necessary, not the convenient. The unnecessary, although it should cost only a cent, is expensive."

Some have criticized Seneca's epigrammatic style for being too terse. The English historian Thomas Babington Macaulay wrote to a friend in the 1800s: "I cannot bear Seneca... His works are made up of mottoes. There is hardly a sentence which might not be quoted; but to read him straightforward is like dining on nothing but anchovy sauce."

Few Spanish cities can boast so many modest and elegant statues of such erudite thinkers as Córdoba. Mosche Ben Maimon, or Maimonides, born in Córdoba in 1135 (d. 1204), is honoured by one of the most beautiful and atmospheric statues of the city, perhaps of Spain. It sits in the tiny whitewashed Plazuela de Tiberiades at the entrance to the city's Jewish quarter, the labyrinth of narrow lanes that twines within the inner walls between the Almodovar Gate and the mosque. The bronze figure, wearing—in Michener's words—the robes and turban of the desert, sits surrounded by a little rose bed, contemplatively holding a book, marking the page with his thumb. The edges of the book and the toes of his tip-tilted pointed slippers are pale against the dark metal, worn creamy smooth by the reverent touch of passers-by. Grasp his slippered feet and draw your hands up and towards you, and feel a satisfying transfer of ancient wisdom. Yes, these tranquil alleys and flower-decked patios prompt profound philosophical reflections.

With the fundamentalist Almohads in power in the city and persecution of Jews on the increase, this cultured and learned man had to flee with this family to Morocco around 1150 while still a teenager. He wandered to Algeria, Tunis, Turkey, possibly to Palestine, accumulating learning as he went. In 1165 he went to Egypt, where he spent his last years as simultaneously private doctor to the sultan Saladin and leader of the Jewish community of Cairo where, his monument in Córdoba reminds us, he died. He is said to have treated Richard the Lionheart while on the crusades, and refused the English monarch's invitation to return with him to England. Maimonides' literary works were translated from Hebrew into Arabic and circulated within the mosques and synagogues of Andalusia. He wrote on biblical and talmudic matters, mathematics, astronomy and medicine. He is best remembered for his philosophical work *Guide for the Perplexed*, in which he tried to reconcile faith with reason. In the book, writes Michener admiringly, Maimonides "takes a bewildered applicant step by step through the religious process, providing rational explanations for the existence of God and for less theological problems. It is a beautifully composed work and explains why Jews consider him the foremost Jewish intelligence since the time of Moses."

Maimonides is said to have lived in a house with two fine patios on the square named after him round the corner from his statue, and which now houses the Bullfighting Museum. A few yards in the other direction, about half-way down Calle de los Judíos—Jews Street—is Andalusia's only surviving synagogue, and one of only three such in Spain (the other two are in Toledo). The synagogue was built in 1314, and is entered through a tiny side court that was originally a house. After the Jews were expelled in 1492, their house of prayer became a rabies hospital, then in 1558 the headquarters of the shoemakers' guild under their patron St. Crispin, and finally a school.

The life of the Muslim philosopher Averroes (1126-1198), known also as Ibn Rushd, paralleled that of his Jewish fellow Cordoban. The jurist, doctor and philosopher was, according to the British historian of Moorish Spain, Richard Fletcher, "one of the most commanding thinkers of the medieval Islamic world." Averroes, like Maimonides, was driven from his home town by fanatical Almohads, Berber fundamentalists who came from North Africa and hated books. When they took over the city in 1148, Averroes was about 22. He initially supported their regime and became an important *qadi* or religious judge in Córdoba and Seville between 1169 and 1184, and the personal physician and trusted advisor of Almohad rulers. But he fell out of favour, possibly through some court intrigue whose details have been lost, and was exiled in 1195. His works were banned and burned. One story tells of how he was ordered to stand by the Gate of Pardon of the city's mosque so that the faithful could spit on him.

Averroes seems to have been one of these multi-talented renaissance men ahead of his time. At the age of 25 he made astronomical observations near Marrakech in Morocco in the course of which he discovered a previously unobserved star. A lifetime's experience as a physician was distilled into this "Generalities" a compendium of medical knowledge completed in 1194. He is best remembered in the western world—where he is more celebrated than in the Islamic—as a philosopher, and in particular as a follower and interpreter of Aristotle.

Towards the end of his life he was rehabilitated, but abandoned the city to settle in the court of Marrakech, where he died. Averroes enjoyed enormous prestige in the Islamic and Christian world during his lifetime, although his doctrines were much disputed. His works were translated in the thirteenth century into Latin and Hebrew and spread throughout the universities of Christian Europe. Averroes was fascinated by Aristotle, and described the Greek philosopher as "an example which nature has devised to demonstrate supreme human perfection ... given to us by divine providence that we might know whatever can be known." He commented on nearly all the master's works—astronomical, biological, meteorological, medical, logical and ethical. But Averroes' ideas aroused strong criticisms, since his Greek idol did not believe in the eternity of the soul. Islam was founded on divine revelation granted to the Prophet and revealed in the Koran, such that all knowledge came from God. To this vision, Aristotle offered a disquieting alternative: the world and its workings may be understood without recourse to the divine. These were, as the historian Fletcher observes, "dangerous and uncharted waters." Averroes argued that men should do good of their own free will, and pursue a higher morality than that fixated on the judgement of the almighty. His work on Aristotelian philosophy had enormous influence on scholars throughout European Christendom in the thirteenth and fourteenth century, including St. Thomas Aquinas (d.1274) who cited him more than five hundred times in his own work. Renaissance thinkers considered him indispensable for an understanding of Aristotle's teachings, and Dante, in his Inferno, wrote of "Averroes who composed the great commentary." Bearded, robed, seated beside the Puerta de la

Luna, near the Puerta de Sevilla, Averroes, like Maimonides, rests a book on his knee.

Córdoba's erudite men are usually portrayed holding a book, which is fitting in a city once renowned throughout Europe as a centre of learning. "When a wise man dies in Seville, they take his books to be sold in Córdoba," an ancient saying goes: "and when a musician dies in Córdoba, they take his instruments to be sold in Seville." The library built up by Abderraman's son, Al-Hakem, is said to have contained 400,000 volumes, making it one of the greatest in the Muslim world. The scholar and poet Ibn Hazm (994-1064) guards the city's Seville Gate. He stands, framed by a Roman arch, also wrapped in his robes and turban and shod in soft pointed slippers, and holds a scroll in his left hand. Ibn Hazm estimated that Al-Hakem's library's catalogue alone ran to 44 volumes of 50 folios each. Ibn Hazm wrote important works on theology, philosophy and jurisprudence—bound together by the unifying theme of the quest of the soul for God. But he is best known for his treatise written as a young man on love and lovers, known as *The Ring of the Dove*. In this work the poet remembers women and men he has loved, praises the spiritual aspects of love, condemns sexual excess and recommends chastity. "It is a work of extraordinary psychological subtlety and penetration, tirelessly illuminating the almost limitless human capacity for self-deceit to which love is so often the trigger," comments Fletcher. The poet's words are nevertheless steeped in the indolent sensuality that clings to this city of flower-decked courtyards, murmuring fountains and quiet, narrow lanes.

Córdoba is considered the capital of Andalusian patios. In no other city in Spain are these little whitewashed squares so numerous or so luxuriant. They are particularly colourful and joyous during Córdoba's patio fiesta every May. Córdobans compete with each other to set out on washed cobbled streets and hang from the walls and wrought-iron balconies as many pots of bright, trailing flowers as they can. Apart from the ubiquitous geranium, patios are laden with pots of scented jasmine, roses and basil, as well as palms and orange trees. Patios were, it seems, a Roman invention that the Arabs refined as a cool, perfumed refuge from the bustle of the street. Ibn Hazm evoked this floral tranquility:

Flowers laughed, and your bracelets moved beneath
the shelter of a diffused shade.
Little birds offered us their most beautiful song.
Some poured forth their pain; others warbled with joy.
Water poured freely between us.
Eyes and hands could meet when they desired.

Yet Ibn Hazm, too, had to flee, and his works were burned, to which his brave riposte was: "Even though you burn the paper, you cannot burn what it contains, because I carry it in my breast..." He wrote a desperate lament for his city destroyed by war:

Now the places where men once lived like lions and virgins like
marble statues amidst untold delights are the refuge of wolves, play-
thing for ogres, amusement for evil spirits and lair for wild beasts...
The ruin of that fortress has appeared before my eyes, and the soli-
tude of those patios that were formerly too small for the crowds of
people that passed through them. I seemed to hear in them the song
of the owl and the barn owl, when formerly you heard nothing but
the coming and going of those multitudes amidst whom I grew up
inside its walls. Before, the night was the continuation of the day...
now the day within those walls is the prolongation of night in silence
and abandon.

One man from Córdoba's Islamic golden age rule left a more lasting, and joyous, cultural legacy, however. The celebrated singer and musician Ziryab was an exile from the eastern Islamic world who established a kind of conservatoire at Córdoba where young musicians and singers could study. Through Ziryab the musical traditions of the east were brought to al-Andalus, enhanced by his revolutionary contributions to them. Ziryab is credited with introducing a fifth string to the four-stringed lute—an instrument brought from the Arab world—said to be an essential step towards the evolution of the Spanish guitar. The musician was also something of a stylist and dandy, an Andalusian Beau Brummel, in Fletcher's view. From him, fashionable Cordobans learned to cook and serve a dinner after the style of Baghdad, with identifiable first and second courses and a dessert, rather than the simultaneous display of all dishes at once. He introduced the

tablecloth, taught Andalusians—and hence the western world—to use a knife and fork. He introduced new hairstyles, encouraged the use of toothpaste, and established the wearing of particular clothes to suit the differing seasons of the year. Until his death in 857 Ziryab was a key figure in the transmission of eastern culture to this far outpost of western Islam.

Plaza del Potro: *Pícaros* and Romantics
The Plaza del Potro, Colt Square, is named after its sixteenth-century stone fountain topped by a lively prancing pony. The spot was made famous by Cervantes who mentions staying at the Mesón or Posada del Potro in *Don Quijote*. Cervantes lived in Córdoba as a child. His family moved there from the Castillian city of Valladolid in 1553, when young Miguel was six, after his father Rodrigo had been jailed for debt. The young Cervantes must have known the inn and the cobbled square that tapers downhill towards the Guadalquivir. The tavern still exists, lovingly restored, a perfect example of a *corrala*: two floors built round a cobbled courtyard, with the upper floor lined with a gallery and a sturdy wooden handrail. It is now a cultural showcase run by the municipality. The area is calm and casual, a pleasant spot to relax and recoup the strength of body and spirit. In their sixteenth- and seventeenth-century heyday, the square and tavern alike were the haunts of picaresque travellers, adventurers, merchants with a nose for a deal, Spaniards fallen to ruin, ready to hire their services for any kind of risky work.

Opposite the tavern is a soberer establishment, the former fifteenth-century Charity Hospital. This too contains pretty courtyards and gardens filled with sculptures, which lead into two linked buildings. One is the provincial fine arts museum; the other the former home of the city's best known artist, Julio Romero de Torres, in what is now a museum in his name. It is fashionable to sneer at Romero de Torres, who despite belonging to art's modern period—he was born in 1874 and died in 1930—has a style that harks back to an earlier romantic age. A contemporary of Picasso, of German expressionism and Art Deco, he stuck none the less to backward-looking nineteenth-century realism. The British writer on Spain, Michael Jacobs, who is also an art historian, is scornfully dismissive: "The Andalucian woman, stripped of personality, intellect, and even clothes, is the constant subject of the turgid and crudely symbolical canvases of the turn-of-the-century artist Julio Romero de Torres, to whom a whole dark and gloomy museum is devoted in his native Córdoba," he writes in his comprehensive *Andalucia*. "These works, in which the female nude is generally portrayed with great candour and set alongside fully clothed guitar players, bullfighters or other such male Andalucian stereotypes, might strike the viewer as being little more than high kitsch, but they are immensely popular in Spain."

Romero de Torres is renowned for his lugubrious *Andaluz* beauties, the dark-eyed, copper-skinned malicious gypsy queen who supposedly lurks within the exploited servant girl. His last painting, one of his best known, is of a bare-shouldered, bare-legged girl sullenly stirring the dying cinders of a brazier used to heat rooms in the winter, whilst fixing the viewer with a challenging look. The painting, *La chiquita piconera*, evokes Victorian-age sentimentality but was painted as late 1930. Still more ludicrously melodramatic, if you share Jacobs' assessment, is the tableau of weeping relatives beside the flower-bedecked, sunlight-drenched corpse of a young girl readied for burial, entitled "Look How Pretty She Was." Other paintings, *Gipsy Muse*, *The Sibyl of the Alpujarras*, continue the theme. But his *Poem to Córdoba* of 1913 is a hymn of praise to the city, a frieze of young female beauties in settings recalling Córdoba's successive Roman, Muslim and Christian ages of glory.

A similarly self-indulgent style, although dating from two centuries earlier, is displayed by the Golden Age poet Luis de Góngora, who was born in Córdoba in 1561 and died there in 1627. Góngora moved to Madrid where he was so mocked by his contemporary, the misanthropic satirist Francisco de Quevedo, that the injured writer crept back to his native land to lick his wounds. It was the celebration of Gongora's third centenary in 1927, organized in Seville by Federico García Lorca, that inspired the Generation of '27, the group of young progressive-minded poets and writers whose flowering was brutally scythed by the Civil War. Among them was the Sevillian poet Luis Cernuda, who wrote the following verse to Góngora:

Weary of long wasted years
In pursuit of fortune far from Córdoba, its plain and its celestial wall
He returns to his native corner to die, tranquil and silent...

Cernuda was referring to a sonnet that Góngora wrote in tribute to his home city, "To Córdoba", which is inscribed on wood in the city's Historical Museum. It begins: "Oh celestial wall! Oh towers crowned/with honor!" and ends, after hyperbolic exclamations of nostalgia and longing: "Oh fatherland, oh flower of Spain!"

The early nineteenth-century romantic travellers who were so enchanted with Seville and Granada were contemptuous of Córdoba. George Borrow's view was typical: "a mean, dark, gloomy place". Richard Ford, who raved about Seville, dismissed Córdoba as "a poor and servile city". He wrote: "Córdoba is soon seen… a day will amply suffice for everything." Gautier was kinder, but similarly disparaging: "One walks between interminable chalk-coloured walls, with occasional windows trellised with bars and gratings, meeting nobody but a few evil-looking beggars, pious women muffled in black veils, or *majos* ["swells"], who ride past like lightning on their brown horses with white harness, striking showers of sparks from the cobblestones. If the Moors could return, they would not have to make many changes in order to settle here again… The life seems to have ebbed away from this great body, once animated by the active circulation of Moorish blood; nothing remains of it now but a white and calcined skeleton." Lorca thought Córdoba was Andalusia's most melancholy city: *sola y lejana* – alone and remote, he wrote, a place to die.

Gautier's assessment is no longer remotely true. Córdoba today is much livelier, though it remains deeply influenced, perhaps overburdened, by its sumptuous history. But with so much of its past expunged, today's Córdoba demands huge feats of imagination to reconstruct its former glory. Except perhaps in one facet of the city's culture—where nothing is left to the imagination.

From Roman Games to the Spanish Beatle
The Museo Municipal Taurino (Bullfighting Museum), in the house once inhabited by Maimonides on the square that bears the philosopher's name, celebrates the city's tauromachy legends, particularly the matador Manolete, who died in 1947. Among exhibits of shocking immediacy are the hide, the head and the tail of Islero, the bull that killed Manolete in the ring, plus the purple and gold cape he twirled as he fell. In the nearby square, the Plaza del Pintor Miguel del Moral Gómez, wall tiles reproduce the poster of that fatal afternoon in

August 1947 when Manolete and his great rival Dominguín faced the bulls in the town of Linares.

For a brief moment in the 1960s, a local bullfighter—El Cordobés—strove to match the fame of Manolete, but became known instead as The Spanish Beatle because of his mop-top haircut. His main claim to fame is *la salta de rana* —the frog leap—a flashy move in which the kneeling matador jumped to reposition himself, still kneeling, to meet the bull as it turned again to follow the cape. El Cordobés, after various comebacks during which his *salta de rana* became ever more laboured, has now finally retired to his luxury ranch. Bullfighting passion lives on, however, which is entirely appropriate: a recent archaeological find reveals once more how modern-day Córdoba has its roots deep in the past.

Just outside the old city centre, in the grounds of the university's veterinary faculty, archaeologists recently uncovered the remains of a Roman amphitheatre they say is the biggest in Europe after the Coliseum in Rome. The find, which they described as being of "transcendental importance", dates from the first century AD, when Corduba was the provincial capital of Betica, which is what in imperial Hispania they called present-day Andalusia. "We initially thought it was a circus, the circular arena the Romans used for horse races and chariot rides," said Desiderio Vaquerizo, Professor of Architecture at Córdoba University. "But we discovered it was an immense oval amphitheatre, 178 metres by 145 metres and up to 20 metres high, which would have been used for gladiatorial contests and similar bloodthirsty spectacles."

The find reveals Córdoba as an even more important Roman city than historians thought, an imperial city built in Rome's image. "The amphitheatre shows that Córdoba symbolized Rome's authority in the west: it was the setting for imperial ceremonies, the place where the emperor showed himself to the plebs and displayed all his power and authority before up to 50,000 spectators," explained Professor Vaquerizo. Less than one-tenth of the arena is visible, but archaeologists plan to uncover one-sixth of it—2,000 square metres— in coming years. The rest of the vast stadium, bigger, more sophisticated and elegant than even that at Italica outside Seville, is likely to remain buried under buildings that have been piled on over the centuries.

Within these oval walls, gladiators were set against each other, or thrown into combat with lions or other wild beasts, or—with the huge space flooded with water—engaged in gigantic naval battles. Such blood-soaked spectacles were all the rage between the first and fourth centuries. Archaeologists found a plaque marking the seats reserved for a prominent Cordoban family honoured by imperial Rome. They also found twenty carved gravestones of fallen gladiators, the biggest such collection outside Rome, which prompts experts to conclude that Córdoba was an important training centre for gladiators. According to the professor, "combatants were between 20 and 25, and it was the custom for their concubines or their families to carve their epitaph on stone tablets. These were than laid on the graves where the fallen were buried inside the amphitheatre." The inscriptions record the category of the gladiator, his victories, the laurels he was awarded, the prizes he won, and the age at which he died.

This was the real historical period in which the fictional private detective Marcus Didius Falco, created by the English crime writer Lindsey Davis, lived and conducted his adventures on the seedy side of Roman life. In *A Dying light in Corduba* Davis's hero romps through the scheming and perilous life of the Roman colony, enjoying the fiestas, the baths, the tapas, olive oil and wine, the opportunism and ostentatious display of wealth, all recognizably echoed in the culture of Andalusian life through to the present day.

Córdoba's Roman amphitheatre was abandoned in the fourth century, when Emperor Constantine, influenced by Christianity, banned the murderous sports as immoral. Then, in the 700s, the Omeyas from Damascus occupied Córdoba, and over the next 200 years built an entire neighbourhood upon the arena's handsome curved terraces, plundering the stonework for buildings of their own. "The discovery is of transcendental importance for the city. It recovers the importance of Roman games, a key aspect of popular daily life," said Professor Vaquerizo.

The ancient stadium reveals the continuity of mass spectator sports in Spain, which descend in a direct line from the Roman empire to today's fiestas and bullfights. "The bullring originated in an amphitheatre; this is the historical thread that links today's popular fiestas to the entertainments of ancient times." The professor's words echo those of the traveller Richard Ford, who added a typical dig at

Jesuit Catholicism. "The sacrifice of the bull has always been mixed up with the religion of old Rome and old and modern Spain, where they are classed among acts of charity, since they support the sick and wounded; therefore all the sable countrymen of Loyola hold to the Jesuitical doctrine that the end justifies the means." The crude relics of modern bullfights, and the celebration of today's garish, savage, compulsive fiesta in Córdoba's Museo Taurino, mark a trail through layers of Christian, Islamic and Jewish culture to the city's earliest Roman origins.

Chapter Eleven
GRANADA

Medieval Alhambra and Modern Mosque

"Give alms, woman, there's nothing in life greater than the pain of being blind in Granada" (*Dale limosna mujer, que no hay en la vida nada como la pena de ser ciego en Granada*). Francisco de Icaza's couplet, inscribed on ceramic plaques in any Andalusian trinket shop, must have been inspired by the medieval Moorish fortress-palace, the Alhambra: there is a breathtaking view of it from the terrace of St. Nicholas church on the Albaicín hillside. One of Europe's best known panoramas, this vista of the "Red Fort" has inspired so much poetic enthusiasm down the centuries that you might feel there is little new to add.

Bill Clinton famously brought Hillary and Chelsea here after the NATO summit in Madrid in July 1997 to share with him what the former US president remembered from his student days as the world's most beautiful sunset. The Clintons watched the Alhambra turn rosy against the glowing backdrop of the snow-clad Sierra Nevada peaks before darkness fell. Clinton had first visited the city 29 years before, during his time as a Rhodes Scholar at Oxford, and had been so stunned by its beauty that he resolved one day to return. "It was the same time in the evening, the same light, the same colours. Everything is the same, exactly as I remember it," he reminisced nostalgically. "Except me. I'm older." And when the journalists tried to question him, he turned to them and smiled: "Don't work today—just watch!"

Dreadlocked hippies who spend their days on this terrace droning ancient Bob Marley classics to an apathetic audience a generation younger were shooed away for the presidential visit. The rest of us must jostle alongside a languid troupe of flautists, pick our way through abandoned beer bottles, and peer over rucksacks for a glimpse of the spectacle.

Gerald Brenan described a curious ritual in *South of Granada*, his Andalusian memoir of the 1920s. He tells of a refined, eccentric old English colonial couple, Mr. and Mrs. Temple, who conducted what they called "the sunset ceremony". Brenan writes: "To explain what this was, I must begin by saying that the Temples had built their house on a hill high above the city so that it might command a view of the snowy mountains. Every evening after tea, at the hour when the sun was getting ready to set, Mrs Temple would marshal her guests towards the verandah, or if it was cold to the large window facing south, and pronounce in her slow, emphatic, careful voice: 'I don't think it will be long now.' We looked and waited. Gradually the smooth, undulating summits, which up to that moment had seemed remote and unterrestrial, began to turn a pale rose, just as though the beam of a Technicolor projector had been turned on them. 'There,' she said. 'Now'. At once a silence fell upon all of us, and we sat without moving, watching the rose flush deepen and then fade away. As soon as it had completely gone everyone began talking with the sense of relief felt by people who have just come out of church, and without any allusion to what they had just witnessed."

Brenan recounts the baffled response of a progressive Spanish intellectual, Fernando de los Ríos, whom he met one afternoon, to the Britons' tight-lipped response. "'Can you tell me,' he asked as we walked down the hill, 'what was going on when we all sat without speaking, looking at the pink spot on the mountain?' 'We were watching the sunset.' 'Yes I know, but why was everyone so serious?' I hesitated for a moment. No one likes to give away his country by revealing its secrets. However, there seemed no alternative, so I explained that this was a mystical rite confined to the higher levels of the British Raj. 'Here it's the sunset on the snow,' I said. 'But in other places it may take the form of watching through fieldglasses some rare bird, a siskin for example, or a peregrine falcon, alighting on its nest. Our viceroys and foreign ministers draw strength in difficult moments from such things.' 'I don't understand,' he said. 'No,' I answered, 'it's not really explicable.'"

The view of the Alhambra is just as fabulous from the garden of the mosque next to San Nicolás church. The Grand Mosque—actually quite a modest building—opened in 2003 as Granada's first public mosque since Spain's Moors were expelled by the Catholic monarchs Isabella and Fernando in 1492. The inauguration of the new mosque, in a ceremony broadcast live on Aljazeera television throughout the Muslim world, was controversial at a moment of international concern over Islamic fundamentalism. But the occasion marked a historic step for Spanish Muslims, many of whom dream of reviving the cultural glories of medieval al-Andalus.

The mosque lies in the heart of Granada's ancient Moorish quarter of Albaicín, and dramatically faces the Alhambra, once the symbol of Islamic power in Europe and today the greatest surviving jewel of Islamic civil architecture. The Albaicín has recovered its Moorish personality in recent years, and the narrow crooked lanes that slip between whitewashed houses are now studded with souks and teashops comparable to anything you might find in Fez or Marrakech. Plans for the new mosque were launched in 1981 when a group of Spanish Muslims, funded by various Muslim countries, bought the small plot between St. Nicholas church and a convent. Squabbles over control delayed completion for 22 years. But the head of Granada's Muslim community, Malik Abderram Ruiz, is proud to have kept the mosque independent from any group. It contains a small apartment for the muezzin who calls the faithful to prayer in the characteristic wailing cry that has been silent in this city for 500 years.

The mosque is surrounded by neat gardens laid out with roses, gravel paths, low stone seats and cool ceramic tiles which, at the behest of Granada's town council, are open to the public. The imam would have liked to reclaim the St. Nicholas church itself, which was built, as they all were in Granada including the cathedral, on the site of a mosque. But the white minaret rising from this historic Moorish quarter, and the proliferation of tea-houses all down the hill, shows that Muslims are slipping back to their old haunts.

Washington Irving, Gautier and Tales of the Alhambra
In his recent book, Robert Irwin explains how the Alhambra's designs were based on principles of ancient geometry combined with mystical references, while the gardens were conceived as an earthly reflection of paradise. Following the Islamic veto on graven images, walls and ceilings were covered with abstract motifs incorporating the ruling Nasrids' motto "No victor save God" and verses from the Koran. But Irwin uncoils a history of what he calls a "poisoned paradise", built by slaves and blighted by poverty and fear, the scene of murderous rivalries when "violence was the chief engine of politics." Of the first nine Nasrid sultans, seven were assassinated, while their two most celebrated

viziers, Ibn al-Khatib and Ibn Zamrak, were also murdered. These poet-statesmen who planned and oversaw the Alhambra were influenced by the Pythagorean ideas that geometrical shapes and numbers indicated timeless truths about the universe. Irwin also traces Jewish and Persian influences in a multicultural realm. Finally, he tells of the Alhambra's rediscovery by the Romantics and its influence on the imagination of writers and artists. Henry Swinburne was the first to alert the world to the dilapidation of the Alhambra in the 1770s. But it was the American Romantic writer Washington Irving who visited Granada in the 1820s and opened the floodgates. Thereafter, the Alhambra became a stop on the Grand Tour.

Washington Irving (1783-1859) was the first and most prominent of a stream of outsiders who elaborated fantasies based on historical traditions and folk legends. His trail was followed throughout the nineteenth century by enthusiasts eager to match his experience of living within the ruined palace itself. Irving's—and Brenan's—experiences still inspire to this day legions of bohemian in-comers to seek out a clutch of picaresque Andalusian locals, and write about life in their midst. Washington Irving's *Tales of the Alhambra* is available everywhere in Granada in many languages, with lovely half-tint illustrations, and is a charming book to graze while you gaze. His motivations must strike a chord with many.

From earliest boyhood when on the banks of the Hudson I first pored over the pages of an old Spanish story about the wars of Granada, that city has ever been a subject of my waking dreams, and often have I trod in fancy the romantic halls of the Alhambra. Behold for once a day-dream realized; yet I can scarce credit my senses or believe that I do indeed inhabit the palace of Boabdil and look down from its balconies upon chivalric Granada. As I loiter through these Oriental chambers and hear the murmur of fountains and the song of the nightingale, as I inhale the odor of the rose and feel the influence of the balmy climate, I am almost tempted to fancy myself in the paradise of Mahomet...

Irving offers a wonderful gateway to the romanticized, glorious and self-indulgent image of the history of Muslim Spain. "How many legends and traditions, how many songs and romances, Spanish and Arabian, of love and war and chivalry are associated with this romantic pile!" In 1829 the writer travelled from Seville to Granada with a Russian diplomat from the embassy in Madrid, and obtained permission to lodge in empty apartments in the Alhambra. "My companion was soon summoned away by the duties of his station, but I remained for several months, spellbound in the old enchanted pile. The following papers are the result of my reveries and researches during that delicious thraldom." He is taken into the care of a peasant woman, Tía Antonia, and meets Mateo, a raffish vagabond who lives in the Alhambra. Mateo attaches himself to the American gentleman and acts as guide to the inhabitants and lore of what amounts to a palatial, if dilapidated, tenement. "Here then," Irving wrote to a friend, "I am nestled down in one of the most remarkable, romantic and delicious spots in the world. I breakfast in the saloon of the ambassadors, among the flowers and fountains in the Court of the Lions, and when I am not occupied with my pen I lounge with my book about these oriental apartments, or stroll about the courts and gardens and arcades by day or night, with no one to interrupt me. It absolutely appears to me like a dream, or as if I am spell-bound in some fairy palace." Mateo has a tale for every tower, every latticed window and every subterranean dungeon of the sprawling site, and often claimed they involved his grandfather.

Whether or not Mateo existed, the character is a perfect literary device for Irving to assemble the legends of the place and pass them on as part of his personal experience. Venal priests eager to swell their purses; Moorish treasures hidden in caves; Boabdil's armies concealed in underground palaces ready to ride forth; princes and princesses locked in towers; magic seals, midsummer rites and symbols from Moorish and Christian legend—all emerged down the centuries from these ancient stones. Finally after three months, as Irving is posted to London and must leave this enchanted world, he hints that not everything he has written is entirely factual: "Thus ended one of the pleasantest dreams of a life which the reader perhaps may think has been but too much made up of dreams."

Dream or reality, the nineteenth-century European traveller wanted more of it. Théophile Gautier, was among those inspired to relive Irving's experience: "We set up our headquarters in the Court of the Lions; our furniture consisted of two mattresses, which were rolled up in a corner during the daytime, a copper lamp, an earthenware jar and a few bottles of sherry which we sent to cool in the fountain... It was not without some slight apprehension that I lay down in my cloak and watched the pale rays of the moon falling through the openings in the vault upon the water in the basin and the gleaming pavement, and mingling, to their astonishment, with the yellow, flickering flame of a lamp." Richard Ford was another enthusiast who was particularly taken by the magnificence of the Alhambra at night "when the moon's wan rays tip the filigree arches and give a depth to the shadows, and a misty undefined magnitude to the saloons beyond." But Ford, always ready with a down-to-earth reflection, wondered if the Alhambra might "disappoint those who, fonder of the present and a cigar than of the past and the abstract, arrive heated with the hill, and are thinking of getting back to an ice, a dinner and a siesta." It is a good idea to conserve your energy by taking the bus to the hilltop.

Weight of the Past

Granada's appeal is inseparable from its spectacular surroundings. The city sits on the edge of the fertile *vega* or flood plain of the Genil river, whose tributary the Darro plunges through a gorge that divides the Sacromonte and Albaicín hillsides from the natural citadel topped by the Alhambra. In the background rises the snow-clad Sierra Nevada, the highest mountain range in Spain. The surrounding rolling terrain, of olive groves and wheat fields lush and green, contrasts dramatically with the arid harshness of most of Andalusia and strongly marks the city's culture and literature. "The river Guadalquivir/flows between orange trees and olive groves./Granada's twin rivers/descend from snow to wheat," wrote Federico García Lorca about his home city. "Green, how I love you, green. Green wind. Green branches." These, the opening words of his "Romance somnámbulo" (Somnambulant Ballad), are probably the poet's best-known lines.

The opening of Lorca's poem "Paisaje" (Landscape)—"The fields/of olives/open and close/like a fan"—were apparently inspired by the view from the Generalife summer palace up behind the Alhambra. Lorca loved his city's fertile hinterland, and images of wide horizons, poplar groves, fields, riversides, flowers, gentle breezes and moonlit nights haunt his work. Lorca was born and brought up in the village of Fuente Vaqueros, west of Granada, and he retained for the spot a passionate nostalgia. "My whole childhood was the village. Shepherds, fields, sky, solitude. Simplicity... I love the earth. I feel linked to it in all my emotions. My earliest boyhood memories taste of earth. The land, the countryside have been big things in my life. The creatures of the land, the animals, the peasant folk, carry associations that reach only a few. I recall them now with the same spirit as in my infant years."

The actual city of Granada, by contrast, he thought a cold, introverted place inhabited "by the worst bourgeoisie in Spain". Lorca's dislike of the city's ruling class was chillingly prescient: these were the people who murdered him, then for decades ignored and spurned his memory.

The Irish writer Ian Gibson, Lorca's biographer, who lived for ten years in a village south of Granada, came to rail against the city. "It's the most depressing city in Spain," he said after returning recently to live in Madrid. "Anyone who doesn't get out goes mouldy and dies. It's secretive, dominated as Lorca said, by the twin burden of two brooding empty palaces of the Alhambra and the palace of Carlos V. Populated only by ghosts, these monuments represent the clash of east and west and weigh upon the city like death. And with its legacy of Arab civilization, Granada should be a great city of reconciliation."

It does not take long to discover that beneath the glory of the Alhambra, and the voluptuous prose and poetry it has inspired down the centuries, plus the intellectual verve proper to one of Europe's great university cities, Granada has a darker, crueller side. It is scarred by its history. This was the last city in Spain whose Muslim rulers fell to the Catholic monarchs Fernando and Isabella on 2 January 1492. The fall of Granada marked the final unification of Catholic Spain, so it is hardly surprising that the city became the symbol of Spain's re-conquest after 800 years of Moorish occupation. Every 2 January Granada celebrates what it calls *La Toma*—the seizure. Guidebooks mark the day as a typical Spanish fiesta, with the brandishing of firearms and flying banners, and noisy processions from the cathedral, but some Granadines consider the occasion offensive, an affront to the city's Muslim heritage that was crushed by the conquering Catholics. The Muslim King Boabdil was forced to hand the keys of the city over to the monarchs as he left to lead Spain's last Moorish rulers into exile. The capitulation treaty the conquerors forced Boabdil to sign guaranteed Muslims the right to use their own language, exercise their religion and their laws. But within a decade, the ruling Catholics, egged on by Queen Isabella's confessor, later the Archbishop of Granada, the fanatical Cardinal Ximénez Cisneros, broke all their promises. They banned Islamic traditions and customs, then forced Muslims—and Jews—to choose between a Catholic baptism or expulsion. By 1609, Felipe II expelled all Moors from Spain, producing a drastic decline in agriculture, crafts and economic activity. The downturn was halted only when Washington Irving's *Tales of the Alhambra* piqued the interest and imagination of Romantic travellers in the 1830s, and installed Granada as part of the Grand Tour.

Lorca lined up firmly alongside those who considered the fall of Muslim Granada a cultural calamity; when asked his opinion in 1936, the poet said: "It was a disastrous event, even though they may say the opposite in the schools. An admirable civilization, and a poetry, astronomy, architecture and sensitivity unique in the world—all were lost, to give way to an impoverished, cowed city, a misers' paradise, a wasteland populated by the worst bourgeoisie in Spain today." Lorca's words prompted a backlash of resentment from those at whom they were directed, and some say Spain's favourite poet was never fully forgiven in his home city for his contemptuous comments. The day of La Toma has been opposed—so far unsuccessfully—for years by a vociferous campaign to replace the celebration of siege and conquest with a Day of Tolerance, which would respect the coexistence of city's triple cultures of Arab, Jewish and Christian.

Granada remains, in other words, a city spiritually divided. And instead of seeking to smooth over the wounds and heal the scars of the past, the city's monuments glory in them, asserting the Catholic supremacy imposed more than 500 years ago. The Jewish quarter where some 20,000 Jews lived before the city fell occupied the neighbourhood around Realejo at the foot of the Alhambra hill. The area is today totally expunged of Jewish remains. Only a statue of a robed and turbaned man stands near what used to be the old frontier to the Jewish ghetto, in an undistinguished corner near the Plaza Nueva. The site is a popular rendezvous. The slender figure lunges forward on to his right foot while brandishing a rolled scroll in his left hand. The energetic pose has earned him the affectionate nickname "The Moor Hailing a Taxi" (*El Moro que llama un taxi*).

But despite his turban and his pointed slippers, El Moro is actually a Jew, the distinguished scholar Yehuda Ibn Tibon. Ibn Tibon is described on the plinth as a son of Granada and Patriarch of Translators who lived between 1120 and 1190, "doctor, philosopher, poet." The statue was financed in recent years by his Sephardic Jewish descendants. If you stand beside Ibn Timon and follow the direction of his gaze you will see, a few yards down the street, not a taxi but the image of his conquerors. The grand bronze monument to Catholic supremacy created by the Catalan modernist sculptor Mariano Benlliure in 1892 is mounted on a huge granite plinth and soars above ground level. It portrays Queen Isabella on her throne handing money to a kneeling, supplicant Christopher Columbus to fund his voyages of exploration to the New World. Around the statue are written the names of 24 nobles who formed the city's first local council—grand Granadine families who still carry weight in the city. The figures of monarch and subject dominate the top of the long main street, the Gran Via, and are backed by the dark glass walls of a spectacularly ugly office building that does not even reflect the monument it so cruelly intimidates.

Granada has two rivers, "one of tears, the other of blood", Lorca wrote. The Genil lazily skirts the city, visible but unremarkable. The other, the Darro, plunges through a little tunnel to disappear beneath the Plaza Nueva and bubble vigorously but invisibly beneath the surface of the city. It is said that if you stand quietly anywhere in Granada and listen, you can hear the murmuring of restless subterranean currents. Do the twin rivers represent the currents, one open and omnipresent, and the other submerged and barely visible, that flow through the city's intellectual landscape. Will the hidden current one day burst forth and cascade into the mainstream?

Lorca: Birthplace and Killing Field

Gerald Brenan loved the Albaicín. He visited it during his seven year stay in the Alpujarras village of Yegen in the 1920s. And when the Civil War was over, he was one of the rare English visitors to venture a journey through Franco's Spain in the early, harshest, years of the dictatorship. He returned to Granada and headed for his favourite spot, then wrote in *The Face of Spain* (1950): "On the morning following our arrival we set off for a walk in the old Moorish quarter known as the Albaicín. Steep cobbled lanes, white houses rising above one another, terraced gardens. A stream of women and children moving up and down, but few men. A feeling of tension. After we had climbed a certain distance, we caught on our right the sound of dogs barking and the harsh jangling of a guitar: they came from the gipsy quarter with its whitewashed caves and grey-green cactus... Far below lay the flat green plain, stretching away to its rim of mountains. From it there rose the crowing of cocks—faint, shrill and charged with distance and memory—into a grey sky that spread over everything.

> *Yes, this was the Albaicín as it used to be—yet why did it seem so changed, so different? As I sat listening to the cockcrows, the answer came to me. This was the city that had killed its poet. And all at once the idea entered my mind that I would visit, if I could find it, García Lorca's grave and lay a wreath of flowers upon it.*

Famed worldwide as Spain's favourite modern poet, Lorca has languished semi-forgotten in his homeland until almost the present day. His murder by fascist soldiers cast such a pall of shame over Spain that enormous pains were taken to conceal the circumstances of his death. The silence lasted long after Brenan tried to find Lorca's resting place in the 1940s, long after Gibson, inspired by Brenan's quest, wrote an award-winning account of the poet's final days, in a book that Franco banned. As recently as 1998 in an exhibition in Madrid to mark the poet's centenary, Lorca's death certificate, attributing the cause of his death to "war wounds", was displayed without comment or

explanation. The certificate says that Lorca "died in the month of August 1936, in consequence of wounds produced by the facts of war, his body found on 20 August on the road between Víznar and Alfacar." This cynical document was actually faked in 1940 at the behest of the Lorca family who needed official evidence of death to claim the poet's royalties.

We know roughly where Lorca lies. Francisco González, who comes from the village of El Fargue, just north of Granada, took me up the winding road that heads north-east from the city; it is the route along which Lorca was driven in a truck to his death. Gonzalez, now retired, was five when his father told him while walking near Granada: "beneath these stones lie thousands who were killed by Franco in the Civil War." The child imagined people lying underground bearing huge boulders on their chest. "It was overwhelming. I've never stopped trying to find out what happened." He added: "My father was forced to enlist with the Falange and was active in the sierra around here, so he knew at first hand everything that went on."

Lorca was 38 in August 1936 and already internationally renowned for poems such as *Gypsy Ballads* and his plays, *Blood Wedding* and *Yerma*. During the years of the Republic, between 1931 and 1936, he had journeyed through Spain with a group of itinerant actors known as La Barraca—students from Madrid University—bringing the glories of Golden Age theatre to small villages throughout the country. He never hid his republican sympathies. By ill luck Lorca had just returned to Granada when Franco declared his coup d'état against the Republic in July 1936. The poet had planned to take a brief holiday in the family home, La Huerta de San Vicente, on the city's western fringes, before heading off on a planned trip to Mexico. Receiving threats, he took advice from members of his family and fled secretly to the house in the city of a friend, the young poet Luis Rosales, whose three brothers were influential *falangistas*, where he thought he would be safe. But someone betrayed him, and he was seized on 16 August and incarcerated by the city's pro-fascist civil governor.

As Francisco González drove north up the winding road out of town, he continued the story of how the next night Lorca was brought to a house outside the village of Víznar that was used during the Republic as a holiday residence for poor children and called La Colonia. The building was taken over by the nationalists who used it as a transit prison. Lorca was kept seated on a wooden bench till dawn. Francisco gestured to the left, to the downward slope of the craggy hillside, from which all trace of this building has been removed. Then he pointed up to the right towards his own village of El Fargue, where you can still see the tall chimney of what was the region's biggest gunpowder factory. Four hundred workers were shot here during the Civil War, he said, as the insurgent nationalists tried to protect their principal source of munitions from attack by the republicans surrounding them. Fighting was particularly fierce around Granada, home of the fascist Falange. "Granada was an island of nationalism in a republican sea," Francisco said.

We stopped, briefly, at the little square of Víznar where, on the left, stands the pretty palace built by an eighteenth-century Archbishop of Granada, which was occupied during the war as a headquarters of the Falange. You can still make out the words *Viva Gil Robles* (the charismatic right-wing Catholic leader) faintly painted in red on the walls. Turning left up the winding lane—known as the Bishop's Way—

as Lorca's captors did early on 18 August, you reach the neighbouring hamlet of Alfacar. There, on the right at the roadside beside an ancient gnarled olive tree pockmarked with what could be bullet holes, the poet was shot before dawn. A few steps further back from the road, an estimated 250 opponents of Franco were thrown into a verdant gulley after being summarily executed. Pines planted as camouflage in the 1940s have grown tall and lustrous, lending a spurious grandeur to the sinister spot. A gravedigger, interviewed by Gibson in the 1960s, told the writer that Lorca had been shot along with a schoolteacher with a wooden leg, and two anarchist bullfighters. The gravedigger confessed that he had bundled the bodies all together on top of each other in a shallow grave.

A rather grandiose park has been laid out around the spot in the poet's memory. A granite block beside the olive tree reads: "In memory of Federico García Lorca and all those victims of the civil war 1936-1939." Francisco plucked a sprig of rosemary from one of the many bushes that flourish on the hillside and placed it on the stone. "We should find his body. Then we can write 'here lies Lorca' on the stone instead of these mealy-mouthed words." In the park a few steps up the hill, the walls of a large semicircular amphitheatre are covered with ceramic plaques framed with wrought iron that bear extracts from Lorca's poems. They all refer to suffering, blood and death. Were these texts chosen for that reason or did they simply reflect Lorca's preoccupations? "Andalusia of his time in the twenties and thirties was a land of much suffering," said Francisco: "He was describing no more than the tragic reality." And he murmured the lines from one of the plaques, from the four-part lament for the bullfighter Ignacio Sánchez Mejías: "I don't want to see it!/Tell the moon to come,/I don't want to see the blood/of Ignacio on the sand/I don't want to see it!... My memory of it burns." Ever since he could read and write, Francisco said, he was aware of the poet. *Gypsy Ballads* was the first book he ever read, in secret. But for forty years "we couldn't say Lorca's name". Francisco recalled the time during the dictatorship when he courted trouble by reciting Lorca in the street. Dry leaves rustled across the pebble-stone paving of this lugubrious spot, the silence broken only by the tinkling of a spring tumbling from an ugly, discoloured fountain set in the wall.

Francisco González is active in the Association for the Recovery of Historic Memory, an organization that aims to recover tens of thousands Franco's opponents dumped in mass graves all over Spain. The hidden slaughter started to surface around the year 2000 as relatives strove to recover the remains of their loved ones thrown into anonymous roadside ditches and common graves. The association says that it is not interested in revenge or raking over past conflicts; its members just want to give their relatives a decent burial in a place where they can mourn. Lorca is just one of legions of Spain's *desaparecidos* (disappeared).

A few yards further on, as the road dips towards Alfacar, rises a spring renowned since the tenth century. The Arabs called it Ainadamar ("the fountain of tears"), because of the force with which the water bubbles from the ground, then courses down the hillside through Granada and the Albaicín. Some take comfort from the thought that Lorca may be buried nearby. In his 1919 poem "Sueño" (Dream) he wrote: "My heart rests there, beside the cold spring." In 1921 he wrote: "I want to die being a spring/I want to die far from the sea." We scrambled through the gorse scrubland, between the poplars and the pines, back towards Víznar, to the most sinister spot on this grisly "tour": the gully or "barranco de Víznar". This is the biggest mass grave hereabouts and contains up to 3,000 bodies of murdered republicans. It is a deep leaf-strewn valley set amidst towering pines. Francisco stood on the gully's edge, to show how the Civil Guard positioned their victims before shooting them, so that they fell backwards into the ditch. And he quoted from Lorca's "Romance de la Guardia Civil Española" (Romance of the Spanish Civil Guard), the poem that made his name: "The horses are black./The horseshoes are black./Upon their capes glitter/stains of ink and wax./Their skulls are of lead,/that's why they don't cry./With their souls of patent leather/they advance down the road./Hunched and nocturnal/they order at will/silences of dark rubber/and fears of fine sand." Stones, flowers, pine cones, and messages written on slips of paper have been heaped on the forest floor in the shape of a large cross.

Francisco Galadí is the grandson of one of the anarchists shot alongside the poet that dawn, and flung with him into a shallow grave. Galadí is keen to recover his grandfather's remains and give him a decent burial. "All his life my father wanted to bury my grandfather with dignity, and he died with his desire unfulfilled. Now I want to honour his memory with a tomb that I can visit and where I can mourn his memory," he said recently. The graves of Americans who died in Normandy in the Second World War are a fitting model, he believes. "Why should those who died defending democracy be abandoned like carrion in a ditch?" he asked. The one-legged teacher's granddaughter, Nieves Galindo, remembers her father telling how he watched his father being driven away to be executed. If she and Francisco Galadí are allowed to excavate the spot, their efforts may also dispel the mystery of Lorca's final hours.

Lorca's descendants, however, do not want to dig for old bones. Elegant Laura García Lorca has the same almond eyes and sober gaze as her uncle. She is the daughter of Federico's younger brother, Paco, and sits at a replica of the poet's desk in her little office at the family's former home La Huerta de San Vicente. In Lorca's day this charming spot, bought by his father in 1926, was on the outer edge of Granada in the green countryside, though barely twenty minutes' walk from the city centre. Now owned by Granada's town council, it is surrounded by high-rise blocks as the city marches inexorably into the *vega*. The distant view of the Alhambra that the Lorcas once enjoyed from their home has long been blocked out. Only the family's swift footwork in the 1980s prevented the whole plot from being compulsorily purchased and swallowed up in urban sprawl. As it is, the natural landscape was trimmed and primped, gravelled, paved and manicured to conform with someone's idea of an urban park. Surrounded by a roaring motorway and overlooked by skyscrapers it may be, but the Parque de Federico García Lorca is nevertheless the only spot in the city to commemorate the poet by name. The house, white with green shutters, remains unchanged.

"We think there's no justification for exhumation," Laura said gravely. "It's an act of violence against a place we consider a cemetery. There's enough evidence about his death, and this cemetery is very eloquent about the brutal extermination, the repression carried out by fascists in Granada." The family respected the wishes of those who wanted to find their antecedents killed with Lorca, "but for us it is just too painful. Let's not try to remake history and re-open the wounds of this tragedy. We must accept that the spot marks his tomb, and that of many others, and it should be left undisturbed."

Lorca wrote many of his finest works at the Huerta de San Vicente, in his little room upstairs whose balcony overlooks the garden at the front of the house. His niece Laura never knew him, but learned everything from her aunts, Federico's sisters Concha and Isabel. Laura describes how the poet loved to work all night, then sleep till midday, when he would eat. Then he would work throughout the siesta—the dead hours of the early afternoon when everything is quiet—and sit out on the terrace downstairs talking with friends until 2 or 3 in the morning. Mature trees still shade the terrace, and one bears blossoms of a heady and beautiful perfume. "An English lady who was a keen gardener told me it was called *Macassar Chimonentis*," Laura said. The house, whose style is comfortable and prosperous, is unpretentious, giving off a simple, cheerful air, with its covered settees and grand piano.

Still more modest, but with the same comfortable feel, is the Lorca family house in Fuente Vaqueros, a half-hour drive north-west, where Federico was born and spent his childhood. This was in Lorca's time a small village surrounded by groves of trees and open fields of tobacco, sugar-beet and wheat. Now it is lapped by workshops and bleak warehouses forming a strung-out industrial park. The small terraced house has been reconstructed with the help of those who knew it, including the poet's former wet-nurse who lived opposite. In 1986, the Granadine poet Juan de Loxa was invited to create and curate a museum here. There is the bed of Federico's parents, with the child's white painted cast-iron rocking cot draped in a blue-and-white lace coverlet, beside it. A little tunnel under the stairs links the kitchen to the living room, an intriguing passageway where the boy ran and played, and beside it the pantry is hung with simple household utensils. Here too is a pair of cushions, embroidered by his two cousins in 1928 on designs that Lorca drew for them, the upright piano at which he played and sang popular songs. Upstairs, in the former storage area for the wheat, barley and quinces of the *vega*, de Loxa has created a museum, with changing exhibitions. And behind—across a pretty patio with a well, a vine, an apricot tree, an orange tree and a couple of wicker chairs and a table—a new building with more exhibits and a small film projection room. Commenting on the polemic over Lorca's resting place, de Loxa said carefully: "We must listen to wishes of the family. But Lorca is different. He belongs to everyone. I think the family could have made more effort to recover him in the years since Franco's death."

Despite the protestations of mutual understanding of different points of view, the families' conflicting demands seem incompatible, and everyone anxiously awaits resolution of the impasse. The mayor of Alfacar, Juan Caballero, wants to help, but is torn by conflicting demands. "I'll give a licence to anyone who asks, but if the Lorca family don't want the site disturbed, a judge must decide," he said. "Both parties have their rights." Meanwhile, thousands of supporters of the campaign to recover historical memory long to know, after decades of fear and silence, exactly where their loved ones lie. They say: "We only want to know where we should weep." By a curious coincidence, two international experts in identifying buried bodies by matching DNA samples happen to be professors at Granada University. Miguel Botella and José Antonio Lorente have worked for decades on identifying those who disappeared during the Chilean and Argentine dictatorships in the 1970s and 1980s. Latterly they were approached to solve the mystery of where Christopher Columbus is buried. But only recently were they invited to tackle the legacy of Spain's own dirty war.

Lorca's "Llanto por Ignacio Sánchez Mejías" (Lament for Ignacio Sánchez Mejías) contains four parts, the third and fourth of which are called "The Body Present" and "the Absent Soul". Lorca in Granada, by contrast, seems to be an absent body but a present soul. There is nowhere that truly commemorates him, not even a grave. But his spirit is everywhere. His favourite Café Suizo on the Puerta Real is now a burger outlet, although the Suizo's marble tables and glinting chandeliers, the ironwork and the mirrors have mostly been retained, to rather bizarre effect. Granada's Arts Society, another familiar haunt, is now a theatre named not after Spain's leading modern playwright, but after Isabella the Catholic.

Manuel de Falla

The musician Manuel de Falla was among those who rushed to Granada's civil governor when Lorca disappeared, unaware that it was already too late. Falla's *carmen* in the foothills of the Alhambra was briefly considered as a possible safe haven for Lorca, as a spot that Franco's troops would never dare violate. But the family mistakenly thought the Rosales' house in the city would be safer. Threatened in turn, de Falla, the sensitive hypochondriac friend of the poet, promptly fell ill and later fled into exile in Argentina.

Manuel de Falla was considered Granada's most distinguished cultural figure during the 1920s and 1930s, and his house and garden—his *carmen*—became, in his words, "like a little Paris". The *carmen* of Granada has nothing to do with sultry cigar girls. "The word, Arabic in origin, denotes a hillside villa with an enclosed garden hidden by high walls from inquisitive eyes, the architectural design expressing, originally, the Islamic notion of the inner paradise, a reflection of heaven," writes Ian Gibson in his biography of Lorca. "From the street outside, the garden is invisible; inside, amid a riot of vines, jasmine, fruit trees and geraniums, splashes the inevitable fountain. Lorca found in the title of a seventeenth-century composition by the Granadine poet Pedro Soto de Rojas the ideal definition of a carmen: 'A paradise closed to many, gardens open to few.' And in 1924 he declared that he adored Granada, 'but only to live on a different plane, in a carmen. All the rest is a waste of time. To live close to what one feels deeply: the whitewashed wall, the fragrant myrtle, the fountain.'"

Falla and Lorca were friends. The musician's maid was aunt to the García Lorca household and the two men were frequently in contact. Gibson even speculates that if they had met sooner, Lorca may have devoted his life to music instead of poetry. The composer's *carmen* has been restored exactly as it was during his lifetime, and admirably fulfills our expectations of what this inner paradise should be. Manuel de Falla was born in Cadiz, into a prosperous merchant family ruined by the decline of the city as a trading port. He was already an established composer when he visited Granada in 1919 after his triumph in London with *El sombrero de tres picos* (The Three Cornered Hat), a ballet version of a tale of the nearby Alpujarras mountains by Ruiz de Alarcón. And he set his 1905 opera *La vida breve* (Brief Life) in Granada long before he visited the city. It tells the tragic love story of a gypsy girl from the hillside of the Albaicín who fell for a fickle downtown Don Juan. His *Amor brujo* (Bewitched Love), premiered in Madrid in 1914, also had an Andalusian and gypsy theme. Already attracted to the city, Falla fell in love with it when he moved there from Paris. He was a reserved man who loved tranquillity and silence. He stayed first in a house on the Calle Real inside the Alhambra with his sister María del Carmen. María del Carmen had a vocation to be a nun but decided instead to devote herself to her obsessive, perfectionist brother. He complained how the fierce north wind of Granada's hard winters whistled down the street and seared his delicate lungs, so in 1922 brother and sister moved into the south-facing Carmen de Ave Maria on Calle de la Antequerela Alta. Falla stayed there until 1939 and was frequently visited by Lorca, the composer Andrés Segovia, Spanish modernist artists Ignacio Zuloaga and Santiago Rusiñol, and other intellectuals.

When he left Spain in 1939 for Argentina he took only a few clothes and his work *Atlántida*, which took him twenty years to finish. For he expected to return: "remember to look after my piano and keep it tuned," were his parting words. But when the Second World War broke out he decided to remain. In 1941, after some silver had been stolen from the house, he asked a friend to dismantle his Granada home and put everything in store. With typical meticulousness, he made an exhaustive inventory, and the friend drew sketches to show where everything went, even inserting a slip into each of the thousand books noting where, and in which bookcase, they belonged. So when Granada's municipal authorities bought the house in 1962 and reclaimed the contents—which the composer had bequeathed to the city on his death—everything could be restored to its original place.

To judge from his neat little house, Falla does not strike you as a cosmopolitan man, but rather an amiable, pernickety introvert. His side table in his monk's cell of a bedroom says it all: piled high with pills and potions, with exercise weights, a prayer book, even a miniature rubber hot water bottle. And, within easy reach, his walking stick. Morbidly Catholic and obsessed by sin, he had simple tastes and hated luxury. The only flamboyant note in this tiny tranquil retreat is struck by some simple locally made wooden chairs, which are painted a vibrant blue; and some fine ceramic bowls and vases that he accumulated when he went around Spain's villages collecting popular songs in 1919. In 1937 Falla became unsteady on his legs, so he commissioned a local carpenter to make him a special wheelchair: a rather comical rustic contraption with little wooden wheels, on which he propelled himself about the house. He was a chain smoker, and there are ashtrays on every surface. On the walls are costume designs for *The Three Cornered Hat*, sketches by Picasso that the painter gave to the composer. And in the little back room an upright piano, a windup gramophone and a typewriter, one of those with a separate keyboard for capital letters. Everything is minute, charming, even a little twee, with thick esparto matting tacked with huge iron nails tp the lower half of the walls to keep out the cold and damp. But the view is sensational. Falla wrote matter-of-factly to a friend, inviting him to stay: "I have the most beautiful panoramic view in the world." From his little balconies, you look over the city to the entire green *vega*, with the snowy mountains beyond, glittering in the pure light.

Falla is remembered in Spain as the man who did most to preserve and revive the traditions of flamenco, fast dying out in his time. Together with Lorca, Ignacio Zuloaga and other prominent figures he organised the *Cante jondo* (Deep Song) competition of 1922. The contest was held on 13 and 14 June in the Alhambra's Patio de los Aljibes ("Fountain Court"), decorated for the occasion by the Basque artist Zuloaga. It was packed both nights by an enthusiastic and flamboyantly dressed audience. The English Hispanist and traveller John B. Trend, who had become a close friend of the composer, described the two unforgettable evenings, the second of which was drenched by a downpour: "Whenever one looked there were exquisite figures in gay, flowered shawls and high combs, while many had put on the silks and satins of bygone days and appeared in the fashion of the [eighteen] thirties and forties—the Spain of Prosper Mérimée and Théophile Gautier, of Borrow and Ford." The great discovery was the performance by an old *cantaor*, all but forgotten, Diego Bermudez Cañete, "el Tenazas" (Pincers) who is said to have hiked across eighty miles of country from Córdoba province. His triumph on the first night was followed by a mediocre performance the second after a day's drinking—sponsored, it was alleged, by his rivals.

"You cannot imagine," Falla wrote to Trend three weeks later, "the extent to which my work and other things put off till later piled up during the long and laborious preparations for the competition." And he retreated to the seclusion of his *carmen*. Falla fled to Argentina in 1939, to the city of Córdoba, where he died late in 1946 shortly before his seventieth birthday. His sister María del Carmen, who had travelled with him, arranged for his body to be brought home and in January 1947 he was buried in the crypt of Cadiz cathedral, his home town, by the water's edge.

Fascist Monuments

From a second-floor balcony on Granada's main Calle de los Reyes Católicos (Catholic Monarchs Street) flutter the twin flags of Spanish fascism. On the left are the scarlet and black yoked arrows, symbol of the Falange, and on the right the red and gold flag of Spain bearing Franco's black eagle insignia.

It is a shocking sight, like seeing a swastika fluttering near York Minster, or the KKK symbol raised on Boston Common. For this is the regional, national and international headquarters of the organization that Franco used to crush his opponents in the Civil War. Repression was particularly savage hereabouts, where thousands of victims lie buried anonymously in mass graves. Critics say Granada's conservative local authorities tolerate the flag because it reflects their secret political sympathies. But the town hall, on the other hand, is dominated by a statue of a blindfold naked man astride a giant horse that prances along the roof. The sculpture, the work of Ramón Ramiro Mejías, was installed by a previous left-wing council, and is said to celebrate the homosexual preferences of the artist who inspired it, Guillermo Pérez Villalta. The figure tacitly alludes to Lorca, whose own homosexuality was undoubtedly an additional reason why Franco's sympathisers hated him. Local cynics wonder which provocative symbol of Granada's political and artistic polar opposites will be hauled down first.

An even more surprising relic of the dictatorship is a monument to the founder of the Falange, José Antonio Primo de Rivera. It adorns a pretty square of orange trees and hedges, just in front of the Bibataubín Palace, seat of Granada's county council. The monument, erected in 1972, is inscribed "Granada a José Antonio" and consists of a circle formed by six right hands raised in the fascist salute, supporting a pair of spread eagle's wings. The arrows and yoke symbol is carved into the plinth, to which some graffiti artist has added the epithet *asesino*. And on the other side, the sculpted A of José Antonio has been encircled to form the anarchist symbol. Beneath, someone has written "*Fachas* (fascists) No!"

Much polemic has been expended over why, decades after the end of the dictatorship, the public boulevard sports a monument to the founder of a movement that included someone who wrote the following: "I have quite distinguished myself in Granada. I was among those who were present, one morning in August, at a firing squad at the cemetery, by the open ditches of seventy reds, all of them bandits, assassins, criminals, rapists, agitators… and I enjoyed it very much indeed, because they deserved it. Among them was the head of the county council Virgilio Castilla; the red ex-governor of Alicante; the red mayor of Granada, Montesinos… we well and truly cleaned up."

These words were written by Manuel Luna to a friend in around 1939. The "red mayor" he mentions was the husband of Lorca's sister Concha. Luna's letter continues: "A few days later, we seized that great scumbag García Lorca—the worst of the lot—and we shot him in the *vega* beside an irrigation channel. What a face he made! He raised his arms to heaven. He begged for mercy. How we laughed at his gestures and miserable grimaces!"

The Cathedral: Enslaved Artist and the Crypt of Kings

It is hardly surprising that Granada's cathedral, built on the site of the grand mosque of the centre of the Muslim kingdom, is perhaps the city's vastest and most grandiose gesture of Catholic supremacy. The cathedral is filled with paintings by the great painter, architect and sculptor Alonso Cano, a contemporary and equal of Velázquez and Montañés. Cano is considered the most modern of Spanish Golden Age baroque artists, whose realistic faces, flesh-and-blood figures and use of light are said to prefigure the Enlightenment.

Cano's story is a tragic one. He married a young girl who one day was found hacked to death. Cano was accused of murdering his young bride and, despite his protestations of innocence, was persecuted by the Inquisition. He fled to Granada and pleaded with the bishop to grant him sanctuary in the cathedral. Granada's religious hierarchy agreed to protect him on the condition that he took holy orders and dedicated the rest of his life to working for the Church. The result was a cathedral full of works of one of Spain's greatest masters, produced under the rigours of life imprisonment. He was said to have a depressive, volatile character, and died in Granada in abject poverty in 1667. When a priest came to his bedside to administer last rites, the artist is supposed to have angrily waved aside the crucifix the cleric offered him, because of its inferior workmanship.

A carved stone deathbed of the Catholic monarchs lying side by side rests in the crypt of the Royal Chapel adjoining the cathedral. The head of Isabella rests deeper on her pillow than does that of her consort, suggesting that she was the weightier figure. The chapel's entrance is dominated by an idealized picture of Boabdil surrendering the keys of the city. And within is a fine collection of truly miserabilist paintings. These include Flemish masterpieces, but are miserable all the same, exulting in chilling images of agony and grief.

Outside the cathedral, across the street is the Madraza, the Muslim university and the Corral de Carbón, once the stopping off point for Muslim traders, then a coal depot, now being renovated as an Islamic cultural centre. It is one of the finest surviving such patios in Spain, a tranquil, majestic place, despite its present decrepitude. An Arab-speaking vendor of posters of the city's jewels of Islamic architecture lays out his wares against the cathedral walls. The Arab and the Christian are always in close proximity in Granada, the geographical legacy of their violent struggle for power. The old silk market, the Alcabaza, just by the cathedral (which used to be just by the central mosque), has been developed as a mock Arab bazaar selling Moroccan slippers, ceramics and tunics. Atmospheric—though apparently a nineteenth-century pastiche of the ancient souk—it none the less represents a deeper truth of Granada's Moorish origins.

Plaza Bib-Rambla: Burning of the Books

A few steps from the cathedral, the Plaza Bib-Rambla was Granada's main square for jousting, flirting and popular festivals during the realm of the Nasrid kings. It was also the site of a historic cultural tragedy that has burned into the collective memory of the Muslim world to the present day. Early in December 1499 the zealot Archbishop Ximénez de Cisneros, confessor to Queen Isabella, concerned that the recently conquered Muslims were not bending sufficiently to Catholic domination, ordered soldiers to enter the 195 libraries of the city and a dozen mansions where some of the better-known private collections were held, and to confiscate everything written in Arabic. The day before, Catholic scholars apparently persuaded Cisneros to exempt 300 manuscripts: Arab manuals of medicine and astronomy. These volumes contained all the advances in science achieved since antiquity, scholarship that had travelled throughout Europe to lay the groundwork for the Renaissance. Cisneros agreed to spare the works, but insisted they be placed in a new library he planned to found in Alcalá de Henares, east of Madrid.

The tragedy that followed forms the starting point of Tariq Ali's novel *Shadows of the Pomegranate Tree* (1992), which charts the decline of the Muslims of al-Andalus after the fall of their last city. "Several thousand copies of the Koran, together with learned commentaries and theological and philosophical reflections on its merits and demerits, all crafted in the most exquisite calligraphy, were carted away by the men in uniform. Rare manuscripts vital to the entire architecture of intellectual life in al-Andalus, were crammed in makeshift bundles on the backs of soldiers. Throughout the day the soldiers constructed a rampart of hundreds of thousands of manuscripts. The collective wisdom of the entire peninsula lay in the old silk market below the Bab al-Ramla," Ali writes.

> *The sumptuously bound and decorated volumes were a testament to the arts of the Peninsulan Arabs, surpassing the standards of the monasteries of Christendom. The compositions they contained had been the envy of scholars throughout Europe. What a splendid pile was laid before the population of the town… Some of the soldiers, perhaps because they never had been taught to read or write, understood the enormity of the crime that they were helping to perpetrate. Their own role troubled them. Sons of peasants, they recalled the stories they used to hear from their grandparents, whose tales of Moorish cruelty contrasted with accounts of their culture and learning. There were not many of these soldiers, but enough to make a difference. As they walked down the narrow streets, they would deliberately discard a few manuscripts in front of the tightly sealed doors… The minute the soldiers were out of sight, a door would open and a robed figure would leap out, scoop up the books and disappear again behind the relative safety of locks and bars. In this fashion, thanks to the instinctive decency of a handful of soldiers, several hundred important manuscripts survived. They were subsequently transported across the water to the safety of personal libraries in Fes, and so were saved.*

Ali describes how the people wailed when a torch was put to their precious books. What they called "the wall of fire" cast a blaze of terror across the coming years, and centuries. He tells of how those Muslims under the pressure of the Inquisition debated three options open to them: to convert to Christianity, to rebel, or to flee. His story is of the destruction of a noble Muslim family living near Córdoba, each of whom choose their fate. The historical tragedy is considerably more dramatic than the language Ali uses to tell the tale, but the novel is a lively account of how Spain's Catholic monarchs from their court in Granada vanquished a proud and cultured people.

The Moor's Last Sigh

A sophisticated, if elusive, evocation of the agony of al-Andalus forms the basis of Salman Rushdie's novel *The Moor's Last Sigh* (1995). This swirling transcontinental saga covers centuries of Muslim, Jewish and Indian history through the extravagant Zogoiby family. Zogoiby is the family name of Boabdil, and means "unlucky". Rushdie evokes Boabdil's "tearfulness" without actually spelling out the legend of the king's ignominious departure from his city as, surrounded on all sides, he had to surrender the keys of the city on his flight to exile. As he rode south taking the last remnants of Islam from Spain, the king paused at a mountain pass and, turning for his last glimpse of his lost kingdom, wept. Boabdil's weakness prompted the bitter reproach of his mother, Sultana Aysha La Horra, the Intrepid, who famously exclaimed: "You do well to weep like a woman, for what you failed to defend like a man." The spot at the top of a slope known as the "hill of tears" is today an unremarkable point on a bleak and untidy motorway. It became known as The Moor's Last Sigh, and was the inspiration for Rushdie's tale.

Washington Irving adds a detail to the legend of Boabdil's flight, revealing the clash of cultures between the vanquished Muslims and the Catholic conquerors: "When this anecdote was related to Carlos V by Bishop Guevara," Irving writes in *Tales of the Alhambra*, "the emperor joined in the expression of scorn at the weakness of the wavering Boabdil. 'Had I been he or he been I,' said the haughty potentate, 'I would rather have made this Alhambra my sepulchre, than lived without a kingdom in the Alpuxarra.' How easy it is for those in power and prosperity to preach heroism to the vanquished!" Irving comments, and makes clear throughout his sympathy for the wronged Boabdil.

As he, too, has to leave the city, the American writes: "I now could realize something of the feelings of poor Boabdil when he bade adieu to the paradise he was leaving behind and beheld before him a rugged and sterile road conducting him to exile." Irving leaves Granada "at an opposite point of the compass" to Boabdil—by the northern road, perhaps alongside the one Lorca was forced down a century later. Lorca was taken before dawn; Irving left at sunset. "The bosky groves and gardens about the city were richly gilded with the sunshine, the purple haze of a summer evening was gathering over the Vega; everything was lovely, but tenderly and sadly so to my parting gaze."

Rushdie celebrates Granada in the closing pages of his novel, as a timeless, universal symbol of the glory of Moorish rule: "And so I sit here in the last light, upon this stone, among these olive trees, gazing out across a valley towards a distant hill; and there it stands, the glory of the Moors, their triumphant masterpiece and their last redoubt. The Alhambra, Europe's Red Fort, sister to Delhi's and Agra's—the palace of interlocking forms and secret wisdom, of pleasure courts and water gardens, that monument to a lost possibility that nevertheless has gone on standing, long after its conquerors have fallen; like a testament to lost but sweetest love, to the love that endures beyond defeat, beyond annihilation, beyond despair, to the defeated love that is greater than what defeats it, to that most profound of our needs, to our need for flowing together, for putting an end to frontiers, for the dropping of the boundary of the self."

Richard Ford condemned Granada for its "bookless ignorance" and often had some quip to deflate the awe and literary extravagance it engendered. But Granada has produced—and attracted—fine writers. Those who visit, even for a short while, usually leave with a pang of nostalgia. But those who live there rarely seem able to throw off the tragedy of the city's violent history.

FURTHER READING

Aguilar Criado, Encarnación, *Las Bordadores de Mantones de Manila de Sevilla*. Seville: University Publications Secretariat, 1999.

Alberti, Rafael, *Antología Poética*. Barcelona: Ediciones Optima, 2000.

Alberti, Rafael, *Marinero en tierra*. Madrid: El País, Clásicos del Siglo XX, 2002.

Alberti, Rafael, *Poemas escogidos*. Madrid: Biblioteca El Mundo, 1998.

Alcolea, Santiago, *Zurbarán*. Barcelona: Ediciones Polígrafa, S.A., 1989.

Ali, Tariq, *Shadows of the Pomegranate Tree*. London: Verso, 1999.

Bécquer, Gustavo Adolfo, *Rimes y leyendas*. Madrid: Espasa-Calpe, 1985.

Beevor, Antony, *The Spanish Civil War*. London: Cassell & Co, 1999.

Bendala Lucot, Manuel, *Sevilla*. Editorial Everest, 1978.

Brenan, Gerald, *Memoria personal 1920-1975*. Madrid: Alianza Editorial, 1977

Brenan, Gerald, *South from Granada*. Middlesex: Penguin Books, 1963.

Brenan, Gerald, *The Face of Spain*. London: Penguin Books, 1987.

Brenan, Gerald, *The Spanish Labyrinth*. Cambridge: University Press, 1969.

Burgos, Antonio, *Guía secreta de Sevilla*. Madrid: Al-Borak, 1974.

Burns, Jimmy, *Spain, A Literary Companion*. London: John Murray, 1994.

Burns, Tom, *Hispanomanía*. Madrid: Plaza & Janés, 2000.

Capel, José Carlos, *Comer en Andalucía*. Madrid: Pentathlon Ediciones, 1981.

Carande, Ramón, *Sevilla, fortaleza y mercado*. Seville: ABC, 2001.

Cascales, Antonio, "Crónica del día en el que Miguel de Cervantes salió de la cárcel de Sevilla", in *ibid.*, *Sombras en la Cal del Muro*. Seville: Luis Cernuda Foundation, 1994.

Cascales Ramos, Antonio, *La Sevilla Americana*. Seville: Ediciones Alfar, 1990.

Cernuda, Luis, *Música cautiva (Antología poética)*. Seville: Town Hall, 2002.

Cernuda, Luis, *Ocnos*. Seville: Town Hall, 2002.

Cervantes, Miguel de, *Don Quixote*. London: Penguin Books, 2000.

Cervantes, Miguel de, *Exemplary Stories*. London: Penguin Books, 1972.

Davis, Lindsey, *A Dying Light in Corduba*. London: Arrow Books, 1997.

De Las Casas, Bartolomé, *A Short Account of the Destruction of the Indies*. London: Penguin Books, 1992.

Díaz-Plaja, Fernando, *El "Don Juan" Español*. Madrid: Ediciones Encuentro, 2000.

Díaz-Plaja, Fernando, *La Vida cotidiana en la España sw la Inquisición*. Madrid: Editorial Edaf, 1996.

Domínguez Ortiz, Antonio, *Autos de la Inquisición de Sevilla*. Seville: Town Hall Publications Service, 1994

Elliott, J. H., *Imperial Spain 1469-1716*. London: Penguin Books, 1990.

Elliott, J. H., *The Old World and The New 1492-1650*. Cambridge: University Press, 1970.

Fernández Bañuls, Juan Alberto, *Semana Santa: fiesta y rito de Sevilla*. Madrid: Guías Artísticas, Tf editores, 1995.

Fletcher, Richard, *Moorish Spain*. London: Weidenfeld & Nicolson, 1992.

Ford, Richard, *Gatherings from Spain*. London: Pallas Athene, 2000.

Ford, Richard, *Handbook for Travellers in Spain*, vols. 1, 2 and 3. London: Centaur Press, 1966.

Fraser, Ronald, *Blood of Spain*. Middlesex: Penguin Books, 1981.

García Lorca, Federico, *Romancero gitano, Poema del cante jondo*. Madrid: El País. Clasicos del siglo XX, 2002.

Garvey, Geoff and Ellingham, Mark, *Andalucía: The Rough Guide*. London: Rough Guides, 2000.

Gautier, Théophile, *A Romantic in Spain*. Oxford: Signal Books, 2001.

Gathorne-Hardy, Jonathan, *Gerald Brenan: The Interior Castle*. New York: W. W. Norton &Co, 1993.

Gibson, Ian, *Federico García Lorca*. London: Faber & Faber, 1989.

Gibson, Ian, *Lorca's Granada: A Practical Guide*. London: Faber & Faber, 1992.

Gilmour, David, *Cities of Spain*. London: John Murray, 1992.

González Troyano, Alberto, *La Desventura de Carmen*. Madrid: Espasa-Calpe, 1991.

Granero, Jesús M., *Muerte y amor: Don Miguel Mañara*. Madrid: 1981.

Guerrero Lovillo, José, *Guías artísticas de España: Sevilla*. Barcelona: Editorial Aries, 1962.

Hemingway, Ernest, *Death in the Afternoon*. London: Arrow Books, 1994.

Hintzen-Bohlen, Brigitte, *Andalucía, arte y arquitectura*. Barcelona: Köneman, 2000.

Irving, Washington, *Tales of the Alhambra*. Granada: Miguel Sanchez, 1994.

Irving, Washington, *Vida del Almirante Don Cristobal Colón*. Madrid: Edicions Istmo, 1987.

Irwin, Robert, *The Alhambra*. London: Profile Books, 2004.

Jacobs, Michael, *Alhambra*. London: Frances Lincoln Limited, 2000.

Jacobs, Michael, *Andalucía*. London: Pallas Athene, 1999.

Jacobs, Michael, *Between Hopes and Memories: A Spanish Journey*. London: Picador, 1994.

Jah, Cherif Abderrahman, *Los aromas de al-Andalus*. Madrid: Alianza Editorial, 2001.

Laffón, Rafeal, *Sevilla*. Barcelona: Editorial Noguer, 1956.

Lafuente, Isaías, *Esclavos por la patria*. Madrid: Temas de Hoy, 2003

Lee, Laurie, *As I Walked Out One Midsummer Morning*. London: Penguin Books, 1971.

Lope de Vega, *El Arenal de Sevilla*. Madrid: Espasa-Calpe, 1962.

Maestre León, Beatriz, "Fábrica de cerámica La Cartuja de Sevilla," in Olmedo, Fernando and Rubiales, Javier, *Historia de La Cartuja de Sevilla*. Seville: Turner Libros, 1989.

Marañón, Gregorio, *Don Juan*. Madrid: Espasa-Calpe, 1958.

Mérimée, Prosper, *Carmen*. Oxford: University Press, 1989.

Michener, James A., *Iberia*. New York: Ballantine Books, 1982.

Molière, *Don Juan*. London: Penguin Books, 2000.

Morales Padrón, Francisco, *Varias Sevilla*. Seville: Town Hall Publications Service, 1986.

Moreno, Isidoro, "De 'bozales' a 'negritos': los negros sevillanos y su cofradía del siglo XV al XIX", in *Palabras de la Ceiba no 3, 1999*. Seville

Morris, Jan, *Spain*. London: Penguin Books, 1982.

Muñoz Molina, Antonio, *Córdoba de los Omeyas*. Barcelona: Planeta, 1998.

Ortiz de Lanzagorta, J. L., *Las Cigarreras de Sevilla*. Seville: JRC Editor, 1988.

Pardo Bazán, Emilia, *The House of Ulloa*. London: Penguin Books, 1990.

Pérez Galdós, Benito, *Fortunato and Jacinta*. London: Penguin Books, 1988.

Pérez-Mallaína, Pablo Emilio, "Sevilla y la Carrera de Indias en en Siglo XVI", in *Navegación,* Catalogue for Expo 92. Seville: 1992.

Perez Olivares, Rogelio, *¡Sevilla!* Madrid: published by author, 1929.

Pérez-Reverte, Arturo, *The Seville Communion*. London: The Harvill Press, 2000.

Preston, Paul, *Franco*. London: Fontana Press, 1995.

Pritchett, V. S., *The Spanish Temper*. London: The Hogarth Press, 1983.

Pulido, Ildefonso, "Historia de la Torre del Oro", in *Museo Marítimo Torre del Oro*. Madrid: Navy Publications Service, 1992.

Rojas, Fernando de, *La Celestina*. Madrid: Unidad Editorial, 1999.

Rosenblum, Mort, *Olives: the Life and Lore of a Noble Fruit*. New York: Absolute Press, 1996.

Ruesga Bono, Julián, *Juan Manuel Rodríguez Ojeda*. Seville: Maldito Seas project, Seville Town Hall, n.d.

Rushdie, Salman, *The Moor's Last Sigh*. London: Vintage, 1996.

Said Armesto, Víctor, *La leyenda de Don Juan*. Madrid: Espasa-Calpe, 1968.

Sánchez Mantero, Rafael, *A Short History of Seville*. Seville: Silex, 1992.

Sender, Ramón, S., *La Tesis de Nancy.* Barcelona: Editorial Casals, 1989.

Seneca, Lucius Annaeus, *Letters from a Stoic.* London: Penguin Books, 1969.

Sierra de la Calle, Blas, "El Galeón de Acapulco y las sedas de Oriente", in *El mantón de Manila.* Madrid: Museo Municipal, 1999.

Silva, Emilio y Macías, Santiago, *Las Fosas de Franco.* Madrid: Temas de Hoy, 2003.

Stella, Alessandro, "Herrado en el rostro con una S y un clavo: el hombre animal en la España del siglo XVI", in *Palabras de la Ceiba, No 1, 1998.* Seville: biennial review of Afrohispanoamerican Culture foundation.

Stella, Alessandro, "'Mezclándose Carnalmente'. Relaciones sexuales y mestizaje en Andalucía Occidental", in Quejia, Berta Ares and Stella, Alessandro, eds., *Negros, Mulatos, Zambaigos.* Seville: School of Hispanic-American Studies, 2000.

Stone, Caroline, *Sevilla y los mantones de Manila.* Seville: Town Hall Culture Department, 1997.

Thomas, Hugh, *The Spanish Civil War.* London: Penguin Books, 1990.

Tirso de Molina (attrib), *El burlador de Sevilla.* Madrid: PML Ediciones, 1995.

Webster, Jason, *Andalus: Unlocking the Secrets of Moorish Spain.* London: Doubleday, 2004.

Webster, Jason, *Duende: A Journey in Search of Flamenco.* London: Doubleday, 2003.

Woolsey, Gamel, *Death's Other Kingdom.* London: Virago, 1998.

Zoido Naranjo, Antonio, *La Prisión General de los Gitanos y los Orígenes de lo Flamenco.* Seville: Portada Editorial, 1999.

Zoido Naranjo, Antonio, *Doce teorías para Sevilla.* Seville: Signatura Ediciones, 2000.

Zorrilla, José, *Don Juan Tenorio.* Madrid: Espasa-Calpe, 2000.

Index of Literary & Historical Names

INDEX OF PLACES